Word Processing Secrets for Writers

ABOUT THE AUTHORS

Michael A. Banks is a full-time freelance writer who also happens to be an enthusiastic computer hobbyist. A computer user since 1978, he bought his first microcomputer in 1980, and since then has written fifteen books and hundreds of articles using a variety of computers, ranging from Apple to IBM to Tandy.

Banks is frequently called upon by writers and publishers for advice in selecting WP and telecomputing systems. He is the author of the standard reference on small computers, *The Modem Reference* (Brady Books/Simon & Schuster).

Banks also writes science fiction novels and short stories and articles on writing and a variety of general-interest topics. He lives in Goshen, Ohio, with his wife, daughter, and son.

Pseudonymous Ansen Dibell, all-around WP maven, is a Senior Editor with Writer's Digest Books. Because she likes to try out and play with software she's become the de facto WP troubleshooter around F&W. In her spare time, she writes science fiction (the five-novel series, *The Rule of One*) and nonfiction (*Plot*). Although the idea for this book came to her in a vision on the stairs just after unscrambling a merge-document mess for F&W's typing center, no winning lottery numbers have yet come to her in her sleep. All the self-inflicted WP disasters described in this book, she admits having committed, but she's getting better and now employs only novel and hitherto-untried methods of fouling files up beyond recognition or recovery.

Word Processing Secrets for Writers

MICHAEL A. BANKS
&
ANSEN DIBELL

Writer's Digest Books

Cincinnati, Ohio

Word Processing Secrets for Writers. Copyright ©
1989 by Michael A. Banks and Ansen Dibell. Printed
and bound in the United States of America. All rights
reserved. No part of this book may be reproduced in
any form or by any electronic or mechanical means including information storage and retrieval systems
without permission in writing from the publisher, except by a reviewer, who may quote brief passages in a
review. Published by Writer's Digest Books, an imprint
of F&W Publications, Inc., 1507 Dana Ave., Cincinnati, Ohio 45207. First edition.

93   92   91   90   89   5   4   3   2   1

**Library of Congress Cataloging-in-Publication
Data**
Banks, Michael A.
   Word processing secrets for writers.

   Includes index.
      1. Word processing. 2. Authorship—Data
   processing.
I. Dibell, Ansen. II. Title.
Z52.4.B36   1989   652'.5   88-33931
ISBN 0-89879-348-3

Design by Carol Buchanan and Barbara Seitz

C O N T E N T S

PART TWO:

Words on Screen:
What Your Manual Won't Tell You

PART ONE

Writer's (Computer) Market: Hardware and Software

What's Out There, What Features It Offers, and What's Important to Writers

INTRODUCTION

This isn't a "this is a cursor, this is a keyboard" book. We're assuming you already know what they are.

We assume that, from your manual, you already know how to do the basics: get your words on screen, save them, retrieve them, print them.

We assume that like us, you're a writer: involved primarily with words rather than numbers. To you, a computer is a step up from a typewriter, not from a calculator. You need a book to take you from "typewriter thinking" into the special shortcuts and tricks that word processing makes possible, and to help you avoid the dreaded data-eaters you never had to worry about with a typewriter: the dangers that can leave you looking at a blank screen where your manuscript was a second ago.

You need a book that goes beyond the basics, beyond your manual, one written in plain language rather than technospeak and addressing the special needs you have as a *writer* rather than someone who's heavily into spread sheets, pie charts, or the gastric details of whatever chips and boards may reside in your computer's innards.

This isn't a book just for users of Apple or IBM, or this or that specific WP program. You may be using any of thousands of possible combinations of computers and software, either brand new or of (relatively) ancient vintage. But no matter what you're using, WP offers certain generic abilities in creating and editing text. All WP systems, for instance, will let you "search" a sequence of letters and locate them in your document; they'll all allow you to designate ("block") a portion of text and relocate it somewhere else; they'll all let you combine the text of two different files into one new combined document. Through taking more thorough advantage of these basic capabilities, the functions that make WP what it is—*regardless of which particular keys you need to hit, with your WP system, to make a given function happen*—you can become a more effective and productive writer.

Generic WP. That's what this book is about: tips, shortcuts, and troubleshooting methods to help you get the most from *any* WP system. We concentrate most heavily on DOS-based systems because that's what most of you will have, but we also discuss the comparable functions and procedures available in non-DOS-based systems. When appropriate, we name names, to pin down an example or cite specific characteristics of particular hardware or software that you ought to know about; but we've made no attempt to rank or evaluate, brand by brand, the current range of computers or WP programs. That kind of news gets stale real fast; and what will be the best total WP package for you depends on your individual needs and budget. Instead, we talk capacities and options: what's available, what it can do, and what advantages it can offer to a *writer*.

Do you need graphics capability or a color monitor? Do you want to get a WP program with a built-in spell-checker, or do you want to find an add-on spell-checker to supplement your current WP software? A modem? A mouse? That's the kind of decision you need to make for yourself.

But we offer some guidelines to help you make those choices. The first part of the book presents an overview of what's out there—hardware and software options—both to help you evaluate your present total WP system and get the most from what you already have, and to guide you when, inevitably, you start to think about trading up to more memory, more powerful software, a better printer, and perhaps the networking and telecommunications capabilities of a modem.

The second part of the book offers hands-on specifics, spelling out writerly WP "secrets" you can use right now in creating, editing, printing, and submitting manuscripts, either as printouts or on disk.

Effectively used, WP can liberate you from much of the drudgery of writing and free you to focus your energy, not on the mechanical techniques of grinding out words, but on the crucial, exacting, exciting process of having something to say and *saying it well.*

With this book, we hope to help you come nearer to achieving this goal.

Good writing!

Michael A. Banks
Ansen Dibell

CHAPTER 1

Computers

OVERVIEW: THIS CHAPTER COVERS:

1. Dedicated vs. computer-based word processing.

2. Basic word-processing hardware: keyboards, monitors, storage, disks and disk drives, printers, memory ("K").

3. Optional hardware elements: mouse, track ball, graphics card, printer interface card, modem.

4. Which computer? Standards and other considerations: manuscripts on disk, disk formats, available software, manufacturer reputation, warranty and service.

5. Buying a computer: gathering data, computer sources, buying a used computer.

6. Taking care of your computer.

EVERYBODY WANTS TO GIVE YOU ADVICE. Whether you're shopping for your first word-processing system or upgrading to a more powerful one, you'll find a lot of people who know nothing about your needs as a writer and who nevertheless are just aching to tell you what you need. Computer salespersons (geared more toward the needs of business users and hobbyists than those of writers) will tell you, in great detail, why whatever they're selling is exactly what you ought to want. Computer-owning friends will tell you to buy what they have, since almost everyone who owns a computer feels that his or her brand is the best, and that those using anything else have either been criminally misled or are folk who need help screwing in a light bulb.

We're going to do it too, after a fashion. In this chapter (and throughout the first section of this book, where appropriate) we're going to show you the more important features available for computers and make recommendations as to why or why not each is useful, and worth the money, for *writers*.

But wherever the advice comes from, remember: the only one who can truly evaluate what you need, want, and can afford is *you*. This first part of our guide aims to give you checklists, overviews, and choices, so you can select the hardware and software that will make word processing more of a pleasure than a labor and maybe keep you from suffering from system envy for years to come.

DEDICATED WORD PROCESSORS VS. COMPUTER-BASED WORD PROCESSORS

When you begin looking at word processors, you'll find there are two kinds: *dedicated* and *computer-based*. Both are in fact computers, but there are important differences between the two—and definite advantages of using one rather than the other. Understanding the distinction between the two will help you choose flexibility over almost instant obsolescence.

A dedicated WP system is just what the name says: a system dedicated to doing one job: word processing. Because of this, dedicated word processors really shine in helping you create and edit text. They usually resemble a computer in appearance, although a few simple ones look like typewriters with small screens.

A computer-based WP system is centered around a microcomputer, more commonly known as a personal computer. Whatever the make and model of the computer, it's distinguished from a dedicated word processor by the fact that it's not restricted to doing just one job. It turns into whatever the software it's currently running directs it to become. Here are some features that make us advise you to choose a computer-based WP system:

•It usually costs less to assemble a computer-based system, whether you do it "piecemeal" (buying the various elements from different sources), or buy everything from one source.

•With a computer-based WP system, you're not stuck with one WP program; using a computer gives you your choice of literally hundreds of programs—and many of them are available at little or no cost (more on this in Chapter 2, when we discuss shareware and public domain software). Choices for dedicated systems are few and there's little incentive for the manufacturers to offer updates and additional software.

•Using a computer gives you access to hundreds of specialized add-on programs, such as style checkers, spelling and punctuation checkers, and other more specialized utilities that can streamline and expedite the processes of writing and editing.

•With a computer, you can usually translate or transfer files from one computer format to another. This is increasingly important as more and more publishers accept (or demand) manuscripts on disk as well as in hard-copy (paper) form. Most dedicated systems make it difficult or impossible to switch formats.

•Most computers are modular, meaning that each element (disk drive, printer, monitor, keyboard, and the computer itself) is a separate device you can easily replace. If something goes bad, just unplug it and replace it with a new one or, if the equipment's in the shop, a "loaner." And because they're modular, you can mix and match the parts as you might those of a stereo system. If, either when buying or trading up, you don't like a particular hardware element of a computer package—be it the keyboard, monitor, or printer—you can usually substitute for it another that's more to your liking. A dedicated word processor doesn't give you this option.

•The resale value of dedicated word processors is far below that of computers. This is because other people have gotten smart. There's more of a demand for computers—that can function either as number-crunchers or as word processors—than for dedicated word processors.

•Finally, a computer is many tools in one. It can be used for word processing, telecommunications, learning, entertainment, bookkeeping, and much more. A dedicated word processor is just that: a word processor. The software available to allow a dedicated system to do other chores varies between limited and nonexistent.

Bluntly, we think writers have about as much use for a dedicated word processor as a fish has for earmuffs. We've used both dedicated machines (in our joint youth: us, and word processing) and computers as word processors, and on almost every front, computers win hands-down.

And it's not just us: if you check around among writers of your acquaintance, you'll find that easily 95% of the writers who use word processors use computers.

You'll find a few dedicated word processors that are less costly than computer-based word processors, but don't let the price seduce you into buying one. The bottom line is this: You'll find yourself very limited by such a system, in word processing as well as in other areas—if not right now, then eventually. About the time you really become proficient in its use, you'll become painfully aware of its limitations.

You decide.

BASIC WORD-PROCESSING HARDWARE

The basic hardware of a computer-based WP system consists of a keyboard, a monitor (screen), storage (ideally, hard or floppy disks), and a printer.

KEYBOARD

Your computer's keyboard is important. You'll have to live with it through literally millions of keystrokes. Thus, you need to consider the following elements carefully.

SIZE

Most computer keyboards are roughly the same size as a typewriter keyboard, with perhaps a little extra width to accommodate certain extra keys. The important element here is whether the keys themselves are smaller than standard typewriter keys, or are placed so close together you have trouble striking just one, and the one you meant to hit rather than its neighbor.

Key size is relative. It depends on what you're comfortable with, like the teeny buttons some pocket calculators have that look as though you ought to be pushing them with pinpoints, as compared to the oversized numerals some phones have that you can dial with your elbow. If the keys are *much* larger than those of a standard typewriter, you'll need to do some reaching, and you'll find some combinations of keys hard to strike. If they're *much* smaller (like those of the Apple Macintosh), you may suffer finger jams and frequent keyboarding errors.

Pick the key and keyboard size best suited to your hands, your desktop space, and how much weight your knees will support comfortably, if you plan to drag the keyboard into your lap and tap away on it in that position for hours at a time. Try a keyboard in various typing positions in the store before buying the computer—at least with *that* keyboard.

LAYOUT

Because all typewriter keyboards look pretty much alike, you'll probably find most computer keyboards confusing at first glance. But if you ignore the extra keys and take a second look, you'll find the letters and numbers on almost all computer keyboards in the right place, in standard QWERTY configuration.

You'll find variations: IBM PCs and their work-(almost)-alike cousins called "clones" or "compatibles," for instance, have a keyboard layout similar to that of the IBM Selectric (the so-called "European standard"), with an extra key (for quotemarks) between the colon/semicolon key and the ENTER/RETURN key. In general, if a keyboard's letters and numbers are in the same places you're used to finding them, the keyboard will be easier for you to get used to. This is true not only of switching from a typewriter to a computer, but in switching from one computer to another: if the special "function" keys have moved from the side to the top, for instance, or the escape or delete key has zipped to a new location, it will take your fingers time to adjust.

There are alternatives to the traditional QWERTY layout, each with its impassioned advocates. Legend has it that typewriter keys were originally laid out the way they are to minimize the frequency of striking two keys together and jamming the little elements that, in a typewriter, spring up and strike the platen. Typists were required to adapt themselves to the machine, rather than the machine being adapted to the capacities of the human hand—what today is called "ergonomics." Since computers have no such elements and key-jamming isn't possible for a printer, advocates of DVORAK, the most popular of alternate keyboard layouts, say the time to change over to a more sensible, more ergonomically-efficient system is *now*.

A DVORAK keyboard can nearly double your typing speed, but first you have to *unlearn* your QWERTY-based reflexes: you have to learn to type all over again. If you're already typing faster than you can think of the words to type, greater speed isn't going to offer you any particular advantage. However, if you've switched over to the metric system and are deeply involved in rational spelling reform, it may be that the satisfaction of having a really efficient keyboard layout will, for you, outweigh the labor of getting used to it. If so, ask about the availability and pricing of DVORAK keyboards: they're out there, though not yet stacked by dozens in every K-Mart. Maybe you'd like the feeling of being the first on your block to have one.

If, on a given keyboard, you find there are individual keys whose positions you simply cannot abide—and this is true for many who use IBM PCs—there are a number of programs available that will redefine keys to suit your typing habits. This key-redefinition can involve one or two keys or the whole keyboard: you can transform a QWERTY to a DVORAK and spend happy minutes pasting on all the tiny letter and number stickers to remind you what all the keys are *now*. (More on this and other special software in Chapter 3.) Add-on keyboards of varying configurations are also available for most high-end computers, sporting things like separate number keypads, graphics touchpads, and other special features.

"EXTRA" KEYS

Besides the familiar QWERTY alphanumeric keys, ENTER/RETURN, and space-bar, you'll find at least one or two (up to about thirty) extra keys on any computer keyboard. These keys can be classed in four groups: control keys, numeric keypads, function keys, and cursor-control keys.

Control Keys The name "control key" is a little misleading because a control key doesn't control anything, nor does it do anything on its own. Rather, it's used in conjunction with other keys to send commands or perform special functions. Press the control key and the letter "H" simultaneously (with some WP software), for example, and the cursor will move back one character. Push the control key and the keypad numeral 1 (with other WP software) and everything left of the cursor is deleted. The control key extends the functions of other keys, making it possible for the keyboard to stay compact while still offering hundreds of optional actions.

The control key on most computers is labeled "CONTROL" or "CTRL." On others, it may have a different symbol, but the idea is the same.

Some computers have more than one control key. IBM PCs and clones, for example, have one labeled "CTRL" and another labeled "ALT," doubling the number of optional special functions, some using CTRL and some using ALT. The Apple IIe has a control key, as well as "Option" and "Open Apple" keys.

Numeric Keypads A numeric keypad is a boon to those who type a lot of numbers. A basic numeric keypad consists of the numbers 0 through 9 and a decimal point. Most, however, also include two or four "math keys" (addition, subtraction, multiplication, division). Some numeric keypads serve double-duty by enabling you to use the numbers (which are appropriately marked) as cursor-control keys; press a key called a "Number Lock" key (or something similar) and the function of the number keys switches to control cursor movement.

Some of the more upscale keyboards sport separate cursor-control keys and number keys, rather than making you toggle between the two functions on the same keys. Although this can be useful if you're working with a lot of numbers, with some keyboard configurations it puts either number keys or cursor keys out of easy reach when your fingers are in normal typing position. For writers, it's more important that the cursor keys be easy to get at than that the keyboard offer "dedicated" number keys. Keep that in mind when some salesperson tries to dazzle you with a custom keyboard the size of an organ console. Less can be more.

Numeric keypads can be a part of an existing keyboard (as with the IBM PC and newer Apple IIs) or added on (as with the Macintosh or the Apple II+). If you want a numeric keypad, we recommend the integrated type, set apart from the main keys—but not *too* far apart.

Function Keys Function keys can be found on IBM and other computers, either to one side of or above the main set of keys. Computers with function keys have either 10 or 12, and they're marked "F1," "F2," etc.

A function key performs one specific operation (save, print, exit, underline, etc.) when pressed either alone or in conjunction with the SHIFT, ALT or CTRL keys. Many programs allow you to define function keys—that is, to change the specific procedure each performs. Note that the functions of function keys will vary, depending on the program you use.

Cursor-Control Keys Cursor-control keys move the cursor around the screen and through a document. Separated from the main keys, they consist of arrow keys for moving the cursor one character or line at a time, and—on some computers—keys to move the cursor a screen up or down, a page up or down, and/or to the beginning or end of a whole document.

Miscellaneous Keys The backspace key is found on all keyboards—normally at the upper right. Like the typewriter backspace key, it moves the cursor one character back (to the left). It's worth noting that many WP programs erase ("delete") the letters left of the cursor when this key is pressed. By contrast, moving the *cursor* back with a cursor-control key doesn't change the letters it passes across at all.

Some computers have a "delete" key, which, depending on the program in use, deletes either the letter it's on or the one to the left. (The decimal-point key on a double-function numeric/cursor-control keypad has this function.)

Almost all computers have a key called the "Escape" key. The escape key is used most often to interrupt, cancel, or "escape from" a program function or command. It's usually labeled "ESC," and may be placed anywhere on the keyboard.

MODULAR KEYBOARDS AND SCREENS
The idea of a separate keyboard or screen (also known as a monitor) may seem strange at first if you still tend to think of a computer as merely a super-smart typewriter with a TV on top. But where word processing is concerned, they offer real advantages and some writers consider them a necessity. The benefits are easy to see:

•Although it's relatively easy to move a typewriter to a more comfortable typing position, it's not so easy to move or adjust a keyboard that's locked to a monitor and/or disk drive housing, not even considering the printer cable. (A typical computer housing has a collection of cords springing out the back worthy of any octopus: they considerably limit the unit's range of movement.) Besides, sensitive electrical equipment doesn't take kindly to being shifted around or bumped—especially the CPU, the box where the computer and its disk drive(s) live. The keyboard and monitor, however, are comparatively hardy beasts

and don't mind the occasional bump and jar.

•An attached keyboard forces you to sit at a fixed distance from its computer's monitor, which can result in eyestrain. Similarly, a monitor that's locked to the CPU has only a limited range of possible adjustments for comfortable viewing.

•A detached keyboard—one on a nice long cord—allows you to change your position while typing—important if you spend a lot of hours writing. You can even hold the keyboard in your lap, or put it on the floor, or tap away in bed, if you want to and your cord's long enough. (You can buy extension cables for some keyboards for extra versatility.)

•A movable monitor allows you to position the monitor and CPU separately—one of us has the monitor below, protected against glare inside a box, and the CPU *on top*—to take best advantage of your available space. Some stands will even let a CPU be positioned sideways, with the disk drive slots vertical instead of horizontal. It takes up much less desk space that way. Also, there are inexpensive "lazy-Susan" stands for monitors that let you adjust height, tilt, and position any way you want, and more expensive affairs that look something like cranes, with the monitor hanging in midair from a jointed arm whose base clamps to your desktop.

So when you're looking at hardware, look at the pieces not only as a unit, but in terms of how—or whether—you can separate them during use. Flexiblity and long cables can mean the difference between steady productivity and a persistent pain in the neck.

KEY TYPES AND "ACTION"
The physical makeup and corresponding "feel" of a keyboard's keys are as important as its layout. Naturally, you want a keyboard with keys that look like a typewriter's keys (some keyboards have keys that are small rectangles and others have literally a *picture* of a keyboard on a plastic sheet

overlaying switches; these are impossible to type on with any speed and are mainly for industrial use, for people with oil-smeared fingers).

The relative sensitivity of the keys is important, too. If you're used to typing on an electric typewriter and switch to a keyboard which requires that you really pound the keys, your typing speed will drop. If you type hard because you have big hands or are used to a less-sensitive electric or manual typewriter, you'll start out making a lot of multiple-letter errors until you get used to the lighter, more responsive touch most computer keyboards offer.

Finally, you should know that some keyboards are noisier than others. Some people like to be answered by a solid click when each key goes down; others find it annoying. For this reason, and because there's a wide range of touch-sensitivity among keyboards, you should try out as many as possible. But keep in mind that it's possible to get used to just about anything.

MONITORS

Despite appearances, a computer's monitor isn't a TV. And shouldn't be. Although you can hook most computers to a standard television set, TV sets aren't designed to display small letters with clarity. (We point this out in case you're new to computing and hope to get by with using your TV as a monitor.)

Since any writer spends a lot of time staring at the screen, monitor quality is important. The factors affecting quality are the size of the screen, the line width and number of lines displayed, and the color.

SIZE

The smaller a monitor, the smaller the letters it displays. Unless you have perfect vision, you're going to want as large a monitor as possible. The standard in monitor sizes seems to be 12 inches (measured diagonally, as with television sets). You can get larger monitors, but as monitor size goes up,

resolution (the sharpness of the images displayed) goes down. The current upper limit on monitors is 14 inches. (NOTE: This applies only to less expensive monitors. Large, pricey monitors with excellent resolution are becoming available to satisfy the demands of desktop publishing software; writers who are working just with text probably won't find the extra expense—currently, equal to that of a midrange PC, including standard monitor and keyboard—justified. Stay tuned, though: prices may come down, and page-at-a-time monitors may become standard equipment and an attractive and inexpensive upgrade item.)

LINE WIDTH AND NUMBER OF LINES

Line width means the number of characters (letters) displayed on one line. The standard is 80 characters per line. This provides enough space to display full lines and margins in the way they'll be printed in your final manuscript. (NOTE: Most monitors can display 80 characters; if a computer displays 40 characters, like the Commodore 64, this is a function of the computer itself, not of the software.)

The number of lines on a standard 12" screen is usually 25, a little under half a standard page (66 lines), including a WP program's "ruler line" or "prompt line."

MONOCHROME AND COLOR

Monitors come in two types: "monochrome" and color.

A monochrome monitor is a single-color monitor, which means that it displays everything in one color against a black background, or in one variation of that color against another—dark blue on light blue, perhaps. Green is the most commonly used and recommended color for monitors because it's easy on the eyes. Amber (yellow) monitors, though slightly more expensive, are even easier on the eyes. (Almost no one sells black and white monitors anymore, and we recommend that you not use one, for your eyes' sake. It's worth noting, however, that the Apple Macintosh's screen displays manuscripts in black letters on a white background—just like typing on paper—and it's very easy to look at. We guess it just goes to show there are exceptions to everything.)

A color monitor is a nice enhancement to word processing. With color, you can set the background- and text-color combination most pleasing to your eyes. Some of the high-end word processors even offer the nicety of displaying special font sizes—small caps and italics, for instance—in a color different from that of the surrounding text. Be warned, though, that the only color monitors worth buying are the very expensive, high-resolution ones. Cheap, low-resolution color monitors work fine with shoot-em-up arcade games, but they have poor focus and show blurred double lines and overlap where colors change.

Unless you're contemplating desktop publishing, a color monitor probably won't offer enough advantages to offset its considerably higher cost.

GRAPHICS

As a writer, you may feel that you don't have much use for graphics. On some computers—mainly IBM PCs and clones—graphics capability of a sort is important because of the way things like literal italics, boldface, and underlining are displayed (or *not* displayed). Special monochrome monitors can display text with these literal features (that is, the italics are *really* slanted, not just underlined or designated with a code; the underlining *looks* like underlining, etc., as opposed to designating the text with varying intensity: green and greener, for instance) if the WP program can handle it, and if you have the appropriate "graphics card" (discussed later in this chapter).

"WHAT YOU SEE IS WHAT YOU GET"

An early and very important innovation in word processing was the "WYSIWYG" display ("WYSIWYG" being an acronym for "What You See Is What You Get"). WYSIWYG elements can vary, depending on the WP program in use and the capabilities of the computer, the monitor and its graphics card. The advantage of WYSIWYG display (which should be "on" during editing, but which you should be able to turn off if you wish) is that you see your manuscript on-screen almost exactly as it will be printed out.

For typewriter users, WYSIWYG display makes the transition to word processing easier. For all writers, WYSIWYG makes word processing less obtrusive to the creative process, since you don't have to try to visualize your manuscript as you type (it's done for you) or try to ignore an assortment of format codes peppered all over the screen. All that's there is the text, looking (more or less) just like a typed page, unless you *choose* to look at the otherwise-invisible codes.

Basic WYSIWYG shows the *result* of page formatting (i.e., margins, indents, tabs, centering, and the like) without showing the formatting codes themselves unless you deliberately requre that the codes become temporarily visible. Basic WYSIWYG is the bare minimum you should accept in any WP system. (We'll explain format codes in more detail in Chapter 4.)

Advanced WYSIWYG display can include alternate-color (or intensity) display of special formatting such as underlines and boldface, or—better still—*literal* display of these features. While alternate-color or intensity display is common and can be handled by most systems, the literal display of italics, underlining, and other features requires a very sophisticated (and correspondingly more expensive) hardware setup. Only the newer computers, such as the Macintosh, Atari ST, IBM PC and OS/2, and Commodore Amiga are capable of literal WYSIWYG display—and then only if the WP program being used supports it.

Of course, literal WYSIWYG isn't an absolute necessity. You can get along fine with literal format display and alternate-color or intensity display of underlining and boldface. The question of whether or not to get literal, advanced WYSIWYG display is easily answered by your pocketbook.

STORAGE: DISKS AND DISK DRIVES

Being able to store your work and retrieve it later for editing or printing additional copies is one of the many advantages of word processing over typing. In almost all computers, storage capability is built in, because the same medium that WP programs come on is used for data storage.

The medium should be disks. Forget cassettes; they're excruciatingly slow and unreliable. The device used to read information stored on disk is called a disk drive.

(NOTE: With rare exception, disks containing files from one brand of computer can't be read by another brand of computer, for reasons too technical to go into here. Thus, an IBM PC can't read the information on a disk created with an Apple IIe. However, there are ways to transfer the information *on* the disks: see Chapter 5. Keep this in mind when selecting your first computer or an upgrade if there's any chance that you will want or need to exchange disks with someone—a publisher or a collaborator, for instance. Nor will disk drives designed to work with one brand work with another brand.)

Disks come in two varieties: "floppy" and "hard."

FLOPPY DISKS

Floppy disks are so named because they are flexible. Physically, a disk consists of a circular sheet of recording medium (mylar with a magnetic coating, just like recording tape) with a hole in the middle (like a 45-rpm record), sealed inside a square, flexible plastic housing. The housing on "standard" floppy disks measures 5-1/4" on a side.

Certain computers, such as the Atari ST, the Macintosh, and newer IBM PCs, use a 3-1/2" disk inside a hard plastic housing. These disks can store almost half again as much as 5-1/4" floppies and are, because of their housing, more durable; but they require a different sized disk drive. Three-and-a-half-inch floppies will

become a new standard in a few years, but 5-1/4" disks won't disappear. Still, if your computer accommodates both types, it might be a good idea to get a drive that uses 3-1/2" floppies as well as one or more that use 5-1/4" disks.

If you're limited to one size drive, go with the five and a quarter inch: almost everyone uses it, and programs are available on disks of this size even if they aren't yet available on 3-1/2" disks.

No matter what the size, floppy disks are your computer's gateway to the outside world. You'll store "backup" copies of your work on floppy disks and may submit manuscripts on them. You'll also use them to exchange work with collaborators and of course, to load programs into your computer. Have lots of them around the house: they're cheap and reusable. One of us has several disks that have been written on and erased thousands of times over a period of almost ten years, and they're still as good as new.

HARD DISKS

A hard disk (also known as a "fixed disk") is in essence a giant version of a floppy disk, although physically it's very different. A hard disk is sealed inside a computer (or inside an external housing); you never touch it.

Hard disks come in two varieties: as physical disks and as cards loaded with microchips inserted in a slot in your computer (these are known as "hard cards").

Either way, a hard disk offers the advantage of being able to store anywhere from 5 to 250 times as much information as a single floppy disk can hold. This means you can store the literal equivalent of 100 or more books without having to swap disks. You can keep your programs on a hard disk, too, and eliminate disk-swapping entirely. And disk access is far faster. All of which is a boon to those who have a lot of text files and programs: no more looking for the right disk before you can work.

You can organize a hard disk into "directories" (in effect, sub-disks) and thereby organize your work and programs into easily-accessible groups, just as though each directory were a separate disk within the machine.

(NOTE: While a hard disk eliminates the need to keep a lot of floppy disks on your desk, it doesn't eliminate the need for floppies completely. You should always make a backup copy of your work from hard to floppy disk, in case the hard disk "crashes" and all its data disappears utterly. Crashes do happen, unfortunately.)

HOW MANY DISK DRIVES YOU REALLY NEED—AND WHY

A minimum WP system configuration should consist of either two floppy disk drives, or else one floppy and one hard disk drive.

If you're using floppy disks only, you may think one is enough, but try telling that to your WP program. WP programs and their associated reference and configuration files (files in which a program stores information you give it on how to operate, which printer you use, and so forth) usually take up most of a disk—and the program and its associated files often *must* be in a disk drive 100% of the time. *Your* files can only get tucked into whatever corners are left, if you have only one floppy drive and your WP program disk has to be in it. It won't take long before you've used up all the available space on the program disk and be faced with a decision rivaling that of King Solomon, the one involving two mothers claiming one child. You'll either have to abandon the document you're currently creating or delete another document from the disk to make more space.

Of course, there are ways to deal with this. You can spend a lot of time copying finished files to other disks and copying them back to the program disk whenever you want to edit or print one of them. Or you can use some of the tips in Chapter 6.

But one of the reasons you switched to word processing is the ease it brings to writing, so why make things hard on yourself? For an extra $100.00 or less, you can at least add a second floppy drive to almost any system—and that investment will pay for itself many times over, just in saved time and unbitten fingernails.

Even if your WP program doesn't require that you keep its disk in a drive to be able to use it, you'll still find an extra drive convenient for accessing disks and moving data from one disk to another. Having more than one drive will also facilitate making backup copies and formatting fresh disks. (Try copying an entire disk's contents with one drive, and you'll know how to get exceedingly sick of messages like "Insert source disk," "Insert destination disk," "Insert source disk," *ad absolutely nauseum.*) Finally, should your lone floppy drive conk out, you'll learn why one of us has *both* a hard drive and *two* floppy drives and can continue getting files into and out of the system even with one floppy drive down. Belt *and* suspenders time.

A computer system with a hard disk requires that you have at least one floppy disk as well, for the simple reason that you have to have a way for your machine to transfer information and programs to the hard disk to begin with. (As just mentioned, some of us feel safer with *two*.)

PRINTERS

The final element (literally and figuratively) in a WP system is the printer. A printer creates manuscripts—the only part of your WP system that most people see. For this reason, we've devoted an entire chapter to printers (Chapter 4). We refer you to that chapter for a detailed discussion of printer features, operation and other considerations.

WHAT'S A K, AND HOW MUCH IS ENOUGH?

No discussion of computing on any level would be complete without that much-bandied-about term, "K." You've read it in spec sheets, and you've heard computer owners and salespersons brag about it, but what is it?

Aside from being a buzzword used to dazzle the uninitiated, "K" is short for "kilobyte," which in turn is a measure of computer memory or disk space or file size. One kilobyte is equal to 1024 bytes, and a byte is one letter, number, space, or control character. Thus, a document with 1024 letters, numbers, spaces, and printer or display control characters would be 1K in size (about 15 lines of text).

How much "K" is enough? Well, at the absolute minimum you should have 128K of computer memory (or RAM, which is an acronym for "Random Access Memory"). That's enough for a long story or book chapter, with enough left over to accommodate your WP program and operating system. Anything less, and you're going to run out of space a lot. Many WP programs require more than this (at least 256K), and 512K is even better. Computers with 640K are also available, but cost more.

Many computers still come with either 64K or 128K of RAM as standard, although the price of more powerful machines has dropped drastically in the last few years and even 512 or 640K machines cost about the same as a decent electronic business typewriter. If you got stuck with a computer that's really a video game with pretensions, you may be able to add on extra memory to bring it to a respectable figure. But it's better to go for the top figure to begin with. Maximum system (RAM) memory still is stuck at 640K, except for the newest OS/2 systems, which promise to explode the existing RAM limit.

Hard drives are a different matter, though. Hard drive capacity is measured in megabytes (a *million* bytes) rather than kilobytes and is *storage* capacity rather than system memory: like a mobile home with a three-story attic.

Good sizes for hard drives begin at 20 megabytes and go up toward the stratosphere from there. We find 20 megabytes perfectly adequate: one of us has the complete text of 6 novels, 2 nonfiction books, and innumerable ledgers, correspondence files, program files, interactive games, etc. stored on a 20 megabyte hard disk and still hasn't used up half the total capacity.

If you opt for a larger hard drive, remember that you're going to need to copy its contents to backup floppy disks on a regular basis for safety's sake. The larger the hard disk, the longer the backup takes. It could mean the difference between a 10-minute backup and one that drags on half an hour or more, even with special hard disk backup software. If longer backups mean, in practice, less frequent backups, you're running increased risk of losing everything stored on your monster hard disk. Weigh the advantages and the practicalities, then decide for yourself how much K is enough.

OPTIONAL HARDWARE ELEMENTS

Additional hardware elements (aka peripherals) that you may want or need to add to your computer-based WP system include a mouse or track ball, graphics card, printer interface card, and modem.

MOUSE

A mouse is a cursor-movement and command device. It consists of a small box with a roller on the bottom and one to three buttons on the top, attached to the computer by a thin cable (the mouse's "tail"). When you move the mouse around a desktop, the roller moves and the cursor moves correspondingly around the screen. The buttons are used in lieu of the RETURN key or control keys to select items from a menu, mark blocks, and perform other functions as dictated by the program in use.

Mice were first introduced to personal computing via Apple's Lisa computer and found wide acceptance in the Macintosh. They've since become available for the IBM PC and other computers.

Using a mouse requires about one square foot of clear desk space and some eye-hand coordination on your part. If you're already using a computer, you may well find using a mouse difficult, because your natural typing reflexes will have to be overcome and because you'll have to remove your fingers from the keyboard to issue commands.

An alternative to a mouse is a "track ball": basically an upside-down mouse, consisting of a ball mounted in a keyboard with approximately one-third of its surface visible. The ball is rotated to move the cursor in the same manner as rolling a mouse moves the cursor.

While some writers (usually those whose first computer was a Macintosh) are in love with using a mouse, most find a mouse rather disconcerting, and it's certainly not a vital peripheral for a writer.

GRAPHICS CARD

In discussing monitors, we referred to graphics cards as a necessary element in displaying formatting such as italics and underlining literally. Such cards are standard on higher-priced computers, but must be added (at extra cost) to lower-priced computers if literal display is a priority.

PRINTER INTERFACE CARD

Before you buy a computer, make sure it has a printer interface card (this should, normally, be what is called a "parallel interface"). See Chapter 4 for more information on these cards.

MODEM

A modem is a device used to send and receive computer data via telephone lines. Today's changing marketplace is moving more and more in the direction of manuscript submissions by modem, about which we'll have more to say in Chapters 5 and 11.

WHICH COMPUTER? STANDARDS AND OTHER CONSIDERATIONS

What with the constantly changing landscape of computer products, we can't recommend a specific brand or type of personal computer over any other for word processing. However, some important considerations can (and should) influence your selection.

MANUSCRIPTS ON DISK: WHICH COMPUTER AND WHICH FORMAT?

Like other businesses, publishers are moving more and more to computerizing operations. This, plus the fact that manuscripts can now be typeset directly from disk, is having a profound effect on the publishing process from the writer's viewpoint. While you must still submit manuscripts in hard-copy (printed out) form, many publishers request or require manuscripts on disk, as well—especially book-length manuscripts.

The question naturally arises as to whether you will have the "right" kind of computer to submit disk files from your computer when requested. (As we pointed out earlier, different brands of computers are incompatible in terms of being able to read one another's disks.) And, you may ask, what is the right brand? What is the standard among publishers?

The answer to all of those questions is "mostly MS-DOS." (This means a computer that uses MS-DOS—an IBM PC or a clone.) IBM started out to capture the business market for personal computers in the early 1980s, and indeed they have. Publishers and typesetters alike are IBM-oriented. However, because of the popularity of Apple Macintoshes among business users, many publishers and typesetters now use them too. (Macintoshes run "Apple" DOS.) As far as other brands are concerned, you're pretty much out in the cold.

But you needn't rush out and buy an IBM PC, clone, or Macintosh for this reason only. It's possible to get the contents of, say, an Atari ST disk transferred to an IBM disk. It's not free, but it can be done. Commercial disk-translation services are available in most larger cities: check your Yellow Pages. And if you have a modem and a friend with both a modem and a computer of the type you need your manuscript transferred to, you can do the transfer yourself (as explained in Chapter 5).

Too, a few computers, like the Atari ST, can read the contents of an IBM disk or write to an IBM disk with a simple program change. And there are disk drives and controllers for many popular computers that let you create files in IBM format on a disk that an IBM (or clone) computer can read.

Finally, in an attempt to get some control over the ambient confusion, many *publishers* are equipping themselves to translate non-MS-DOS files and acquiring modems for phone-transmission of at least accepted manuscripts, if not submissions. Things should sort themselves to something more workable, in terms of non-compatible formats, as the months and years pass. If your computer is the basic Brand X, a modem and associated software may be all you'll need to survive the transitional period and still deliver your manuscripts on time and in an acceptable form.

SOFTWARE AVAILABLE

The type of computer you use dictates the types and brands of WP software you can run, which in turn partially dictate the features available to you. But the features available with a particular IBM WP program, for example, can often be found in software for Commodore, Apple, and other brands of computers. Too, you'll find that some software publishers provide the same program for different kind of computers (WordPerfect and Word for the IBM PC and the Macintosh, WordStar for IBM PC and CP/M computers, etc.). So you don't necessarily have to buy a certain computer to get specific features; you can probably find all the features you want in a program for any computer if you look at enough software packages (more on that in the next chapter).

You should take note that the largest variety of software is available for the major computer brands: the Apple II series, the Atari ST, the Commodore Amiga, IBM PC and clones, and Macintosh.

MANUFACTURER REPUTATION, WARRANTY, AND SERVICE

The reputation of a manufacturer is important in buying a computer system, particularly since some manufacturers appear only to disappear with alarming speed. Apple, Atari, Commodore, and IBM aren't likely to disappear anytime soon, but smaller manufacturers—especially those who make clones—come and go. So you want to select a computer brand with some assurance that the manufacturer is going to be around as a source of information, service, and upgrades. There are no guarantees; but if a computer brand existed two years ago, chances are better it will still be around two years hence.

Although computer failure is relatively rare, it's still nice to have a warranty. It's even nicer to have service available—warranty or no. Service is not usually provided by the factory, but by dealers and authorized service centers. It's rare to find service for one of the computers that aren't among the major brands listed two paragraphs back, by the way—a very important consideration, indeed.

BUYING A COMPUTER: TIPS

Throughout the process of evaluating computers, you should be gathering information on each from as many sources as possible. Read ads and reviews in computer magazines, question fellow writers about what they use, and visit computer stores for hands-on demonstrations. Write or call manufacturers for general information or even answers to specific questions. You can't have too much information.

The form below should help you in the evaluation process. Copy it if you don't want to write in this book. Write the brands of computers you're considering in the blocks at the top of the chart and check off each feature below.

Table 1.1 Computer Selection Chart

Computer brand and model						
FEATURES	How much RAM?					
	Dual floppy disk drives?					
	Hard disk?					
	Monitor type and color					
	Keyboard quality					
	Software availability					
	Serial and/or parallel cards included?					
	Peripherals included? (mouse, etc.)					
	Graphics capability?					
	Local service?					
	Manufacturer support?					
	Warranty?					

Eventually, you'll have a list of specific brands and models that provide exactly what you need. Then it's time to make the final choice—and decide where to buy it.

COMPUTER SOURCES

You have several choices in buying a computer: computer stores, discount stores, and mail-order houses. (And you don't have to buy all the components of your computer system from the same source, although doing so may or may not save you some money; single-sourcing, however, *will* simplify a service contract, if you get one.)

COMPUTER STORES

The first place you thought of looking when you decided to buy a computer was probably a national computer store chain. We don't want to alienate anyone, but we do have to say that such chain stores aren't really oriented to the needs of the individual computer user. They typically charge full retail price (or higher!) and—perverse as it seems—their salespeople often know less about how a computer works than you do at this point. Such stores are geared more toward high-volume, high-price sales of complete computer systems (hardware, software, and maintenance packages—and maybe training) to corporate and small-business customers. So it's unlikely that you'll find much technical help at such stores (like car dealers, they push specific makes and models), and it's even less likely that you'll get a price break.

(NOTE: We've not named names here for the reason that not all national chains are like this. And we'd like to cite one overall exception to this trend: Tandy. Without getting into an unpaid ad here, it's worth mentioning that almost all Tandy stores have personnel on hand who are very familiar with their computer products and how to use them, and who generally will not try to sell you on a "package"

you don't need. Of course, they sell only Tandy computers . . .)

Independent computer stores, on the other hand, tend to be more inclined to meet the needs of the individual, which means they'll not only be excellent sources of advice on what to buy, but also good resources on using the equipment. And the salespeople in many such stores are computer users first and salespeople second. Couple these facts with the prospect of being able to do some bargaining on price, and you'll probably find that an independent store suits your needs.

One caution, though: small, independent stores are more apt than large chains to vanish, leaving only an empty storefront. You needn't care . . . *unless* you had a service contract with that particular store. Although you can take your computer to another dealer for service, no other store will honor your service contract, unless *your* store was taken over by another, which *may* be persuaded to transfer your contract. Check on how long *your* store's been in business: that will be a fair, if not absolute, indicator of how long it's apt to last. If you don't intend to buy a service contract, though, the whole question becomes moot.

DISCOUNT STORES AND MAILORDER HOUSES

Discount department stores such as K-Mart and Service Merchandise have become major outlets for computers and peripherals in recent years. You can save 25% or more on the list price of a computer at one of these stores, but be advised that you will receive little, if any, help in selecting or using the equipment you buy. If you want to buy a computer from a discount department store (or any other non-computer retailer, for that matter), be prepared to work out problems in its operation for yourself, or rely on long-distance telephone calls to the manufacturer. Discount department stores usually offer a warranty-exchange service, but make no provision for servicing equipment.

WRITERLY ALTERNATIVES TO PAYING RETAIL PRICE FOR HARDWARE

1. GROUP DISCOUNTS

Several national writers' organizations have group discounts with certain computer manufacturers and/or national retailers. If you're planning to buy a new WP system, it's worth the cost of joining an organization to be able to take advantage of such discounts. (And if you belong to a large writers' organization that doesn't offer members this kind of discount, press the officers to set up a discount program with a manufacturer or retailer. It costs the organization nothing.) In volume is power—and bargains.

2. LEASING

Leasing a computer is no different from leasing any piece of business equipment, be it a 10-ton delivery truck or a typewriter.

It works like this: You agree to pay a certain amount per month to lease the equipment and commit yourself to leasing the equipment for a set number of months or years (typically, three or four years). When the lease is up, you have (or should have) the option to buy the equipment at a "salvage" price, usually 25% or so of the original list price. Or you can renew the lease with new equipment.

You may have to come up with a deposit up front (a couple months' lease payments) and penalties may be involved if you turn in the equipment and terminate the lease agreement early.

Now, if you look at the lease cost of equipment, you'll see that X number of months times X dollars per month usually equals the cost of the equipment, or more. So where's the advantage?

Actually, the question should be "What are the advantages?" (plural), because there are several advantages to leasing. For openers, the equipment isn't yours (until/unless you buy it at the end of the lease term). This means that you're guaranteed working equipment—either on a "swap" basis or via a service contract that's figured into the cost of your lease.

Not owning the equipment also means that you're not stuck with disposing of it if you decide to upgrade at the end of your lease; just turn the hardware in and lease or buy newer and better equipment.

And there can be substantial tax advantages. Provided you can demonstrate the lease is a legitimate business expense, every lease payment is 100% deductible. In most cases this will be a more substantial deduction than is possible through depreciating equipment you buy outright.

Be warned, though, that in recent years, the IRS has taken a tough stand on computers as deductions. Restrictions on deductions for computers in home offices have become tighter. If the question ever arises, you'll be required to supply proof of business use of your computer—manuscripts sold or at least submitted, letters to and from editors, and

Mail-order houses offer computer equipment at wonderful prices and usually have someone on hand who can answer technical questions but, like discount department stores, offer no follow-up help. Too, you'll often find that getting warranty replacement or service through a mail-order house is a difficult proposition.

BUYING A USED COMPUTER

Buying used computer equipment is like buying any used piece of hardware or electronic gear. While you have no guarantee against there being something wrong "in-side," or a problem about to develop, you *can* determine the relative quality of the equipment.

The first element you should examine is cleanliness. A dirty computer housing can be indicative of careless use, and a paper dust-filled printer interior means that the owner hasn't bothered to keep the inner workings clean.

Worn spots around keys and disk drive doors are indications of heavy, extended use, as are a worn print head or worn-down letters on a printer.

See if you can persuade the seller to

all the other paperwork that would demonstrate you're a working writer, not a hobbyist. And the deduction will be applicable *only* against your income as a writer, not against income from any other source. So unless you're raking in an annual amount at least equal to the lease payments, it may well not be worth it to you to go this route.

With all that in mind, check with your friendly tax preparer on whether you can save money by leasing. If you can, seek out a firm that supplies leased equipment to small businesses. An established computer store ought to be able to suggest a name or two of such firms they've dealt with.

3. GETTING A COMPUTER FROM (OR THROUGH) YOUR PUBLISHER

It's not uncommon nowadays for writers to receive complete WP systems as full or partial payment on a book contract (the advance).

Now, before you get too excited, understand that the WP systems weren't *in addition* to a cash advance, but *part* (or all) of the advance. An author might receive a computer valued at $2,000 plus $2,000 cash to fulfill a contract that called for a $4,000 advance.

Why are publishers doing this? Well, it's to their advantage to put better working tools in the hands of someone they're paying to write a book. And if the publisher in question is one of the "biggies," it can actually save the publisher money—thanks to something called a "corporate discount." Consider: Enormous Publishing, Inc., is buying computers for all of its locations—several in Manhattan, branch offices in Chicago and Los Angeles, etc. In exchange for buying the same kind of computer for all its offices (a smart move), Enormous has a direct-buy deal with a volume retailer or a manufacturer. So Enormous can buy a $2,500 system for $1,500.

Along comes Will Writer, who'd love to have a WP system. Enormous signs him to write a book with a $7,500 advance, gives him a $2,500 WP system and $5,000 cash. But the computer cost Enormous only $1,500, so that $7,500 advance is actually only $6,500. (Incidentally, Will would have to pay income tax on the full value of a system obtained this way.)

The moral: If you're offered a WP system as complete or partial payment on a book advance, ask what the publisher actually pays for it and see if you can't take your advance completely in cash and then buy a system *through* the publisher, taking advantage of the large-business discount while getting your advance *in full*—in both cash and merchandise. The publisher may agree since it actually costs them nothing extra, wins your smiling goodwill, and is likely to produce a manuscript the publisher's typesetter can read directly from disk, saving typesetting costs. Such a deal still may be worth the publisher's while, and you again cash in on a volume discount that would otherwise be unavailable to you.

agree to a limited, handshake service contract: if you find anything wrong with the equipment within a specified period—between one and three months, say—the seller agrees to pay for the repair. It's virtually impossible to *enforce* an agreement like that, even if it's written on your bill-of-sale or receipt, but it can't hurt and it's better than no guarantee at all.

Computer equipment depreciates at variable rates, depending on the original manufacturer, whether new, upgraded models of the same equipment have been introduced, and other factors. While there have been some attempts at creating price guides to used computers (in the tradition of the price guides used by automobile dealers and banks in evaluating automobiles), there are no valid price lists for used computer equipment because the price is generally whatever someone is willing to pay. In general, however, the price of used computer equipment should be no more than half its original retail price, unless it's almost new (and the owner has a dated sales receipt to prove it).

Your best (and safest) source for a used computer is a friend who is upgrading to newer or better equipment (a friend whose word you can trust, that is).

TAKING CARE OF YOUR COMPUTER

Good computer care begins by selecting a good location. It should be in a location that avoids temperature extremes (don't, for example, place a computer near a window where it's likely to be exposed to strong sunlight; like all electronic equipment, computers operate better when they're not overheated). The computer should also be in a relatively dust- and moisture-free environment.

Other considerations in selecting a location include a solid supporting surface, and minimizing the chance of heavy objects falling on it (or small objects into it). You should not plug a computer into an outlet that's already being used by electrical equipment that uses a lot of power. (If you overload a circuit by plugging too many things into it, the result is low voltage, which can affect electronic components adversely.)

Computers require very little maintenance beyond keeping them clean. Clean the outside surface periodically with a mild cleaning solution. Use a small *plastic* vacuum cleaner attachment to clear dust and other debris from the keyboard and any vents.

CHAPTER 2

Word-Processing Software

OVERVIEW: THIS CHAPTER COVERS:

1. Software media; software on disk, in ROM, and other packaging.

2. Software operating modes; menu- vs. command-driven software, and hybrids.

3. Basic software features (the necessities).

4. Advanced software features: the bells and whistles—what you're most likely to want or need, and why.

5. How and where to buy a WP program.

IN FORM AND USE, WP SOFTWARE is no different from other types of software on disk; it may be written in any of a number of computer languages (the language in which a program is written normally doesn't matter for the user), and may be copyable for backup purposes (copy it *right away*: never use your originals if you can avoid it). Running a WP program involves the same basic commands and protocols as running any other type of program.

More likely than not, the WP software you buy will be provided on disk. But because software offerings vary from computer to computer, you may find that there's software available for your computer on cassette tape, in a plug-in "ROM pack" or microchip, or even built into your computer.

SOFTWARE ON DISK

Floppy disks—either 5-1/4", 3-1/2", or, in the case of some older computers, 8"—are the standard medium for desktop microcomputer software. Which size disk your software comes on depends on which size disk drive your computer has. Each has relative advantages and disadvantages, as discussed in Chapter 1.

(NOTE: Some WP software packages for the IBM PC and compatibles include both 5-1/4" and 3-1/2" disks, to accommodate users of either type. This is a plus, as you may well require a different disk size if and when you upgrade to a new computer or change one of your present two 5-1/4" drives for a 3-1/2" drive—a possibility you should not discount.)

SOFTWARE ON CASSETTE

Except for a very few low-end (and mainly old) computers and some laptop portables, software on cassette is almost extinct. This is mainly because cassette software takes a long time to load. Of course, if you don't have disk drives (because your computer doesn't accommodate them or because you

haven't bought any yet), you may have to find your WP software on cassette.

We recommend against cassette software—even if it means spending to add one or more disk drives (or, in the case of a laptop computer, buying software in ROM). A program on cassette can take up to ten minutes to load on some computers, and the reliability of cassette-based software (and file storage) is minimal at best.

DO IT YOURSELF: PLUG-IN ROM SOFTWARE

Software in ROM (Read-Only Memory, which can't be changed) is provided for a number of popular laptop computers, among them the Radio Shack Model 100 and its compatibles and successors. Such software comes in the form of a "chip" with appropriate programming, which is plugged into a designated socket inside the computer.

The major advantage of having WP software available within the computer is the fact that the software doesn't have to be loaded from a cassette or a disk—extra baggage that most owners of laptops *bought* their laptops to avoid carting around.

Installing such software usually requires you to open the computer's case, but the installation process isn't difficult for the minimally handy, and the chips usually come with easy-to-follow instructions. Or, of course, a computer store's service department can do it for you.

A very few desktop computers (like the Commodore 64) accommodate plug-in cartridges with software programmed in ROM in addition to software on disk. However, getting software on disk is less expensive and far more practical where desktop computers are concerned. Disk software also gives you a far wider range of choice than plug-in software.

"BUILT-IN" SOFTWARE

Built-in software can be found in portable

computers and some desktop computers. Like plug-in ROM software, built-in software is preprogrammed on a chip. The main difference between built-in software and plug-in ROM software is that built-in software is factory-installed.

The one overwhelming advantage of built-in software is this: it's designed to work perfectly with its host hardware.

Desktop computers with built-in software are extremely rare. As we said, floppy disks are by far the most common medium for desktop computer software. So it's unlikely that you'll find a desktop computer with built-in WP software.

A number of portable computers—especially laptop models—come with software already in ROM. Built-in software in a portable computer offers the same advantage as plug-in ROM software: loading it is fast and easy. However, if you find such software difficult to use or becoming outdated, you may well be stuck with it, depending on the kind of computer you're using. Remember, in Chapter 1 we warned you against dedicated WP systems: a computer with built-in WP software you can't easily switch or upgrade to take advantage of newly available features. We still say, steer clear.

MENU-DRIVEN VS. COMMAND-DRIVEN SOFTWARE

MENU-DRIVEN SOFTWARE

As you might expect, menu-driven WP programs require you to select commands from a menu or menus: a list of choices on the screen. A program may provide one menu containing all choices. Or it may use a main menu from which submenus are selected, in which case the actual commands are selected from the submenus. A variation on this allows you to bypass the main menu and select submenus directly.

Once you're familiar with a menu-driven

program's operation, watching the menus come up every time you want to issue a simple command (like marking a block of text) can get annoying. So you should be able to turn off the menus if you wish, and perhaps set varying levels of menus. (NOTE: Menus are sometimes referred to within a program's nomenclature as "Help," and settable menus as "Help levels.")

The main advantage of menu-driven software is its "user friendliness." You're offered a series of specific choices, and you choose whichever you want. So it's easy to get started with a menu-driven WP system. Its disadvantage is that it adds one or more extra steps in performing the actions the menus control (printing, for instance) and rouses impatience in experienced users who just want the action done without being obliged to stare at a menu and poke extra keys in order to set the action going.

COMMAND-DRIVEN SOFTWARE

Command-driven software displays no menus; rather, you issue commands in one of three ways. You can press a a designated "command key" (usually ESC or a control key) which switches what you type to a command or status line. (The command line is usually the absolute top or bottom line of the screen display, so it's not in your way.) The command line is normally visible during editing sessions, but with some WP programs can be turned off. The cursor moves from the display area of the screen to the command line when the designated command key is pressed, and commands can then be entered on the command line.

The second way to issue commands in command-driven software is to press a function key (on those computers that offer function keys).

A third way is to press a command key followed by a letter or letters which constitute a command. (The command key tells the program that the next letter is going to be a command.) In this setup, the commands are normally mnemonic. This means they consist of letters that are easy to relate to the command in question—"C" for "copy," for example. Thus, in a command-driven WP program using this type of command entry, you would press the command key and then "C" to copy a block of text.

The main advantage of command-driven WP programs is speed and maintaining a relatively "clean" screen, eliminating the need to switch from your onscreen document to one or more levels of menus to do what you want done. Their disadvantage is that they require you to memorize a more or less lengthy series of command key-letter(s) sets and don't "walk you through" your choices as simply as a menu can. Athough they're comparatively harder to get started with, command-driven WP programs are quicker and feel less cumbersome once the command-key combinations have become second nature to you.

HYBRIDS

A number of WP programs are both menu- and command-driven. Final Word II for the IBM and WordStar for IBM, CP/M and other systems are prime examples of this kind of software, which offers the option of entering a command directly or selecting it from a menu.

This is the most efficient setup for many users, as it allows you to quickly enter those commands you know and use often, while still permitting you to "look up" commands that you use less frequently. (This feature is obviously helpful when you're learning a program.)

MAJOR FEATURES

The first thing you should know about WP software features is that you won't be able to use some of them. Some (like using

twenty different type styles) depend on printer capabilities, while others (like color or WYSIWYG display) are useless unless your computer system supports them. Some require a minimum amount of system memory—364K, for instance. And some are designed to work only with MS-DOS rather than, for instance, Macintosh format (though most of the major WP programs sell versions for each—just be sure what you buy suits your computer).

Too, whether or not you use certain features and options depends on what you want to do and what you find comfortable and useful. Because of this, we haven't listed the features in any order of importance. The idea of this summary is to show you what each feature is, rather than to advise you on what to look for. On the other hand, some features, like the ability to delete, move, and copy blocks of text, are prerequisites to successful word processing. We'll discuss those necessities first.

Since we're trying to give you an overview here rather than dictating you buy this or that particular program, we've added, as Appendix A, a list of the top WP programs currently available. This list may help you narrow your search, but which one you'll prefer depends so much on your personal needs and taste that the choice *has* to be yours. All good WP programs offer certain basic functions—block/move, save, search, etc.—yet each differs from the others by a little or a lot. It's features you should be looking for—the features *you* want—rather than a given brand name that we or anybody else happens to recommend. Any of the listed programs will serve you well.

Finally, we haven't included every possible WP software feature, for several reasons. Some possible features are merely subsets of features discussed here, while others are too trivial or limited to discuss (and there are probably a few obscure features of which we're unaware for the same reasons). Others don't currently exist, but may be introduced after this book is published. For comprehensive information on a particular software package's features, refer to its user manual and, if you can, talk to somebody who has used it.

CURSOR MOVEMENT

How and where you can move the cursor is very important.

The "how" of cursor movement is pretty much dictated by the makeup of a computer's keyboard, and usually involves cursor-movement or control keys, as described in Chapter 1. However, different programs make use of keys in different ways, and you should pay attention to whether a WP program uses a cursor-movement key marked "Home" to move to the beginning of a document or the top of a page. What you prefer the keys to do is up to you, but make sure you know what a program does with each cursor-movement key—and that includes more than the compass-point East West North South arrows.

The "where" can vary greatly, but at a minimum you should be able to move the cursor, without scrolling the text on the screen, in the following ways:

•One character (letter or space) to the right or left.

•One word to the right or left.

•One line up or down.

•To the beginning of a line.

•To the end of a line.

•To the top of the screen.

•To the bottom of the screen.

•One screen forward or back. (Note that this means a screen's worth of text—usually 25 lines—not an actual printed-page's worth.)

•To the beginning of the document.

•To the end of the document.

Other standard cursor movements include scrolling the text one line up or down

while keeping the cursor fixed in one location (the cursor moves up and down the screen with the text), and keeping the cursor in one location (halfway down the screen, for instance), while lines of text scroll past.

More advanced WP programs offer these cursor-movement options (again, this is movement of the cursor without scrolling the text on the screen):

•One printed page forward or back.

•To a specified page number (as the pages would occur when the document is printed).

Ideally, all such cursor movements should be accomplished by pressing a single function key, cursor-movement key, or control-key combination.

INSERT/OVERWRITE MODE

You should be able to switch between an "insert mode" (in which letters to the right of the cursor are shoved along ahead of the cursor as you type new letters), and an "overwrite mode" (in which what you type replaces, or overwrites, existing text). (NOTE: We find it much easier to use the insert mode; apparently the rest of the world does, too, so most WP programs start up in insert mode.)

WORD WRAP

Word wrap is what happens when you reach the end of a line and the cursor, along with the word you're currently typing, jumps down to the next line without your having to press the ENTER/RETURN key. This is an absolute must in a WP program; even though you may be used to hitting RETURN at the end of every line on a typewriter, you'll find that it's an easy habit to break, and your typing speed and concentration are greatly improved when you're not constantly on the watch for the end of a line. Most current WP programs offer word wrap automatically, but it can't hurt to check before you buy.

FORMATTING FEATURES

Because every manuscript is different (and because you create documents other than manuscripts), you'll need the capability to change margins, line-spacing, and other formatting elements. Look for these basic formatting capabilities in a WP program:

•Variable margins and line-spacing—even within a document.

•Underlining and boldfacing.

•Centering.

•"Hanging indents." This feature allows you to reset the left margin on a paragraph-by-paragraph basis, so the first line of a paragraph starts at the left margin and the remaining lines are indented.

•Running headers, footers, and page numbers (discussed in detail over the next few pages).

•Variable tabs. Tabs composed of spaces should be settable—just as on a typewriter. If you're using "true" tabs (technically, a single "tab" character, as opposed to a certain number of spaces), you should be able to specify the number of spaces to be used for the tab. And you should be able to switch between space tabs and true tabs.

Other formatting elements offered by WP programs include right-justification, flush right and flush left text alignment, and automatic hyphenation (not really useful unless you must produce a right-justified manuscript, and we recommend against that unless for some odd reason it's mandated). You may also find handy the ability to insert non-printing comments (notes to yourself that appear in the document onscreen, but aren't printed). These are discussed in Chapter 10.

All such formatting elements should be saved with the document. Many, such as margins, can be preset to the same value each time.

Formatting entry should be via function key or simple commands.

SCREEN-EDITING VERSUS LINE-EDITING

Don't buy a WP program that is billed as a "line editor!" A line editor is an extremely cumbersome approach to word processing that allows you to work on only one line at a time. Each line is numbered, and, although several lines are displayed on the screen at a time, you have to use complicated commands to move from one line to another, add or delete text, etc. Imagine word processing as it might be portrayed in "The Flintstones," and you'll have a good idea of what a line editor is like.

There are fewer and fewer of these lurking on the market every year, but they *are* out there. So make sure the program you select is a "full-screen" editor that lets you move easily around your onscreen text.

ONSCREEN DISPLAY

What is displayed on your computer's screen is as important as how it's displayed (which topic we'll get to in a couple of pages). You naturally want to see as much as possible of the text you're working on, in both directions; there are, therefore, certain minimum requirements involving the number and width of lines displayed.

It's also important to see certain information about the document onscreen. Among other things, you often need to know exactly where you are in the document (which page number, etc.).

THE LONG AND THE SHORT OF IT: LINES PER SCREEN

A WP program should display a minimum of 22 lines of text on your computer's screen. Anything less and you're going to feel really cramped, once you're used to a program. A display of 22 lines allows for a status or command line at the bottom of the screen and a "ruler line" (which marks margins and tab locations) at the top of the screen, if the program uses one. It's helpful to be able to "turn off" the ruler or status/command line, too. (NOTE: The screen may display fewer lines if the program offers optional menus—and you should be able to turn those menus off. Menus are like training wheels: You won't need them forever, and once you're proficient at using a program, they get in the way.)

The maximum display for standard monitors is 25 lines. To get more lines, you'll have to buy a special monitor (see Chapter 1) or use a program designed to squeeze more onto the standard screen by displaying very tiny letters (not recommended, for the sake of your eyes).

SCREEN WIDTH

Screen width is sometimes limited by the computer in use, but the standard is 80 columns (letters) of text. Avoid computers—and programs—that display fewer than 80 columns.

INFORMATION PLEASE

Because you can't immediately look at an entire document (or, usually, an entire printed page) while you're writing or editing a document, information on its status is important. Such information comes in several forms. At a minimum, a WP program should keep you informed of the page, line, and column number of the cursor. Many programs also let you know whether you're in insert or overwrite mode, the current line-spacing setting, whether or not your caps lock key is down, and perhaps how much disk space is left. All such information is provided on a status line or by a running tally at the top or bottom of the screen. It's nice if the display of such information can be turned off, to have a completely "clean" screen, but most programs don't offer this feature.

WYSIWYG (WHAT YOU SEE IS WHAT YOU GET) DISPLAY

"WYSIWYG," (also called "virtual" or "literal") display is increasingly affordable and therefore nearly a must.

At the very least, a document should be displayed with the literal margins and line-spacing you specify. Centering, paragraph indents, and hanging indents should also be displayed literally.

Other formatting elements may be marked by control characters (such as $^\wedge$S for underline and $^\wedge$B for boldface), or displayed as shaded, highlighted, or in color.

True WYSIWYG—at present highly dependent upon special hardware but becoming more common—displays underline and boldfacing literally, using a computer's graphics capability.

A WP program should display any literal elements as you create a document, rather than requiring you to go into a "preview" mode to view your manuscript in its finished format on its screen. Optionally, literal formatting may be turned off, to enable you more easily to locate and/or change formatting marks that are otherwise invisible.

BLOCK OPERATIONS

Block operations are, as the name implies, operations that involve blocks of text. Special markers are used to mark segments of text in what are called "blocks" (or, sometimes, "marked text"). Lest you get the wrong idea, we hasten to add that a block of text isn't necessarily a rectangular or square section of your document. A block can be a single letter, a sentence or portion thereof, a paragraph, a page, or even the entire document.

How a block is marked varies from one WP program to another, but the job is usually done by moving the cursor to the beginning of the section of text you want to mark, pressing a designated key or control-key combination, then moving the cursor to the end of the section and, in some cases, pressing another designated marker-key to indicate where the block ends. Most programs color or highlight a block to set it off from the surrounding text.

What you can do once you've marked a

block is nothing short of incredible. You can delete a block, move it from one location to another within the manuscript (instant "cut and paste"), copy it within a manuscript, print it, or even make a separate file out of it (saving or "writing" a block).

And those are just the basics—any WP program you consider should offer those block operations *and* allow you to recover a deleted block of text.

More sophisticated block operations offered by certain WP programs include the ability to spell-check a block of text, move a block between two documents (if you have windowing capability), and move or copy blocks as columns or rectangles. Yet another option you may encounter is the capability to change the case of all the words in a block to all lower-case, all caps, or initial caps. Some programs, like XyWrite, provide function-key assignments (macros) that mark the current line, sentence, paragraph, or page, so you don't have to zero in on the exact beginning and ending of your block to mark it. We'll discuss ways of using the block/move function in Chapter 10.

FILE MERGE/WRITE

File merge and write capability go hand-in-hand with block operations. We've already mentioned file writing, which is nothing more than marking a block of text, then telling your WP program to save it on disk as a new file. This is useful when you decide that a paragraph in the document you're currently working on ought to go in another document—say, in Chapter 9 rather than Chapter 7. Mark the paragraph, tell the WP program to save it on disk under an appropriate file name ("ADD.9", perhaps), then delete the block from your screen.

Calling one file into another is the opposite of writing a block to disk. It allows you to call a file from disk into the current onscreen document. The file in question—whether it's a paragraph or thirty pages—is brought into the document you're editing at the present cursor position, pushing the text that already exists "below" the cursor down into new pages.

(NOTE: Some programs call this process either "reading" or "merging" one document into another. It may also be called "importing" a file. We won't use "reading" because we want to avoid confusion with the common meaning—using your eyes—and won't call it "merging" hereafter since *merge* is also a specialized term for creating two files—for instance a letter and a list of names, address, etc.—which *automatically* combine when a special merge command is given. More on this in Chapter 8.)

This process can be illustrated using our hypothetical example from the first paragraph under this heading. Say you've saved Chapter 7 and moved on to Chapter 9. You remember that you wanted to put that paragraph you removed from Chapter 7 (and then saved) into Chapter 9. Move through the document to the spot where you want to add the paragraph, issue the appropriate command to tell your WP program to retrieve, from disk, the file "ADD.9" and zip, there it is. Saves a lot of retyping.

TEXT SEARCH AND SEARCH/REPLACE

Search and search/replace—also known as "find" and "find/replace"—are functions that enable you to quickly find any set of letters or string of words in a document and/or replace them with other letters or words.

Because the search function is at the core of all this, we'll discuss it first.

SEARCHING, SEARCHING

When activated, a WP program's search function asks you to enter what is called a "search string" at a prompt. This may be one letter or other character, or—with some few programs—up to eighty letters or characters. After you enter the search string, the WP program prompts you for search options, then moves the cursor to the first place in the text that the string occurs.

Software designers have thought up a variety of options for the search function. The desirable options are:

•Single-command search repeat. When you enter a search string, the WP program stores it anyway, so you should be able to "replay" the search with a single command, without having to re-enter the string to be found.

•Specifying that the program find only incidences of the search string that exactly match what you entered with respect to capitalization, or that the program find *all* incidences of the string regardless of capitalization of individual letters. This can save you time if you want to find a word like "the," which may begin a sentence or occur in the middle of a sentence. At the other end of things, it can save time when you need to find only those occurrences of a word that are capitalized.

•Searching backwards. If you don't have this feature, you'll have to move to the beginning of the document every time you want to find a word.

•Finding whole words only. This avoids sitting through long search sessions while the program finds and shows you words that contain the string you're seeking. For instance, finding "return" when you were searching for "turn."

Additional search-function options include specifying that the program find the "nth" (2nd, 3rd, 4th, or other) occurrence of the search string, rather than the first; that it go to the beginning (or end) of the file on its own and search for the specified string from there (a macro can supply this function, if it's not built in: more on macros in Chapter 9); and specifying control-characters as a search string or portion of a search string (this is a necessary feature if your WP program inserts control characters as printing format marks, as will be explained in Chapter 4; for instance, it should be able to find where you changed margins or tabs).

As indicated earlier, you'll find that the possible length of a search string varies from one program to another. Longer search strings are generally better, as the more characters you can enter as a search string, the more likely you are to find exactly the phrase or sentence you're seeking.

Note that almost all WP programs are limited in searching in that they cannot "see" a search string unless it's all on the same line. Thus, while a search will find the string "jumped over the lazy" in this line:

The quick brown fox jumped over the lazy brown dog.

It can't find that string in these lines:

The quick brown fox jumped
over the lazy brown dog.

But if you just specified "lazy" as your search string, both would have been found. Sometimes short strings are better, although it's nice to be able to enter a long string if you want to.

"OUT WITH THE OLD AND IN WITH THE NEW!"

Search/replace is a logical extension of the search function. When a search/replace command is given, the program not only finds the search string, but replaces each instance of it with a string you specify.

A search/replace operation begins with you entering a search string ("to be replaced"), after which you are prompted for the string to replace the search string. Then you're prompted for options.

Search/replace options include the same options provided for the search function alone, as well as these:

•Global search/replace. This tells the program to find and replace every incidence of the search string.

•Confirm. This tells the program to ask before it makes a replacement, whether you're doing a search/replace on a one-time or global basis.

A few WP programs will let you reverse the search/replace with a single command, undoing the replacement and ending exactly as you begin.

AUTOMATIC PAGE HEADERS, NUMBERING, AND FOOTERS
GETTING AHEAD OF THE GAME

As you know, each page of a manuscript intended for submission must include a header. This consists of the title (or a keyword therefrom), your last name, and the page number, all on one line at the top of each page. Virtually all WP programs will print a header like this, automatically on each page, along with the proper page number. You only have to enter the header once, and the program takes care of things from there.

There are two ways a header can be entered. The first—and best—way is to enter it as a part of the document, preceded by special control characters, dot commands, or other characters to identify it as a header. This kind of header is entered just once, at the very beginning of the document, and is saved with the document, but will appear on every page (except those where you cancel it) when the document is printed.

The second way is to specify the header at print time, when you enter other printing instructions. This is inconvenient because you have to enter the header each time you print out the manuscript. Fortunately, this technique is used by only a very few programs.

A few programs—like ScreenWriter II for the Apple II series—allow you to create headers either way. And there are some programs that require you to select a menu item to add a header.

Most WP programs that offer headers also offer the option of "footers" which give a specific line of text and/or page number at the bottom of each page: the same as a header, only lower. Writers aren't apt to need this feature much, but if you want headers, footers tend to come as an alternative form of this function.

BY THE NUMBERS

Page numbers are an obviously vital manuscript element, and we know of no commercial WP program that doesn't provide them automatically, on request. However, some programs don't allow you to put page numbers where you want them. Some insist the numbers be printed centered at the top or bottom of each page, which gives you a nonstandard manuscript format; stay away from these.

THE GAME'S AFOOT!

The need for footnotes is rare, except among those who write for scholarly or technical journals. But when you need this capability, you *need* it. If you use footnotes, make sure your WP program allows you to create footnotes of whatever length necessary—and to make the line-spacing different from that of the main body of the manuscript, if necessary. Some WP programs give you the option of printing your footnotes either at the bottom of the page or at the end of a section—a chapter, for instance. Some will automatically renumber all succeeding footnotes if one is added or deleted. Considering how tedious footnotes can be, if you're obliged to use them in your writing give yourself the maximum possible simplicity and freedom in creating, editing, and managing them.

WINDOWS

Windows are extra screens in the sense that they allow you to view and/or edit more than one document at a time. Some windows overlay one document with another, via a split screen, while others allow you to flip from one screen to another, like turning the pages of a book. Some WP programs allow you to edit only one document and view others, while other programs allow you to edit as many documents as there are windows and to copy or move text between documents.

Windows are especially useful when you're working on books, as you'll frequently find yourself needing to view and edit more than one chapter at a time. (See Chapter 3 for more information on windows.)

MACROS

The ability to generate macros is a very popular WP software feature. These are discussed in more detail in Chapters 3 and 9, but, in brief, a macro is a "recording" of a command, series of commands, or string of text that you can call up with one or two keystrokes or by "invoking" it by name. Macros eliminate the tediousness of having to enter frequently-used commands or phrases, as well as the chance of mistakes in entering them. They can also allow you to self-program, in effect, certain capacities your WP system lacks. For instance, if your present WP program will search but not replace, you could construct a macro that *would.*

Depending on the program, macros may be stored permanently on a work disk or temporarily stored in your computer's memory (to disappear when you exit the WP program or turn off your computer). Either way, a macro may be used as many times as you find it handy.

This isn't an absolutely vital feature *for your WP program*, because supplementary macro-generating software is available for almost every kind of computer, but macros created by a WP program are easiest to use with that program.

SIMULTANEOUS PRINTING AND EDITING, AND PRINT SPOOLING

The ability of a WP program to read and

send a file to a printer while letting you continue to work on screen can be very important. There's nothing more frustrating for a productive writer than having to wait for a file to print, and few things more satisfying than having the printer print one manuscript while working on another.

Some programs accommodate simultaneous editing and printing, and some don't. Those that do accommodate it either handle the job by accessing the file being printed while you're working (bad, because it slows down the response time of the editing portion of the program) or by creating a special area in your computer's memory in which it stores the file to be printed so that it can be accessed in such a manner that you are not interrupted. The latter method, called "print spooling," is more desirable.

For programs that don't do print spooling or don't accommodate simultaneous printing and editing at all, there are software and hardware solutions. These are discussed in Chapters 3 and 4, respectively.

OPERATING SYSTEM AND DISK ACCESS

Although you may not think you'll need operating system commands, there will come a time when you have to erase a file from your work disk to make room for saving a document you're editing, or copy a file from one disk to another without leaving your WP program. These and other commands and disk operations are often convenient and sometimes vital. So make sure your WP program allows you to at least erase and move files while you're editing.

DOCUMENTATION

As you may already know, software user manuals are something of a joke among those in the computer industry. Unfortunately, the joke is a cruel one for unsophisticated computer users. All too often, you have to be a real "hacker" to figure out a program's operation—especially if it's what the Banks half of this writing team refers to as "user-belligerent" software. Poorly-planned and -written manuals abound and can be found among even the best WP programs.

The main reason is that software user manuals are typically written by people who are computer whizzes first and writers last . . . or not writers at all. To be fair, a number of software publishers have begun to take the problem seriously and are striving mightily (with the help of real writers) to produce manuals that actually teach the user something. However, the sheer complexity of many programs makes creating an effective user manual for them an imposing, if not impossible, task—as evinced by the large number of guidebooks available for various specific WP programs. (Many of those, unfortunately, are written by computer whizzes too.)

If you're set on a particular program because it has the features you want, and that program has poor documentation, you'll have to take what you get and maybe buy a $25.00 book about the program. But if you have several programs in mind, look for these features in the documentation:

•A good index. (Read: "A *large* index." The more entries, the better!)

•A "quick start" section or manual.

•A step-by-step tutorial, heavily illustrated, that *shows* you how to use every function and feature of the program.

•An alphabetical reference to functions and commands that contains detailed explanations, with examples.

•A quick-reference section or tear-out card that lists commands by category or alphabetically by function.

SELECTING WORD-PROCESSING SOFTWARE

You should by now have a good idea of which features your WP software should offer. But features are not the only elements to consider in selecting a WP program. Computer compatibility, compatibility with peripherals, software compatibility, price, technical support, and warranty also figure in the equation.

COMPUTER COMPATIBILITY

We can't overstress the need to assure compatibility between your computer hardware and the WP software you select. Because most dealers won't allow you to take a software package home for a test drive, it's important to investigate a program completely before you buy it. Find out how the software will operate with your printer and with any special elements of your computer hardware. Ask detailed questions or, better still, ask to try out the software with a computer like yours in the store. If a given dealer doesn't have a computer like yours, go to one who *does* and deal with that one.

COMPATIBILITY WITH PERIPHERALS

If you plan to use a hard disk or an extended memory card with your WP software, make sure the software you're evaluating will accommodate such hardware.

With reference to hard disks and memory cards in particular, you should stay away from copy-protected software. Copy-protection schemes quite often require that the original program disk be accessed while the program is running, and this can't happen if you're trying to run the program from a hard disk or RAMdisk (discussed in Chapter 3).

If you're using a "clone" of a popular computer brand (a Kaypro PC in place of an IBM PC, or a Franklin clone of an Apple), make sure that the program in question will operate with that computer.

SOFTWARE COMPATIBILITY

That's right—*software* compatibility. As

you'll learn later in this book, you may have occasion to use what are known as *memory-resident* programs concurrently with a WP program. (These are also called RAM-resident, or TSR—terminate-and-stay-resident—programs.) Or maybe you already use one or more memory-resident programs, like Borland's Sidekick. (Such programs supply onscreen notepads, calculators, *et al.*) You certainly won't want to give up the convenience that these programs offer.

Either way, you'll have to do some research to determine the feasibility of using WP software with such programs. First, find out how much memory the WP program requires. If it's more than is usually left after you load your memory-resident programs, you're either going to have to give up some memory-resident software, or look for another WP program, or buy more memory for your computer.

Next, try to find out whether the memory-resident program's operation will interfere with the operation of the WP program you're considering. This is a little more difficult—sometimes it involves *which* keys do *what*, in the WP program and the memory resident program—and you may end up just taking what you can get and hoping for the best. But do check with your computer dealer and friends who use the programs, as well as the publishers of the software involved. No matter how strange a software combination you're considering, chances are someone else has tried it. If you're lucky, one of the above sources will have the information you need.

PAYING THE PRICE

Software pricing is quite a bone of contention, and something we could discuss for a good many pages, so we'll avoid editorializing here and discuss sources *vis a vis* price. Where are the bargains? Are the bargains risky?

If you've seen ads in computer magazines and mass mailings for discount-priced software, you know it's possible to save 50% or more on the price of some software packages. So why go to a walk-in store and pay more (or even full retail)? After all, the software publisher's warranty is the same no matter where you buy the software.

Well, for openers, if you deal with a P.O. box or a WATS number, you may not have anyone to go back to if there's a problem with your software, or if you just need some coaching to get started. A computer store, on the other hand, usually has someone on its staff who knows how to use the software—someone who can help you *after* you've taken the software home. And there's always the possibility that you can try out the software in the store before you buy it. Finally, if you buy a computer *and* software from the same dealer, you may be able to get a nice package discount and still have the benefit of service after the sale.

PRODUCT SUPPORT

Product support on the part of a software publisher is not a requirement for a good software package, but it's a big plus! If you've ever had to learn to use a complex program of any kind, you'll appreciate the availability of product support.

Quite a few software publishers offer telephone customer support teams whose job it is to answer questions about their products (even "dumb" questions like, "How do I load the program?"). These customer support people are generally better informed about a particular program's operation (unlike computer retailers, they have to know only one product!) and can handle just about any software problem you might have. Many publishers charge for this service, though.

Be advised that public domain programs are not supported, beyond what you can learn from other users (or from their authors, who often include contact information with their documentation). "Shareware" program authors do provide support, but only if you become a registered user. This means paying a registration fee, but it's not a bad idea if you like the program; the more money a shareware author makes, the more likely he or she is to improve the program and to create new and equally useful software.

WARRANTIES

If you've ever read the legal agreement that accompanies a commercial software package, you know that software publishers spend more time explaining what their programs will *not* do than what they *will* do. Of course, nearly all programs do what their publishers claim they'll do, but the publishers want to be sure that you don't mistakenly think that a program will, say, make a better writer out of you.

The one thing that can—and should—be guaranteed is the software media. It sometimes happens that a disk is faulty, due to problems during manufacture or exposure to heat or magnetism during shipping or storage. As rare as such an occurrence is, you should be protected against it.

It's customary for a software publisher to replace a disk or other software medium if it won't load (read: work) when it comes out of the package. Further, most software publishers offer to replace a faulty disk for a period of 30 days after purchase. Many, unfortunately, charge for disk replacement (a bit of piracy that is entirely unjustified when you consider software prices). Usually, however, if you get a bad disk, the dealer who sold you the program will replace it.

Beyond 30 (or 60) days, a fair guarantee is to replace faulty medium for a set period of time for a small percentage of the original purchase price. Unless the software is copy-protected, however, you shouldn't have to worry about this (you *do* make backups, don't you?).

Software publishers extend such warranty coverage *only* to registered users—which is why you should fill out and send in warranty registration cards.

UPDATES

Software publishers usually offer product updates when they bring out a new version of their software. The cost for such an update should be no more than half the original purchase price of the product. This, like warranties, will vary from one publisher to another. The important thing is that the publisher agree to make updates available to current users at some discount.

Updates are, of course, available only to registered users (which is yet another good reason for sending in the registration card that accompanies a commercial software package—or for paying the registration fee for a shareware package).

SOFTWARE COMPARISON SHOPPING

Comparison shopping is the easiest way to see how various software packages measure up to your needs. You'll find the software comparison chart provided here (Table 2.1) helpful in making comparisons. Write the names of the software packages you're considering in the blank row at the top of the chart, highlight the features in the left hand column that are of interest to you, and check off those features offered by each software package. (Make a copy of the chart if you'd rather not write in this book).

Table 2.1 Word-Processing Software Selection Chart

WP Program					
S Media?					
Menu- or command-driven?					
E Full cursor movement?					
Screen or line editor?					
R Word wrap?					
Insert/overwrite?					
Formatting commands?					
U Variable tabs?					
WYSIWYG display?					
T Page/line number status?					
80-column display?					
A Block operations?					
File merge and write?					
E Search/replace?					
Automatic headers, footers, and page numbers?					
F Macros?					

F E A T U R E S					
Windows?					
Print spooling?					
Operation system and disk access?					
Documentation quality?					
Computer compatibility?					
Peripheral compatibility?					
Software compatibility?					
Publisher support?					
Warranty?					
New version update?					

SOFTWARE SOURCES

Where you get your software will depend on whether it's commercial, public domain or shareware software. There are several sources for each type of software. Selecting a source involves weighing tradeoffs between price and product support.

COMMERCIAL SOFTWARE SOURCES

As we said, computer/software retail stores are the way to go if you want the convenience of local product support and don't mind paying full price. If you want to save money, you can go with a mail-order operation. Of course, you have *publisher* support no matter where you buy a software package (including from the publisher—which is usually going to cost you full retail price).

Local computer clubs or other organizations sometimes arrange for software discounts as a membership benefit. In this kind of deal, the software normally comes direct from the publisher.

PUBLIC DOMAIN AND SHAREWARE SOURCES

You won't find many retailers offering public domain or shareware because selling it doesn't offer the enormous profits of peddling commercial software. (Too, some shareware is distributed on the basis that it not be resold for profit.)

You can get PD software from your friends, a computer users' group, or from small mail-order operations that specialize in distributing PD software. PD distributors usually charge a nominal fee per disk (anywhere from two to five dollars), but may sometimes hit extremes of fifteen dollars or more.

If you have a modem, you can download PD software from an electronic bulletin board or online service.

Shareware is distributed via the same channels as PD software. In addition, the publishers of shareware will mail their products to you for varying fees. Some charge the full registration price for a program on disk, along with printed documentation. Others offer you the option of paying a nominal fee—ten dollars or so—to cover handling and mailing a disk, after which you may pay to become a registered user if you like the program. (Remember, registration has a number of benefits: you may receive a printed manual and you'll get program updates at a discount. You'll also be able to get answers to your questions about the program from the developer.)

CHAPTER 3

Extra Software & Utility Options

OVERVIEW: THIS CHAPTER COVERS:

1. RAMdisks: using an "imaginary" disk to speed up file access and program operation.

2. Spelling, grammar, and punctuation checkers.

3. "Online" thesauruses; programs that find alternate words for you when you're stuck for a meaning.

4. Windowing systems that let you run more than one program at a time or edit multiple documents.

5. Memory-resident programs that operate simultaneously with your WP software.

6. "Desktop accessory" software that puts important tools from your desk—notepads, calculators, and more—on your computer screen.

7. Printer-control software.

8. File-conversion software, for converting your program's output to something your editor can use on his/her computer.

9. Hard-disk utilities that can make your hard disk faster, more efficient, and prevent a lot of work and potential grief.

10. File-compression utilities to save disk space.

11. Keyboard-redfinition programs and macro programs, to change keyboards you don't like or say it all with one keystroke.

12. Other utilities to recover "trashed" files, change screen colors, and more.

THE UTILITY OF UTILITIES

STRICTLY SPEAKING, ALL YOU NEED for word processing is a good WP program. But what if you need to convert text from one WP program's format to another (*not*, notice, from one *computer* to another: that takes modems or special cables, software, and two computers) for delivery to a publisher? And what do you do when you have to look at a document other than the one you're editing? You'll be interested to know that there are a number of programs that can take care of these problems for you, as well as others that can enhance word processing in ways you may not have imagined.

Among other things, such programs (called utilities) can:

•Convert documents from one WP program's format to that of another.

•Reduce the size of files to save disk space.

•Check your spelling during writing or editing.

•Allow you to view and edit more than one file at a time and transfer text between files.

Some supplementary programs are merely useful enhancements to word processing while others (especially hard-disk utilities) are vital.

RAMDISKS

A RAMdisk, sometimes called a "virtual disk," is a temporary "imaginary" disk carved out of your computer's Random-Access Memory (RAM). It can be a very useful addition to your WP system software, especially if you intend to use an online spell-checker or thesaurus (which we'll discuss in a minute).

The major advantage of using a RAMdisk is speed. Reading files from a RAMdisk is faster because there's no mechanical disk head to direct and move. (Wear and tear on floppy and hard disk mechanisms is reduced, too.) This can be important when your computer has to search through a very large file (such as a spell-checker or thesaurus dictionary). If you have a lot of memory in your computer, you speed up the operation of programs by placing them on a RAMdisk, too.

For those who don't have a hard disk, a RAMdisk is a viable alternative since it provides a "third disk." A RAMdisk provides a place to temporarily store merge files or files that you must reference frequently without worrying whether your work or WP program disks will be filled up. However, because the RAMdisk vanishes when you turn off your computer, it absolutely shouldn't be used to store data or text files: they'd vanish along with it! But a RAMdisk is wonderful for running programs on. The program remains the same, on its disk, while its duplicate is running on your RAMdisk. When the RAMdisk vanishes, no data is lost.

RAMdisks can be created using special RAMdisk software—available commercially or as public domain or shareware. The necessary RAMdisk files also come built-in on MS-DOS. In either case, you install the program once, and thereafter a RAMdisk is created for you every time you boot up your computer using the disk with the RAMdisk program and *voila*, a third drive, of whatever size you define within the available RAM.

Note, though, that your computer really ought to be 364K or better to support a RAMdisk; with less memory, you'd be limited to a RAMdisk too small to use, or would be tying up so much of your system's memory in the RAMdisk that the remaining memory might not be able to carry on normal WP functions, like handling a big file or merging two middle-sized files.

SPELL-CHECKERS

Spell-checkers are a natural and vital element in word processing. They automate a portion of an important mechanical process—proofreading—and free the writer to concentrate even more on the creative process of writing.

A spell-checker operates by scanning words in a document, comparing them with a "dictionary" file, and displaying, marking or changing misspelled words. Depending on the program used, the spell-check can be done on command while you're editing a document or externally after the file is saved. (A few spell-checking programs, such as Borland's Turbo Lightning for MS-DOS computers, will check each and every word as you type it, a feature that will definitely drive you crazy: the words *distraction* and *galloping paranoia* come to mind.) Some spell-checkers operate in an "online" mode, meaning the program is always available to check a word or a portion of a document on command. Others have to be run from the operating system rather than directly from the WP program.

Almost all WP programs include spell-checkers nowadays, so you probably won't be looking for a spell-checker as a separate program. However, if you don't like the spell-checker that comes with your WP program or have an older WP program that doesn't include one, here are some basic features you should look for in a spell-checker:

•The dictionary should be large. Forty thousand words may seem like a lot, but a good spell-checker needs a dictionary of at least 100,000 words (and 200,000 is better). To a dictionary, *you, you're, you'll, you'd* and *you've* are five different words; each tense and number (singular, plural) of a single verb is a separate word. You need a *big* dictionary.

•Provision should be made for you to add words—names, special nouns, etc.—to the dictionary and take others away—either singly, or as lists.

•The spell-checker should be compatible with your WP program (make *sure* of this). If you're in doubt, call the manufacturer of either the spell-checker or your WP software to confirm compatibility.

•The program should be interactive; it should not make corrections without asking you.

•Capitalization and punctuation (apostrophes, for instance) should be retained when replacements are made.

•Some sort of "preview" function should be available to allow you to look at and make a judgment about what the spell-checker thinks are misspelled words. Otherwise, you could spend half an hour or more wading through a fantasy story, okaying character names (or the same in a technical document, confirming esoteric terms that don't happen to be in the spell-checker's dictionary).

•You should have the option of letting individual occurrences of "misspelled" words pass while correcting others.

Other features offered by spell-checkers that may or may not interest you include catching incidences of double words, looking up individual words, optionally marking words so you can check them in context later, automatic reformatting when a replacement word changes a line's length, the ability to work with more than one WP program, and the capability to search for proper spellings based on how words sound when they are pronounced.

Some spell-checkers include lists of technical words (for instance, legal terms). Several software publishers sell separate auxiliary dictionaries that consist of lists of technical terms for various fields (medicine, chemical engineering, etc.). If you're using a lot of specialized language, you might want to check out whether an auxiliary dictionary might save you time and trouble.

Spell-checker dictionaries sometimes take up an entire disk. If you're working with a system that has two floppy disk drives and have your WP program in one disk drive and your work disk on another, you aren't going to have a place to put the dictionary. Thus, if you intend to use the spell-checker in online mode, you'll have to swap disks whenever

THE LIMITATIONS OF SPELL-CHECKERS

The chief problem with spell-checkers is that a misspelled word may, through the misspelling, have become another legitimate word that the spell-checker recognizes (after all, it's in its dictionary) and passes by without question. If you meant to type "word" and instead typed "work" or "ward," the spell-checker will think it's OK. And English being what it is, the change of a single crucial letter can turn dozens of words into dozens of others. Consider "though" and "through" or "want" and "went." Or think about *find*, *bind*, *kind* or *life*, *lift*, *left* and you'll begin to see the proportions of the problem. The spell-checker doesn't know what you meant to say; it only knows which of the words in your document doesn't match its word list.

Not only can the "wrong" word be ignored; a missing word can be ignored, too. There's a lot of difference between "The singing was a sensation" and "The singing dog was a sensation." And if what you wanted was the latter sentence, that difference could be important. But a spell-checker would pass either by without a beep. Although the better style-checkers (which we'll talk about in a minute) might note a sentence without a subject, not even a style-checker would have found anything to question in either sentence. Sometimes what you actually typed is not what you meant; and neither a style-checker nor a spell-checker can help you with that.

Finally, you can evade all protections by forcing your own bad spelling on the program. For instance, one of us was dead certain that the right spelling was *wierd* (based on the mnemonic—but, in this case, *wrong*—rule, *I before E except after C*). When the spell-checker questioned the word, the key got punched to tell the program, "That is too a real word!" on the assumption that the word simply wasn't in the dictionary. So the wrong spelling got added to the dictionary and went unquestioned thereafter for nearly a year. Weird.

Sure, you can remove wrongly-spelled words from your dictionary, but first you have to realize they're wrong. And if you told the spell-checker to regard them as correct to begin with, the chances of your noticing the wrong spelling later, with the spell-checker confirming it as correct, are vanishingly small. Therefore, don't add any dubious words to your dictionary unless you've checked them, that minute, in a decent dictionary. If you make a habit of doing that, you should be able to regard the spell-checker's confirmations as reliable.

Because of the limitations of spell-checkers, it's vital to do a hard-copy (read: printed out pages) readthrough after you're done checking over the document with any spell-checking and/or style-checking programs you use.

It also helps to overcome the limitations of spell-checkers to bypass them to check on known problems, using simple search/replace instead, confirming each replacement. For instance, one of us has a bad habit of typing "nothing" for "noting." Searching for all instances of "nothing" and replacing the wrong ones with "noting" takes care of the problem nicely.

We'll have more to say about proofreading your pages in Chapter 11, but for now, what's important is to realize that no checking program, invaluable though it may be, can substitute for the acuity of the human eye controlled by a writer's mind. Adding the stubborn persistence of a fanatical proofreader is also a good idea.

you want to use the dictionary. It's therefore best to have the dictionary on a hard disk or a large RAMdisk.

STYLE-CHECKERS

Style and grammar checkers are a rather strange element in the world of word processing. A style-checker scans a document and looks for mechanical problems (such as no close parenthesis after an open parenthesis or missing quote marks) as well as grammar problems. Grammar problems may include lengthy sentences, passivity in sentence structure or verb choice, and repetition of a word or phrase.

As it scans, the style-checker either

SPEEDING THINGS UP: RAMDISKS AND HARD DISKS

The one thing that may push you into upgrading your system—adding extra memory, a hard disk drive or hard card, or actually going out and buying a more powerful computer—may very well be how slowly the more powerful programs, like spell-checking software, can run on a computer whose capacities are stretched to the limit just running the software, to say nothing of running it quickly.

A hard disk runs programs faster, by its increased storage capacity (no disk swapping!) and relative speed accessing any part of its contents, as compared to a floppy drive. But if you already have a computer with a hard drive, or even a computer of good capacity (500 + K RAM) without a hard drive, you can increase many times over the speed at which your spell-checker runs by copying it onto a RAMdisk. (Since the RAMdisk disappears when the computer is shut off, you'd of course want to copy your auxiliary dictionary file to the floppy or hard disk before turning things off, so that new words you've added wouldn't be lost.)

Copied to and then running on a RAMdisk, the spell-checker program doesn't have to move a physical read/write head (think of it as a phonograph needle) to different locations of an actual disk, hard or floppy, or sift all the a's to reach *axolotl*. Instead, it has all the available words in your dictionary almost instantly accessible. So it will check and confirm all the ordinary words like "the" and "that" almost instantaneously, spending its time on what matters: letting you look at and either confirm or change the offbeat words, the ones it doesn't recognize.

You'll really notice the change in speed with programs that offer guesses as to what an offbeat word should be, or which look words up phonetically, because either process requires that a program access different parts of its internal files and run a separate subprogram to find words similar, even though composed of different, and different numbers of, characters. Waiting for your spell-checking program to offer alternatives can be a long wait on a floppy drive system.

Just remember that the RAMdisk disappears—and so does everything on it—every time your computer is turned off. So never NEVER keep data files there.

stops and asks if you want to change or mark a problem area, or marks the problem on its own (with or without annotations). At the end of the scan, the style-checker adds a brief report, citing the number of words and sentences in the document, the number of unique words, and the reading level. (There are variations on these elements, but this is how it usually goes.)

The problem with style-checkers for experienced writers is this: without exception, all style-checkers look for problems based on the requirements of business writing (and on what their designers think good writing *should* be). Thus, a style-checker will flag a line of dialogue as "sentence too long" without even recognizing that quotes and attribution are involved.

Or it may look at a highly lyrical sentence in a fictional narrative and decide it's too passive. Or it may object to a sentence fragment where you *wanted* a sentence fragment. *This, for instance.*

Even nonfiction writers may find style-checkers annoying. We used a grammar checker on one of the shorter chapters of this book and, believe us, had we written the entire book based on the kinds of recommendations we got, you would have found the reading about as exciting as a corporation's annual report.

Because they're so unimaginative, style-checkers shouldn't be considered a quick fix for writing style. But in a limited sense, a style-checker *can* identify recurring problems in your overall style. Style-checkers can be helpful in identifying any over-repeated "pet" words and phrasings. They can also help any writer judge whether the level of writing is suitable to its intended audience by determining sentence length and complexity, number of difficult or long words, and similar factors that have a direct impact on readability to a given readership. Writing below your audience can seem either patronizing or ignorant; writing above them seems arrogant and pedantic—like somebody who "swallowed a dictionary." It's important to find the right balance, appropriate to the intended audience; a style-checker can help give you the objective overview that will help you make the best choices for effective communication, no matter whom you're writing for.

Once you've checked your style with this kind of software a few times, you'll probably find you've outgrown this utility. True, you can use it to check punctuation, but punctuation checkers (few though they are) can do the job faster. And even they will overcorrect your intentional sentence fragments.

We don't recommend day-to-day use of style-checkers—and won't, until one designed for writers (and *by* writers) is available, one that wouldn't blow its tiny circuits over a passage by Faulkner or e. e. cummings.

THESAURUSES

An electronic thesaurus (or online thesaurus) is a convenient, albeit limited, enhancement to any WP system. Like a thesaurus in book form, it lists alternate choices for specific words. The problem is that, if you're a writer, you undoubtedly know a hundred times the words the thesaurus does and a thousand times more about the flavors and shadings of every one of them. You know *red*'s associated with both anger and heat; the thesaurus hasn't a clue. One of us has a top-of-the-line thesaurus that can't recognize the word *red* at all—*not a headword*, it announces haughtily—(nor crimson, carmine, fuchsia, vermilion, etc.). In this respect, the mind's a better computer than anything you can buy.

In operation, an electronic thesaurus looks at a specified word in a document and searches a special dictionary for an entry matching that word. When it finds the word, it displays synonyms and, in some cases, definitions. (The word to be looked up is specified by placing the cursor on it, or by typing it in.) After displaying alternate words, the thesaurus program will replace the specified word with a new one of your choice.

Some thesauruses are more "intelligent" than others. The best ones offer a list of similar words if they don't find the word you specify and allow you look up further synonyms for the synonyms they present. Examples of thesauruses offering these capabilities are Webster's New World On-Line Thesaurus, for Apple and IBM, and Word Finder for IBM. Such a thesaurus also comes as part of the WordPerfect package. So far, we haven't yet found one that's half as satisfactory as a good spell-checker.

Like a spell-checker, a thesaurus requires a lot of memory for its dictionary; if you're not using a RAMdisk or hard disk to hold the dictionary, you may have to swap disks whenever you want to look up a word. This can get tedious. You may do as well, and conceivably better, on your own, without the so-called help of an electronic thesaurus.

DOING WINDOWS

"Windowing" means overlaying one program or document with another or flipping between two such programs or documents—either on the same screen, partitioned into sections, or on a spare blank screen you can switch to whenever you want without affecting what's on your "main" screen. The overlaying or alternating screens of different programs or docu-

TIP #1: THESAURUSES DON'T GIVE WARNINGS

There's an important difference between the way a thesaurus program works and the way either a spell-checker or style-checker works: it offers no way whatever to prevent or locate errors. It gives no guidance on appropriate usage of the words it lists as related. All it offers is groups of roughly equivalent words whose connections are all pretty much on the literal side, and maybe the kind of definition you'd get from a *very small* pocket dictionary. The program has no way to help you know whether or not the word you select is appropriate or effective in the context in which you'll be placing it.

So don't think that by using an online thesaurus, you'll magically expand your working vocabulary. It doesn't work that way, and it won't tell you when you're wrong. And chances are you know more words, and more subtle connections between the implied meanings of words, than the thesaurus program does. So take this warning: it's the only one you'll get.

ments are called, appropriately enough, "windows." Windows were first used for Apple's Lisa and Macintosh computers and are, unlike memory-resident software, not programs, but an operating system that controls programs running within it.

Because of the popularity of Macintosh's window "environment"—which allows you to run several programs at once and jump between them—software developers have leaped on the bandwagon to develop window operating systems for other computers. Thus far, such efforts have met with limited success, due to technical difficulties that involve variances in computer hardware, key function, and programs. WordPerfect, for example, doesn't handle Microsoft's "Windows" operating system for the IBM PC (conflict between the designated function keys), although it likes "Sidekick" fine and also comes with built-in switch-screen and windowing capacity.

Actually, the term "windows" is open to discussion, as far as its definition is concerned. Many programs offer another version of windowing that has nothing to do with an operating system. XyWrite for MS-DOS computers allows you to move among up to nine documents at once, and FinalWord and Sprint (again, for MS-DOS computers) perform similarly. Ditto for a number of Macintosh word processors. In each case, you can move text directly from a document in one window to another document.

For those computers and/or programs that don't offer windowing, memory-resident notepads (more on them in a minute) offer some of the same capability.

MEMORY-RESIDENT SOFTWARE

Memory-resident software (also called "RAM-resident," or "Terminate-and-Stay-Resident [TSR]," or "Pop-up" software) is software that you load into your computer before you start your WP program. Thereafter, the memory-resident program or programs remain available, called into action by pressing a designated set of keys (such as Control and Shift or both Shift keys).

When called, a memory-resident program either completely overlays whatever is on your computer screen or appears as a small "window" (a "screen in a screen"). The program you were running is temporarily suspended, but you return to it once you exit the memory-resident program.

The most common uses of memory-resident software are discussed in the next few pages.

(NOTE: Depending on how they use your computer's memory, some memory-resident programs may conflict with your WP software or with other memory-resident programs. Such conflicts may cause your computer to "lock up," or cause erratic operation in one or more of the programs in use. Or your WP program may require so much RAM that none is left to accommodate memory-resident programs. In any of these cases, you may not be able to use a particular memory-resident program, or any at all.

Remedies for this problem include sacrificing one memory-resident program to accommodate another, either temporarily or permanently, switching to a different WP program, or adding more memory [RAM] to your computer.)

"DESKTOP" SOFTWARE

Desktop accessory software—a category of memory-resident software that includes electronic notepads, calculators, calendars, and more—is a popular addition to word processing. The idea behind such software is to provide computer versions of desktop tools, and it's an excellent idea, indeed—one more step toward the (relatively) paperless office. If you aren't now using such software, give it a try; you'll find it extremely useful in virtually all computer applications.

NOTEPADS

If your WP program doesn't include windows, you'll probably want to get a memory-resident notepad program to substitute for windowing capability—especially if you'll need to view one file while you're editing another. You'll also find that such a program is an excellent note-taker. We both use Borland's Sidekick notepad (for the IBM PC) nearly every time we're working. It's much handier to pop up Sidekick's notepad to make a note than to try to find a piece of paper and pencil, and with Sidekick you can save notes on disk, where you actually can *find* them a week or a month later.

Because some notepads' editing features

are fairly powerful, you can also use them to create letters or even brief articles, which you can save or print out immediately. And if you want to use a paragraph (or more) from one document on disk, it's an easy operation to call the document into the notepad, mark the text in question, write it to disk, then exit to your WP program, then call up the text in question. (With the more powerful notepads, you can directly copy a marked section of a document between the notepad and your main WP program.)

Commercial and PD/shareware memory-resident notepads are available for many popular computer brands. Here are a few:

- •Apple IIe/IIc: Pinpoint and Timeout.
- •Atari ST: CornerMan, DeskCart, and Deskpak.
- •CP/M: NOTEPAD.LBR.
- •IBM: HomeBase, RHM, Sidekick, TSR Notepad, and PC-DeskTeam.
- •Macintosh: Various desk accessories (MockWrite and MiniWRITER, among others).
- •TRS-80 Model 4: DeskMate.

CALCULATORS

Having a calculator available is handy for all sorts of calculations that come up while you're working. Here again, we use Sidekick—it provides a calculator with a memory and other features for simple or complex calculations. (You can even insert the results of a calculation into a document with a few simple keystrokes.) Most of the other software listed just above offers calculators too.

CALENDARS

If you have trouble finding a paper calendar when you need it, a pop-up calendar can be handy because it's always there. Most allow you to check more than just the current year's dates. Some pop-up calendars (like Sidekick's) include an appointment file, which is a *very* useful accessory.

PHONE DIRECTORIES

While you can use a notepad to keep a list of phone numbers, some desktop programs provide a special phone directory element (here again, Sidekick is an example). A phone directory is not only searchable by number or name, but in many cases will dial a number for you for a voice call, if you have a modem.

PRINTER-CONTROL SOFTWARE

If you use a dot-matrix printer, you may have occasion to change the type style, turn on or off features like emphasized or boldface, send formfeeds, etc. Pop-up printer-control programs are available for some computers—MS-DOS computers in particular—that allow you to select printer commands from a menu.

FILE-CONVERSION SOFTWARE

Some word processors use their own special methods to store documents. Apple's AppleWriter, for instance, uses what is called a "binary" format, and WordStar on the IBM PC uses what is called "8-bit ASCII" storage. And almost all use their own special print-format codes.

The technical ins and outs of what these formats are and why they are used (usually to conserve disk space) are superfluous; the important thing is what these differences mean to you. And what these differences mean is this: many word processors produce files that can't be edited by other WP software even if it's being run on the same computer. So if your editor wants a manuscript on disk and you use WordStar while your editor uses XyWrite, you're going to find that you are incompatible, as it were.

Too, if you need to deliver text by modem, it will often need to be in standard 7-bit ASCII format.

So what do you do? Retype the entire manuscript using the other word processor? Not at all. If your word processor has a provision for outputting text to an ASCII file (sometimes called "print to disk" or "DOS text mode"), you can produce docu-ments that can be edited with any other word processor on your kind of computer.

If your WP program doesn't do this, you'll have to use a file conversion program (like XWORD for the IBM PC) to convert files to ASCII or to the format used by the other word processor.

(By the way, if you convert one WP program's file directly to another program's format using a program like the aforementioned XWORD, you get the bonus of having all the formatting commands converted, too. We're doing quite a bit of that in writing this book—both as an experiment and to be practical. One of us uses WordStar for most work, while the other uses WordPerfect; we use XWORD and ASCII output to make our files mutually compatible for trading back and forth.)

An ASCII translation is the capacity of some WP programs to save a document in "generic" WP mode. Most of the formatting codes are stripped out (*not* tabs or underlines, though!), including the excess "hard returns" and spaces which ASCII adds to retain the document's format. Yet like ASCII documents, a "generic WP" document can be read by a WP system other than the one which created it, assuming the *disk* (not software) format is compatible .

HARD-DISK BACKUP AND OPTIMIZING UTILITIES

As you learned in Chapter 1, hard disks can store massive quantities of information—as much as 60,000 pages of text! But as we also mentioned in Chapter 1, it some-times happens that hard disks "crash" (a general term for a catastrophic malfunc-tion that causes data loss). Because of this, it's absolutely vital to make, on a regular basis, backup copies of all work stored on a hard disk.

But, you may ask, doesn't this take time? How long does it take to copy 60,000 pages of text from a hard disk to a slower-access floppy disk? And won't this take up a lot of disks? Well, it will take hours—and a lot of floppy disks—if you use normal copy commands. But you don't have to use normal copy commands to back up files on a hard disk, not with the special backup programs that are available for this purpose. These programs (of which FASTBACK for MS-DOS computers is only one example) copy hard disk contents at super speed and compress them to take up less space on a floppy disk as they go. (MS-DOS also comes with a hard disk backup utility that's slower, but still better than copying the files one at a time.)

Another less visible problem that hard disks present has to do with how they organize and access the information they store. As you might imagine, locating specific files among this much data requires that the hard disk be well organized. If it's not, the hard disk can take a long time to find and retrieve information. Too, inefficient storage can result in significant amounts of a hard disk's storage being wasted. Fortunately, there are a number of "disk-optimization" utilities available for "cleaning up" hard disks and arranging the data on them in the most efficient format. And many of these programs not only arrange data in an efficient manner, but also catch potential trouble spots of "confused" data and thereby help prevent disk crashes. (More discussion on disk backup and optimization in Chapter 6.)

And if a hard disk does crash—or if you accidentally delete a file or copy one file over another—all is not lost. You can use any of several hard-disk utilities to recover all or most of such files.

FILE-COMPRESSION UTILITIES

File compression programs (sometimes called "archiving" or "library" programs) are useful to those who have a lot of text to store, especially backups or archive copies of old work. A file compression program does these basic jobs:

•compresses files to their smallest possible size.

•combines several files into one file, reduced in size, called an archive or library.

•decompresses compressed files so they can be edited or printed.

The benefits of using these programs are obvious. Since a file is smaller after it's been compressed, it takes up much less disk space. (A long novel can thus be stored on one disk instead of two.) This means you use fewer disks and save money.

Any of several "packing" or "archiving" methods are used to reduce files to as little as 40 percent of their original size. Some file compression utilities can perform specialized operations on archives, in addition to their basic functions. These include displaying a directory of the contents of an archive, displaying or running a file from an archive, and deleting or copying files in an archive.

A significant percentage of the program, data, and text files available for downloading via modem on bulletin board systems (BBS) and online services are in compressed format. So if you intend to do much downloading—that is, accepting data from a computer network or database—you should make it a point to get one or more of the more popular file compression programs used with your brand of computer to save online costs and storage problems.

Almost all file compression programs in common use are public domain or shareware programs. Programs for various computers include:

•Apple II+/e: The File Librarian and Binary Library Utility, or BLU (ProDOS version of LU, compatible with MS-DOS, CP/M and UNIX LU programs), and ProPacker (DOS 3.3).

•Atari (8-bit): ARC.TTP and SCRUNCH.

•Atari ST: ARC.TTP, EZSQUEEZ.PRG, and TINY.PRG.

•Commodore Amiga: ARC, PKARC,

Squeeze, LIBRARY, PAK, TRACKER, and ZOO.

•CP/M: CRUNCH24.LBR, UNARC16.LBR, and NULU152A.LBR (the latter does not compress, but combines files for storage).

•IBM: ARC.EXE, LU.EXE, PKARC.COM, SQ.COM, and USQ.COM.

•Macintosh: PackIt III and StuffIt (a special version of the latter is available for IBM users to unpack files—like VCO face libraries—compressed on a Macintosh using StuffIt).

•OS-9 (CoCo, Atari, and others): AR.BIN and PAK.BIN.

•Tandy Color Computer: PIXCMP (CoCo 1 & 2 graphics only), TC12 (CoCo 1 & 2), and TC3 (CoCo 3).

•TI-99/4a: ARCHIVER, SARCEXE, ACRIIv2.3, and ARCIII.

•TRS-80 (I/III/4): LU/CMD, SQ/CMD and USQ/CMD.

KEYBOARD-REDEFINITION AND MACRO UTILITIES

As noted earlier in this book, some keyboards may be fine in all respects—except for the location of one or two keys. If this is all that's keeping you from buying a particular computer (or if you've found after buying it that the key in question is intolerable) it's possible to change how that key operates. All that's required is a keyboard-redefinition program. Such a program can take the tilde key on the IBM PC keyboard (which is where part of the ENTER/RETURN key is located on most keyboards) and make it function as a ENTER/RETURN key. Or, as mentioned in Chapter 1, it can switch your whole keyboard from QWERTY to DVORAK.

Macros, which we'll discuss in detail in Chapter 9, are commands (simple or complex) that you can set going with a couple of keystrokes or by "invoking" the macro by the name you've given it. They're useful when you have to type long or complex commands or phrases more than a couple

of times in a manuscript. If you have to type "Allied Publishing and Iron Works" repeatedly in a manuscript, assigning this phrase to a macro can cut the tedium of repetition and reduce the potential for error.

Macros are created by assigning the command or phrase desired to a unique key combination, such as CTRL-Y. Then, when the keys to which the macro is assigned are pressed simultaneously, the macro is executed just as if you had keyed it all in each time.

Some word processors have macro-creation capability built in. For those that don't, macro programs provide this capability. Examples of such programs for MS-DOS computers include NEWKEY (shareware) and Smartkey (commercial). (By the way, macros can be used to redefine keys on a keyboard, too.)

OTHER UTILITIES

Other utilities that you may find useful include programs that do the following:

•Change background and foreground screen colors. (These are useful even if you have a monochrome monitor; you can, for example, change a WP program's display from green letters on a black background to light green letters on a dark green background—a combination that is much easier on the eyes).

•Recover damaged, "trashed," or accidentally-deleted files from a disk.

•Rearrange disk directories on floppy disks to suit your method of keeping track of things.

•Search through multiple files on a disk to find specific words or phrases.

SOURCES OF SUPPLEMENTARY PROGRAMS

As you've probably gathered, most of the programs in the categories discussed in this chapter are PD or shareware. Commercial versions of some of the programs (such as online spell-checkers) are available; these usually offer extras that don't come with PD software or shareware.

In selecting supplementary programs, your best course is to try some likely PD or shareware programs before looking at commercial programs. (You'll probably find what you need on your local electronic bulletin board system or favorite online service, or from PD/shareware distributors, as discussed in Chapter 2.) The only category of programs we suggest you consider in commercial versions first are spell-checkers, thesauruses (do you *really* want one?), hard-disk utilities, and windowing systems. For such complex software, you very well may get as much (or as little) as you pay for.

CHAPTER 4

The Bottom Line: Printers

OVERVIEW: THIS CHAPTER COVERS:

1. How a printer interacts with the other components of a word-processing system; how a printer communicates with a computer; controlling a printer.

2. Types of printers and how they work, with the major advantages and disadvantages of each, from the writer's perspective; what "letter quality" means to the writer.

3. Printer features—the various features that come built into printers: type faces and sizes, graphics, justification and proportional spacing, and more.

4. Printer hardware options, including sheet- and bin-feeders, tractor feed, internal and add-on buffers, external controls, character font cartridges and chips, and keyboards.

5. How to select a printer. Determining what you as a writer need (versus what sales brochures and ads say people who use word processing want); should you buy now and trade up later, or wait until you can afford the top-of-the-line model?

AN EDITOR'S FIRST IMPRESSION of your work is largely determined by the kind of printer you use (and how you use it). If your printed words look bad, your writing looks bad.

You may have heard that the paperless society is here. No more paper. Just zip your electronic manuscripts to publishers on disk or over phone lines, after which the publishers obligingly convert them to books and magazines for the benefit of low-tech types. Bad news: it hasn't happened yet. Virtually all publishers—even the ones who accept manuscripts on disk or via modem—require a manuscript on paper ("hard copy") for editing. They also require that initial manuscript submission be on paper.

More bad news: it's going to stay that way for years to come. Nobody really enjoys reading a manuscript as tiny lights on a screen instead of nice crisp black typed letters on a solid, white page of 20-lb. bond paper. And in the writing game, what editors want, editors get.

Anyway, you'll always want hard copy to proof before submission. There's always something you'll catch on a hard copy that will pass right by you unseen on screen. So start out knowing that printers are here to stay.

At this point you may be thinking of upgrading your printer—moving up from dot matrix to daisywheel or even considering the newest thing in laser printers, whose output can approach the resolution of typesetting. You need to evaluate what's out there, what it does, and which printer features are apt to be important to you and which ones are relatively useless and aren't worth the money for writers. You'll find the requirements of your work differ from those of business people. Be sure your system offers features you need, rather than too few features, or features you'll pay for but never use. Evaluate what you have now and decide whether add-ons such as a tractor feed or a memory buffer might be enough to make you perfectly content with your present printer.

PRINTER BASICS

Before getting into the "hands-on" aspects of printers, we're going to take a few pages to explain not only how printers work in general, but also how they relate to and interact with computer hardware and software.

How a printer works is important because it may or may not interfere with your work on screen, the printer's output, and your mental health—and that of your neighbors in the next apartment, if you're in the habit of doing printouts at three in the morning.

COMMUNICATING WITH YOUR PRINTER

Computer-to-printer communication is fairly straightforward. Your computer, directed by your WP program, sends data (information) to the printer in the form of electrical signals along a wire (the printer cable).

The data carried by the signals is in the form of bits. Now, you can write happily for the next fifty years without the least idea what bits are, but you'll find that understanding exactly how your words are broken into bits (literally!) and reassembled by your computer and printer is really helpful, both in using your printer and in handling any problems that may arise.

That said, let's take a closer look at bits. Bits are the smallest unit of information handled by a computer and, for reasons we needn't go into here, the most efficient way for computers to handle information.

Alone, bits are meaningless to humans. To come up with human-readable information, a computer assembles bits—seven or eight of them—into larger units called bytes. "Byte" is technospeak for a character, characters being the letters, numbers, etc., that you see (and don't see) on your screen. Every alphanumeric symbol on your keyboard is a character. So is a space. So is any kind of formatting code for margins, tabs, whatever. So is every printer control code, which—again—you can probably live and write happily without knowing intimately.

To recap, every single mark or space, visible or invisible, in any document on screen, or any file on disk, is a character. And a character is a byte, which can be composed of seven or eight bits.

Now it starts getting technical.

THE PRINTER/COMPUTER CONNECTION

The basic steps involved in printing a document with a WP system go something like this: your WP program directs your computer to read a file stored on your floppy or hard disk, then sends all the characters (bytes) in the document to the printer through the printer cable. Alternatively, some WP programs provide the option of making what is, in effect, an instant snapshot of an onscreen document (even the parts of it you can't see at any given moment: the whole document), putting it in a temporary printer file, and then sending that to the printer through the cable.

At the receiving end, the printer translates the bytes into letters, numbers, and spaces and puts them on paper.

Serial and Parallel There are two ways a computer can send this series of bytes to a printer—in serial or in parallel—and printers are categorized as one or the other. Most computers have both serial and parallel "ports," or hookups where the printer cable plugs in.

There's a technical difference, too: with a serial printer, the bits that make up each character come in one at a time—in a series, like tiny beads on a string. Serial is slow. Parallel printers, by contrast, receive all seven or eight bits that make up each character together, at the same time. Parallel is therefore faster.

But what's really important is that parallel printers are the *de facto* standard for WP programs. Virtually all WP programs talk with parallel printers, but getting them to talk with serial printers is at least difficult and often impossible. So stay away from serial printers. Make sure the printer you buy is a parallel printer, and you will have little—if any—trouble getting your software to communicate with it.

THE PRINTER/SOFTWARE CONNECTION

A few lines back we noted that a character may be a letter, number, space, or punctuation mark. We also mentioned characters that you don't see. These are called format codes.

Format codes include the tabs, margin sets, and other elements that define how your document is printed out. You key these codes in before, during, and/or after creating the document. They may be invisible on your screen, but you see the results: tabs, "hard" returns, etc. When you save the document, the embedded codes are saved, too. When you print the file, the format codes are sent to the printer along with all the other characters, telling the printer how to print: where to move to a new line, tab in, end a page, add a header or a page number, and so forth.

Most basic format codes are the same for all printers. Other format codes, as you'll learn in a minute, aren't.

Format Codes Embedded format codes can't do all the work of formatting a printout because many formatting jobs require more than one character, and parallel printers accept only one character at a time. When this happens, a WP program acts as a "translator," turning the codes into a series of commands the printer recognizes and separates from the "printable" characters it receives.

Format codes take one of two forms. One form is that of an identifying character followed by two or more letters that constitute a command. The identifying character is usually a period, a]], or a /, and when it occurs at the beginning of a line it acts as a "flag" for the WP program. That is, when the flag appears, the WP program knows that the letters immediately following are a formatting command it has to translate into a command sequence for the printer. A typical command of this type might be ".lm 10" which would mean, "set the left margin to 10." Another might be ".HM 5" which would mean, "leave five spaces between the header of this document and the main body of the text on each page." (Examples of programs that make use of this type of formatting command are ScreenWriter II, for Apple II computers, and WordStar.)

The other form of format codes is similar, with the difference that the codes aren't normally visible on your screen and don't have to be placed at the beginning of a line. This type of formatting (which XyWrite and WordPerfect for the IBM PC use) causes the document to be displayed on your screen in a "what you see is what you get" (WYSIWYG) fashion—which means that the document on screen is fairly close to what the printed version will look like.

Some programs (for instance, WordStar) use both types of format codes.

Installation Extra Because the vast majority of printers share only a few format codes, a WP program must send a different set of commands to, say, change margins or underline to an Epson MX-80 than it sends to a Diablo 630 printer. This holds true for both kinds formatting instructions—embedded, invisible format codes and visible format codes that start with flags.

The program knows what to send to a printer thanks to modifications it makes in itself when you first install it. During the installation process, one of the things the system wants to know is what kind of printer you'll be using. Once the program has this information, it modifies itself to

send the right commands to that particular kind of printer.

But if and when you buy a different printer, you'll need to re-install your WP program, or at least that part of it that designates the printer being used. Redefining your printer lets the WP program modify itself again to suit whatever kind of printer you've chosen.

KINDS OF PRINTERS AND HOW THEY WORK

Now, to business: what's out there, what it does, and what you should be looking for in shopping for a printer.

The finished product of word processing—your manuscript—can vary greatly according to how the printer actually goes about putting the characters on the page. The three basic kinds of printer are daisy-wheel, dot-matrix, and laser. There are other kinds of printers, but these are of little interest or use to writers, so we'll discuss them only briefly.

The quality and nature of printout varies with each type of printer. Each has its pros and cons. We'll consider the varieties of printers available in descending order of popularity.

DAISY-WHEEL PRINTERS

A daisy-wheel printer works about like a typewriter. A letter is produced by pressing (banging, actually) a metal or plastic image of the letter against an inked ribbon, behind which lies a sheet of paper. The letters are mounted at the ends of the "spokes" of a print wheel, which the printer rotates to select the proper letter. The configuration, shown on page 55, looks much like a flower, with the letters at the ends of the "petals." Hence, the term "daisy-wheel."

Many newer typewriters use this method of printing too. In fact, the printout of a daisy wheel printer is indistinguishable from that of a standard typewriter.

Variations on the daisy-wheel printer

use a thimble-shaped printing element or the famous "golf ball" printing element used by the IBM Selectric. These variations tend to be a bit slower than the daisy wheel configuration, but the net effect is the same: you get true typewriter printout.

ADVANTAGES

A major advantage of using a daisy-wheel printer is the quality of printout. In using a daisy-wheel printer, you are guaranteed an easy-to-read manuscript and avoid possible conflicts with editors who abhor word-processed manuscripts (and there are a few of those).

Changing the print style (from pica to elite, for instance) is relatively simple with a daisy-wheel printer. You don't have to learn something new (i.e., which commands to send to the printer to select a particular type style) as you do with other types of printers. With a daisy-wheel printer, you simply change the daisy wheel—it's not much different from changing the printing element in a typewriter. (You will, however, need to adjust your margins if you'll be getting more characters per inch: elite is smaller than pica.)

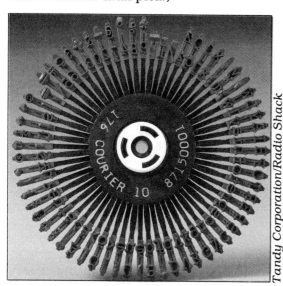

Figure 4.1 A Daisy-Wheel Printer's Print Wheel

DISADVANTAGES

When compared with the second-most-practical type of computer printer (dot-matrix), the major disadvantage of a daisy-wheel printer is price. Daisy-wheel printers have quite a few precision-made moving parts, and this keeps the cost at a level that is typically 30% to 50% higher than a quality dot-matrix printer.

The large number of moving parts also means a daisy-wheel printer is more likely to break down. However, a quality (expensive) daisy-wheel printer won't break down often—less frequently, in fact, than a good typewriter, since the printer has no keyboard to clog or letter buttons to break.

Another comparative disadvantage of daisy-wheel printers is lack of speed. A "fast" daisy-wheel printer prints 55-60 characters per second—which translates into nearly one minute to print a page. This may not seem like much time, but when you have a 440-page novel to print and no print buffer (more on that in a minute), you may find your computer tied up for six or eight hours.

DOT-MATRIX PRINTERS

Dot-matrix printers print by knocking pins against a ribbon hundreds of times per second as the print head moves across the paper. The end product is a set of tiny dots in horizontal and vertical rows, creating a pattern in the shape of a letter. In the case of the letter "I," the pattern printed might be seven dots in a vertical column with five horizontal dots at the top and bottom of the column, as shown in figure 4.2.

The pattern of the dots is called the "ma-

Figure 4.2 Dot-Matrix Letter (Enlarged)

trix"; hence the term "dot-matrix." These dots can be placed anywhere on the paper, and can be made to overlap or print twice. This offers some obvious (and not-so-obvious) possibilities, as you'll see.

The quality of print you get from a dot-matrix printer will vary according to the number of pins used (more pins mean smaller dots placed more closely together and darker print) and how the printer is placing the dots (some dot-matrix printers can be instructed to print two sets of overlapping dots for each letter, which eliminates the "dottiness" of the character by filling in the holes that otherwise would be left).

Higher-quality dot-matrix printers can, when operating in "letter-quality" or "near letter-quality" mode, produce a printout that's as good as that of the best typewriter around. (Quality dot-matrix use more pins—24 is the maximum currently used—and overlap the dots.)

ADVANTAGES

The two major advantages of dot-matrix printers over daisy-wheel printers are speed and price.

In draft mode (plain, dots visible), dot-matrix printers can print three to five times faster than daisy-wheel printers. This is an important consideration for those of you who may have to print several drafts of a manuscript for editing or showing around to your 200 closest friends and trusted critics. When printing in letter-quality mode, even a low-end dot-matrix printer can print two to three times faster than a daisy-wheel printer—important if you're printing lots of long articles or novel chapters.

The cost of a typical dot-matrix printer is generally one-half to two-thirds that of a daisy-wheel printer.

Usually, a dot-matrix printer has only two major moving parts: the print head and the paper-feed mechanism. Because of this, there is less likelihood of breakdown.

DISADVANTAGES

There's a knee-jerk reaction against dot-matrix printers on the part of some editors who have, unfortunately, been exposed to the printout of some of the poorer quality dot-matrix printers. And those printouts can be really bad. But if you use a quality dot-matrix printer, you shouldn't run into problems. If an editor can't tell the printout from typewriter type, who's going to object? (In the "quality" group, we'll list Epson, Toshiba, and Star Micronics printers.)

The only other disadvantage of dot-matrix printers is the fact that most of them—even the quality models—cross over the descenders of lower-case letters when underlining. This means that letters such as "y" or "p" can end up looking like "v" and "o" when underlined! (If you don't do a lot of underlining and are willing to add underlines to your manuscripts by hand, this isn't a problem.)

LASER PRINTERS

Although it's by no means an entirely new technology, the laser printer is a fairly recent innovation in word processing. Simply described, a laser printer prints using techniques similar to those used by a high-quality photocopier. But instead of scanning a page for an image to reproduce, the laser printer's electrostatic print head is fed the image by a computer.

To actually place a page of characters (which it "sees" as one whole graphic image—a picture—rather than as a series of letters) on paper, a laser printer uses a special powder, called "toner," which is electrostatically "welded" to the paper where the letters go.

The printout of a laser printer is very good, its quality approaching that of typesetting machines. (By way of comparison, the graphic density of the average dot-matrix printer is perhaps 1/10 that of a typesetter's output, while that of a laser printer is 1/4 that of a typesetter's output. But where a writer is concerned, it's not typesetting quality but readability that counts, and a laser printer certainly offers that.)

Laser printers also offer graphics capability and an endless variety of typestyles. But unless you're involved in desktop publishing, you really don't need such amenities.

ADVANTAGES

As just mentioned, laser printers provide unparalleled quality of output (although once you've seen a few laser printer pages, you'll find it easy to recognize when someone is using one). It's letter quality plus. While not quite identical to daisy-wheel printout, laser printer pages are eminently readable.

The new generation of laser printers are fast—so fast that their speed is measured in pages per minute rather than characters per second. They can print an average of eight pages per minute (compared with three pages per minute for dot-matrix printers and one page or less per minute for daisy-wheel printers).

Laser printers are quiet, too. No pins or letters banging against the ribbon and paper.

DISADVANTAGES

The major disadvantage of laser printers is price. A typical low-end laser printer costs between $1,500 and $1,800—twice the price of a top-quality daisy-wheel printer, and eight times what you'll pay for a decent dot-matrix printer.

The toner used in the laser printing process is not inexpensive, either (this is the biggest complaint that users have).

Another disadvantage of laser printers is the fact that not all WP programs (and not all computers) can communicate with them. Any IBM PC, IBM PC clone, Macintosh, or Apple II computer can be used with a laser printer, and most IBM and Macintosh programs are set up to accommodate laser printers. Ditto in terms of hardware

and software for the Atari ST and Commodore Amiga. However, not many Apple II word processors speak laser. (Actually, because of their complexity, laser printers have built-in computers, which is the source of many compatibility problems.)

OTHER TYPES OF PRINTERS: INK-JET AND THERMAL

Ink-jet printers were introduced a few years ago and were precursors of the laser printer. They operate by squirting tiny jets of ink to create letters on paper in much the same manner as dot-matrix printers. They're fast and quiet but expensive to operate, thanks to the special ink cartridges they use in place of ribbons.

Except for the most expensive models (like the Hewlett-Packard "Think-jet"), the quality of ink-jet printers really doesn't approach that required for manuscripts. So we can't recommend ink-jet printers with much enthusiasm.

Most thermal printers work by heating points on a special thermal-sensitive paper to darken those areas and create an image. If you have a printing calculator, it most likely uses a thermal printing device.

Most thermal printers are very cheap—in every sense of the word. No writer should use one to produce manuscripts for submission. Because of the type of paper used and the printing process itself, the printout is of extremely poor quality and actually deteriorates with time. If you've seen the output of a calculator's printer, you already know that. If not, trust us; don't buy a thermal printer.

But there's one exception worth noting. Although IBM Quietwriter series printers work by thermal transfer, they don't require the special paper just mentioned. Instead of heating the paper directly, they heat a printing element that looks like a big staple, which in turn heats a ribbon and fuses each character to the page. These printers produce images as lasting, sharp, and smudge-free as those of daisy-wheel printers. They therefore escape our general condemnation of thermal printers and, indeed, are recommended.

TYPEWRITERS AS PRINTERS

It's probably occurred to you that if you could use a typewriter as a printer, you could avoid certain problems. Unfortunately, you can't. It only makes things worse.

You'll find a number of typewriters on the market that are designed to connect to a computer, just like a printer. The majority of these typewriter-printers produces poor-quality dot-matrix printouts. Those that are capable of producing quality dot-matrix or daisy-wheel printouts are usually difficult to use with the majority of WP programs. (Most WP software packages don't provide for their installation.) So it's best to steer clear of typewriters masquerading as printers. You can have a typewriter. You can have a printer. But when they mate, the offspring tend to be sterile and virtually useless.

WHAT "LETTER QUALITY" MEANS TO THE WRITER

We're sure that the phrase "letter quality" has been running through your mind throughout this discussion—along with the fear that you'll end up selecting the wrong printer. After all, aren't letter-quality printers the way to go?

The answer is "Certainly!"—but letter quality is a rather slippery term nowadays. It used to be that only daisy-wheel or similar printers were letter-quality printers. Things have changed, though. We now find ourselves in an ongoing revolution in printing technology and quality—a revolution that began in the early 1980s when the first true letter-quality dot-matrix printers were introduced for personal computers. Costing more than daisy-wheel printers, these early "LQ" printers could produce characters with near-invisible dots, offering the advantage of speed and quality. (In 1983, one of us tried out an LQ dot-matrix printer—a Toshiba P1350 that cost well over $2,000. The characters in the printout were so smoothly printed that the dots couldn't be spotted—pun intended—with a magnifying glass. Today, a dot-matrix printer capable of producing similar quality printout is available for less than $500.)

Laser printers also provide what is essentially letter-quality printing, but what *is* letter-quality printing, exactly? That's a difficult question, because it's far easier to say that this printer or that printer produces letter-quality printout than it is to provide a strict definition of what letter quality is.

In the end, letter quality is a judgment call, rather than a style of print or the output of a particular type of printer. You can either read a printout easily or you can't. If a printout is difficult to read and varies in density, it's safe to say that it's not letter-quality. (And if an editor says, "Yeah, I'd call this letter-quality print," then the printout in question is letter-quality, for your purposes!)

To emphasize the point that letter-quality is not strictly daisy-wheel printout, consider these facts:

One of us uses a Daisywriter daisy-wheel printer while the other uses a Star Micronics dot-matrix printer. Both are trusty old-line machines, and each has printed hundreds of thousands of published words for its owner with a minimum of maintenance. Both of us have had similar acceptance among book and magazine editors of our printers' output (the same editors in some cases). Letter-quality, like Beauty, is strictly in the eye of the beholder.

So what's the difference in whether you use a dot-matrix or a daisy-wheel printer? As we've demonstrated, there are several differences, having to do with price, speed, and performance aspects. The major consideration is whether a printer produces dark, crisp, readable print. If it does, it's adequate for a writer's needs.

PRINTER FEATURES

The full range of printer features is so vast that we simply can't cover them all here. But we will focus on those that have a bearing on producing a quality manuscript or making the writing process easier. We'll also highlight a few features that may seem necessary, but aren't.

BIDIRECTIONAL PRINTING

A printer with bidirectional printing literally prints coming and going. It prints not only from left to right, but also from right to left (but the output is not backwards!). This is an important feature for both daisy-wheel and dot-matrix printers; a printer's print head has to move from the right edge of the paper back to the left every time it prints a line from left to right, so it might as well be doing something on the return trip. If not, the printer is wasting half its time.

CONTINUOUS UNDERLINING

This is a minor but important feature. With it, an underline is printed as a continuous line that includes spaces between letters (which is how typewriters underline). Without it, underlines have an odd, choppy appearance. It looks funny, and if it looks funny, you don't want it.

BACKSPACING AND OVERSTRIKING

A printer should be able to backspace in order to print some special characters, do underlining and boldfacing more efficiently, and to do special effects such as character strikeover. (That last is important if you include odd characters in a manuscript, like the cent sign, which can be produced with a "C" overstruck by a slash: ¢.)

SUPERSCRIPT AND SUBSCRIPT PRINTING

If you use superscripts and subscripts in your manuscripts, you'll welcome this capability. It's built into most dot-matrix printers and available on appropriate print wheels for daisy-wheel printers. You'll find it particularly useful if you produce documents containing footnotes.

MICROJUSTIFICATION AND PROPORTIONAL SPACING

Among the more esoteric terms you'll hear bandied about when printers are discussed are "microjustification" and "true proportional spacing." These printer features aren't as complicated as they sound (nor are they really important when it comes to producing manuscripts).

Microjustification is a method used by some printers to spread out the white space between words (and sometimes between letters) as evenly as possible. This makes for right-justified text that doesn't contain extra spacing between words.

True proportional spacing is the ability of a printer to print letters a varying distance apart, proportionally according to their width. A lower-case "i" is given less space than a lower-case "n," and an "m" gets more space than either.

Conventional typesetting machines use both techniques to make type flow smoothly on the printed page. Unfortunately, all printers except laser printers create a poor imitation of a typeset page when these features are used—an imitation that is very hard on the eyes. The irregular spaces between words make for bumpy reading.

While both microjustification and proportional spacing are obviously desirable traits in some situations, neither is of much use in producing manuscripts. The reason? Editors generally find right-justified and proportionally-spaced text difficult to read. That's one very important count against these features. Moreover, most editors are used to scanning pages in a certain manner, and these features throw them off. (And let us not forget the standard manuscript format, which dictates ragged right margins.)

FANCY FONTS AND OTHER SPECIAL EFFECTS

Daisy-wheel printers have interchangeable printing elements, offering a variety of fonts and type sizes. Dot-matrix and laser printers can produce graphics and an astounding range of type (laser printers are in fact used to typeset flyers, brochures, and even small books by some printing companies). Not surprisingly, some writers are tempted to use these "special effects" in their manuscripts. The results range from literal italics and fancy type styles to large type for headers and even graphics.

Whether this is done in an attempt to gain attention for the writer or to make things "easier" by providing an editor with a manuscript that looks typeset, it's a very bad idea. You should stick with a standard pica or elite typeface (the former is preferred because it's larger) and limit the special effects to underlining to indicate italics and maybe superscripting and subscripting, if there are footnotes. Anything else is superfluous and a distraction from the manuscript content—not to mention a deviation from standard manuscript format.

If you don't believe this, try submitting a manuscript with nine different type styles and maybe a few pictures thrown in. You'll get it back—fast! Save the fancy stuff for club flyers or letters to your friends.

Despite our apparently grim view of fancy type sizes and styles, you'll find them useful in letters and in creating letterheads, so they're not a bad feature to have. They're just not worth extra money if you're expecting them to earn their keep in sold manuscripts.

COLOR

Color is another printer feature writers don't need. There's really no use for color in producing manuscripts (you never used green ribbons in your typewriter, did you?). And color printers are expensive! The only realistic applications for color

printers are producing business documents and desktop publishing operations where *small* print runs are involved. Color printers do shine in reproducing color graphics and text for one-shot presentations, and in creating transparencies. But black on white is manuscript color.

MULTIPLE PRINTING MODES

The better dot-matrix printers—those offering letter quality or near-letter quality printing—often give you several printing options: letter-quality mode; standard "draft" mode (which prints in standard dot-matrix format); or "fast" mode (which prints in an extra-fast, though less legible format, with the minimum dots-per-character). You'll find uses for each, so if you buy a letter-quality dot-matrix printer, be sure that it offers multiple printing modes.

ARE GRAPHICS IN YOUR FUTURE?

After bad-mouthing printer graphics, we'll now redeem them a little. Graphics do have a place in writing—and not just for desktop publishing. If you're writing nonfiction that requires illustration, you'll find that dot-matrix and laser printer graphics are accepted by some book and magazine publishers. And if you don't draw very well, you'll find a new world of personal artistic "talent" in computer graphics. (Even if you don't produce finished art with your printer, you can at least provide some sensible roughs for the publisher's in-house artist to work from.)

If you need fancy letterhead, computer graphics can help. It's a simple matter (given the right program) to create letterhead graphics (and text) that look good when reproduced on a dot-matrix or laser printer. Once you've created the basic letterhead, you can store it and simply merge it in at the beginning of every letter you write. This eliminates switching between fanfold computer paper—the kind with the holes in the sides—to single sheets when you want to use letterhead stationery.

PRINTER HARDWARE OPTIONS

The hardware options and add-ons available for printers are almost as numerous as printer features, so we'll again focus on those most of interest to the writer.

FEEDING YOUR PRINTER (WITH PAPER)

Speaking of fanfold paper . . .

One of the great advantages of using a printer rather than a typewriter is not having to crank in a new sheet of paper for each page. Oh, you can put in paper one sheet at a time if you want; a printer's platen works just like a typewriter's. But feeding paper to a printer by hand is almost as silly as pushing your car instead of driving it.

There are two ways to automate the process of getting paper into a printer. It can be done one sheet at a time, using a sheet- or bin-feeder, or by using continuous, perforated sheets of paper that are fed to the printer using what's called a tractor feeder.

SHEET AND BIN FEEDERS

A sheet feeder is similar to the device used to feed paper to a copier. It's a Rube-Goldbergish mechanism that pulls sheets (if you're lucky) one at a time from a box, and conveys the sheet by any of several techniques to the printer's platen. A bin feeder is gravity-driven, allowing sheets of paper to fall (again, with luck) one by one to the printer's platen. Once a sheet of paper arrives at the platen, it's pulled through by friction as the platen is advanced.

Both sheet and bin feeders allow you to use any kind of standard-sized paper—letterhead, high-quality bond, or even colored paper. Both devices also offer a lot of potential headaches—headaches that we feel far outweigh any advantage in being able to use different kinds of paper. (And the advantages are few; as a writer you're going to

be using plain, 20-lb. bond for almost everything.)

The proper operation of a sheet or bin feeder depends in large part on the exact alignment and performance of mechanical devices. If a sheet of paper is even 1/32 of an inch off when it's delivered to the printer, you'll end up with either a jammed printer or a page with lines printed at an angle or outside the designated margins. Sheet and bin feeders are expensive, too (typically, three to four times the cost of the alternative, a tractor feeder). Finally, not all WP programs accommodate sheet or bin feeders.

For these reasons, we discourage the use of these paper-feed mechanisms. (NOTE: All laser printers use sheet or bin feeders. It makes you think . . . of all the jammed photocopiers you've wrestled with.)

TRACTOR FEEDERS

A tractor feeder advances paper through a printer rapidly and in perfect alignment. It consists of two wheels with rounded spikes (one wheel at either side of the platen, but typically movable to accomodate different paper widths and sheets of labels), which turn as the platen turns. The rounded spikes extend through holes on the outer edges of a special type of paper, pulling the paper through the printer in increments corresponding exactly to the movement of the platen. There's no slippage and no misalignment.

The paper used with tractor feeders is called continuous or fanfold paper, or more commonly, computer paper (the term we'll use here). The holes in the edges are not in the sheets themselves. Computer paper has an extra strip of paper on both sides and the holes are in these strips, at half-inch intervals. The strips are of course perforated for easy removal.

This paper comes in continuous sheets: the sheets are attached to one another (actually, they're perforated, but the idea's the same). This in turn means that a continuous stream of paper rolls through the printer, with the printer keeping track of the top and bottom margins. This is obviously faster than feeding the printer one sheet at a time—manually or automatically.

Tractor feed is an option on many printers, but it's becoming more and more an accepted standard. (Incidentally, *All Things Considered* on National Public Radio had a contest to name the strips with the holes: one we liked was *perfetti*. They're also called, more mundanely, tear strips.)

The average cost of a tractor feeder is low—below $150—but be sure to figure this in when shopping for a printer.

Paper Chase Computer paper is cheap and easy to work with. When you remove the perfetti, you're left with a width of 8-1/2 inches. Horizontal perforations between the sheets are spaced eleven inches apart. Thus, the paper separates into conventional 8-1/2″ × 11″ sheets.

As with typing paper, you'll find computer paper in various quantities and weights. You can get computer paper in quantities of 100, 250, 500, 1000, and 2500 continuous sheets, and the price is comparable to or (if you don't mind doing a little shopping) below that of standard paper. The paper comes in weights of 15 or 20 pounds, and we recommend using the latter.

There are two kinds of perforations. Standard perforations leave paper edges that look as if they were torn from perforations. The more common "microperf" or "clean edge" computer paper, however, leaves an edge that is all but indistinguishable from a cut edge. So be sure you buy microperf paper. And remember to take off the tear strips and separate the sheets before you submit anything. Don't laugh. We've seen it happen.

BUFFERS

Computers are fast, except when they have to deal with external devices to which they are connected (aka peripherals). When a computer has to exchange information with a peripheral, its speed of operation drops dramatically, to the rate the peripheral is able (and willing) to work.

This is true of printers, too. Although the contents of a file are fed to a printer literally at the speed of light, a printer's print head operates at a speed far below that.

Too, most printers accept a file from a computer in segments and electronically store each segment in a tiny, built-in memory area called a buffer. A printer must print the contents of this buffer (which may be less than half a page) before it can accept more of the file from the computer. This slows things down even more, since the entire WP system must pause to send more data down the pipeline when the buffer is empty. And if you're using a printer that has no buffer at all, the process gets even slower.

This bottleneck can cause other problems, too. Depending on what WP program you're using, you may be unable to edit a file while printing a document. Or if your program accommodates simultaneous printing and editing, you may find that the WP program responds more slowly to your commands while it's printing. And if you want to run a different program while you're printing, forget it: no WP program will cease operation while printing without scrapping the print job in progress (it will tactfully warn you first).

Fortunately, there are solutions. You can expand the printer's buffer (this usually involves adding microchips) or buy a device called a printer buffer, which is essentially a small box that goes between the computer and the printer. In either case, the larger buffer accepts the data as fast as the computer sends it. The buffer then feeds data to the printer at a speed the printer can accept.

In the meantime, the WP program is "fooled" into thinking that the document in question has already been printed, which frees it up for other tasks.

A minimal buffer size is 8K (8,000 bytes of memory); a practical buffer size is 64K (or 64,000 bytes of memory). This will accommodate most files you need to print. If you can, buy a printer with a good-sized buffer already built in.

EXTERNAL CONTROLS
Almost all printers have external controls (buttons) of some sort. The basic controls you should find on any printer include a button to take a printer offline (i.e., disconnect it from the computer without turning it off—important if you have some special format commands in the printer you don't want lost, or you don't want to lose the portion of the document stored in the buffer while you're, say, changing ribbons); a "line feed" button, which advances the paper one line each time it's pressed; and a "form feed" button, which advances the paper to the next page.

The more pricey printers offer additional controls used to set certain printer features. These can be convenient—even though most of the work of controlling a printer is done by software—because, as you've gathered by now, to get the software to tell the printer what to do requires that you tell the software what to do. This is fine in most instances, as putting format codes in a document usually causes the document to be displayed on the screen in close-to-printed format. But if you want to change printing modes—from "draft" to "letter-quality" with a dot-matrix printer, for instance, or from standard to all bold-face with a daisy-wheel (and there may be times you'll want to do this)—it's far easier to simply press a button on the printer than to insert a command in a document. So you may want to investigate the availability of such external controls when shopping for a printer.

OUT-OF-PAPER SIGNAL
Even a 2500-sheet stack of computer paper will run out eventually, and it may well happen when you're not in the same room as your printer. A printer will continue printing (on the bare platen!) if it doesn't have some means of telling whether there's paper there or not. Fortunately, most printers have a "paper out" alarm, which simultaneously stops printing and makes the printer beep to attract your attention. This is worth having.

DIP SWITCH ACCESS
You may want to change certain elements of a printer's operation without going to the trouble of sending software commands every time you print—elements that external controls don't handle. These include switching the paper out alarm off or on, using extra-wide paper, having the printer add line feeds after carriage returns, etc. Many printers have what are called external DIP switches, which make changing such elements easy (if you follow the printer manual's instructions). They're worth having.

REPLACEABLE PRINT HEAD (DOT-MATRIX PRINTERS)
Because it's the most active moving part on a dot-matrix printer, the print head is the element most likely to wear out. Many printers are designed so that the user can replace the print head, and this is a real plus if you like to save money. You can usually buy a replacement print head for less than $50 and save far more than that in labor costs (not to mention reducing the amount of time your printer is "down" for repairs). Sure, you're a writer, not a repairperson, but if you can use a screwdriver, you can replace a print head. Most printers' manuals give instructions. Some of the easiest kinds simply snap out, once a restraining latch is flipped out of the way—easier than changing most typewriter ribbons. Though not a must, easily replaceable printheads are worth considering.

CHARACTER-FONT CARTRIDGES AND CHIPS

A few dot-matrix and almost all laser printers offer plug-in cartridges and/or microchips that enable the printer to print additional type sizes and styles. Normally, the standard fonts you'll use in manuscript preparation are already built into the printer, so you'll find no real use for these add-ons unless you're doing desktop publishing.

KEYBOARDS

A rather early "innovation" in computer printers was the keyboard. The idea was to offer the user the benefits of both a typewriter and a printer and to provide a back-up way to use the printer in case the computer was out of commission.

We're back to halfbreed typewriters again; like the printing typewriter, this wasn't a good idea. For one thing, switching from one keyboard to another is difficult. Then there's the fact that printers with keyboards tend to have a larger "footprint" (amount of space taken up on a desk top) than normal printers. Most lack buffers. Finally, they cost much more than conventional printers.

If you really need typewriter-style response from a printer, some WP programs offer a "typewriter" or "type-thru" mode that makes a printer echo what you type immediately. (There are also a number of special programs that will do the same thing.) But why would you want to use a word-processing system as a typewriter to begin with? Aside from addressing envelopes, using a computer printer as a letter-by-letter typewriter is self-defeating; you can't edit! Forget this one.

HOW TO SELECT A PRINTER

At this point, you probably feel you know more about printers than you ever wanted to, and surely have enough knowledge to make an intelligent selection. But there are a few other considerations in printer selection that we'd like to pass along.

Before getting into those, this piece of advice for those who are shopping for their first WP systems: if you don't buy your computer, software, and printer from the same source, it's best to buy the computer and software first. Even though the printer is the most important element in your WP system as far as the outside world is concerned, it is in some respects the least important element to you, as a writer putting words on the screen. A printer has very little to do with how you create and edit documents—which is what you'll spend most of your word-processing time doing and which most of the rest of this book is about—whereas the computer and WP software you use directly determine the ease and efficiency with which you'll produce those words. First things first.

DETERMINING WHAT YOU NEED

Printers cost. And your printer is a purchase you'll probably live with for quite some time. So it's a good idea to determine exactly what you need before you begin shopping (and don't put much weight on a salesperson's "it's just like . . ." "it's as good as . . ." or "you'll never notice the difference"). Combine what you've learned about printers thus far with the considerations we're about to discuss.

Make a list of the features and options you feel are absolutely necessary to you. Then visit computer stores and ask to see these features demonstrated on various printers. Don't take anybody's word for what the printout will look like: see for yourself. If you can't spot the dots, an editor's not likely to either. (There's a lot of nonsense talked about letter quality, especially by people selling non-letter quality.)

You may modify your list as you go, but you'll know exactly what you're looking for.

Be firm. Don't eliminate a feature or features just because someone says you don't

TIP #2: TRADEOFFS

The major considerations for a writer in buying a printer are print quality and speed, tempered by budget. So you may have to eliminate something of what you want in a printer in favor of what you *need*. For instance, a daisy-wheel printer that can print a page in under four minutes (and there are some that slow!) may be out of your price range, in which case you'll have to look at dot-matrix printers. Conversely, if you're just not satisfied with the print quality of dot-matrix printers, you may have to save up a little more money to buy a daisy-wheel printer and wait while the pages grind out. Then, too,

you may find that you can live with either a slower daisy-wheel printer or a letter-quality dot-matrix printer, depending solely on the price.

In general, if you can't afford the printer you want but have the option of buying a lower-priced printer that offers a minimum of compromise (buying a dot-matrix printer instead of a daisy-wheel, perhaps) you should go ahead and buy now. You can upgrade later and sell your old printer to recover part of your investment. In the meantime, you'll be enjoying the unlimited benefits of word processing.

---

need it, or because a printer that offers all the features on your "must" list except one is available at a good price. Shop around. And remember that your needs as a writer are not those of the market at which printer ads and sales pitches are normally aimed (business users, casual users, and others who need—or think they need—features that you don't). Modify your list of necessary features only when you've determined, by trying out a feature, that you can live without it.

Now let's take a quick look at the elements that will determine what you include on your list of printer features.

PRINTER FEATURES AND OPTIONS

By now you should have a good idea of what features will be useful to you. You've probably eliminated color from consideration, for example. Or you might be considering graphics capability for letterheads or your monthly writers' club newsletter. And maybe you've decided that computer paper just isn't for you, in which case you've eliminated tractor feed from consideration. We'll leave that up to you—you're the best judge of what you need.

If you think you can do without certain features we've recommended, however, at least see them in action before you eliminate them. And remember that some features add to the price of a printer, so you may well have to eliminate one or more of them.

PRINT QUALITY

Don't decide that you must have one type of printer rather than another based on print quality until you've seen examples of the best of each. It's easy to find a daisy-wheel, dot-matrix, or laser printer that will produce an acceptable printout. Make "print quality" a defining rather than a limiting criterion. It's important, but it's not the be-all and end-all—speed, reliability, and price are important, too.

SPEED

Speed is relative. If you've never used a printer, a 22 character-per-second daisy-wheel printer will seem fast—especially if you type at 10 characters per second (60 wpm). If you've been around computers for a while, though, daisy-wheel printers will seem really slow. Dot-matrix and laser printers are the real speed demons in the printer world and always will be. But you need to ask yourself how important speed is to you.

If you're a prolific writer, speed is going to be very important (and even more important if you don't have a print buffer to speed things up—though there's a way around that, as you'll learn in Chapter 5). If you aren't concerned that a novel will take ten hours rather than six to print, or if you're working primarily on short stories or articles that can be printing out while you walk the dog or let the cat in/out/in, then you'll probably be happy with a daisy-wheel printer or with one of the slower letter-quality dot-matrix printers.

Consider carefully whether speed will be on your list of necessary features; if you sacrifice speed for top quality, you may regret it later as you watch your printer while away the hours on a lengthy manuscript. At the other end of the scale, you may end up unhappy with the fact that you could have had better print quality for the same money, whereas you opted for lightning pages that look like junk.

PRICE

The one constant in the personal computer market is the fact that prices continually bob up and down. This is partly the result of competition, and partly the result of perfectly useful equipment becoming "obsolete" as new models are introduced. (Obsolete means it's six months old and people are trading up to the new stuff in droves.) Because of this, the prices we've quoted here are for comparison only. But it's safe to say that the relative prices will stay the same, which means that the low-cost printers are dot-matrix, with daisy-wheel printers next and laser printers at the top end of the price scale.

When budgeting for a printer, think of price *ranges*. Determine ranges for each type of printer and use these as a guide in eliminating or including a particular type of printer on your list of possibilities. If, for example, you can afford a laser printer, then you can afford a daisy-wheel or a dot-matrix printer. If you can't afford a daisy-wheel printer, then you can't afford a laser printer, but you *can* afford a dot-matrix printer. (Used printers are a different matter—one we'll get to in a minute.)

Once you have determined the type(s) of printer you can afford based on general price ranges, you can add or eliminate various features and options based on their price ranges.

OTHER CONSIDERATIONS

Other elements worth considering include hardware compatibility, software compatibility, warranty, and the availability of service.

HARDWARE COMPATIBILITY

Obviously, a printer must be compatible with the computer you intend to use. With many computers, insuring compatibility is a simple matter of making sure the seller provides the right connecting cable for you. However, you may find it necessary to buy an adaptor or card to connect the printer to your computer. (And remember—stay away from serial printers.)

SOFTWARE COMPATIBILITY

Software compatibility is a major issue in buying a printer. Many printers aren't accommodated by a particular WP program, though most programs are frequently updated to include more printers. In general, avoid any printer you're not sure your WP software will support (work with). However, some printers can behave like any of several different printers, according to the way their DIP switches are set. If a printer emulates (acts like) a printer listed as supported by the WP program you want to use, it may work with that program. To be safe, however, contact the printer's manufacturer or the publisher of your WP program if you have any questions about compatibility.

WARRANTY AND SERVICE

See our comments on warranty and service for computers in Chapter 1; these apply to printers as well as computers.

GATHERING DATA

As with computers, you should gather information on printers from as many sources as possible. Read ads and reviews in computer magazines, quiz fellow writers about the printers they use, and visit computer stores for hands-on demonstrations. Write or call printer manufacturers for general information or even to get answers to specific questions. You can't have too much information.

The evaluation form below will help you in the selection process. You may want to photocopy it, to have it ready when you're considering your next printer.

TIP #3: IS A CHEAP PRINTER REALLY CHEAP? QUALITY VS. PRICE

Quality is an all-important consideration in buying computer equipment. And "quality" usually means a reliable, full-featured machine made by a reputable manufacturer. You can find bargain-priced printers of all types, but we all but guarantee a better than 90% probability that off-brand, low-cost printers are going to cost you more than their original price. Such printers tend to show up in the marketplace only to disappear within a few months, leaving hundreds or thousands of owners with no support (read: the repair shop is in Singapore). Equally bad, many of them use obscure, difficult-to-find, or expensive ribbons. Many bargain-priced printers are basically junk, good for a few thousand pages (if that) before they literally fall apart.

In the end, such a bargain will cost you time, money, and incipient ulcers—and you'll have to replace it with the quality printer that you should have bought in the beginning.

Table 4.1 Printer Evaluation Chart

Printer brand, model, and type					
S Bi-directional printing					
E Continuous underlining					
R Backspacing/ overstriking					
U Super- and sub-scripts					
T Micro-justification					
A Proportional spacing					
E Multiple printing modes					
F Graphics					

F E A T U R E S						
	Tractor or sheet feed?					
	Built-in buffer? (size)					
	External controls					
	Out-of-paper signal					
	DIP switch access					
	Replaceable print head					

Eventually, you'll have a list of printers that provide exactly what you need and fit in your budget. Then it's time to make the final choice—and decide where to buy it. When you're ready, review our comments on buying computer equipment (new and used) in Chapter 1 to see if you might be able to acquire your dream printer for less than full retail price.

TIP #4: TAKING CARE OF YOUR PRINTER

Printers require the same setup and care as discussed for computers. Avoid temperature extremes in the printer environment, and be sure to select a location that is relatively dust- and moisture-free.

Your printer should have a solid supporting surface, and you'll want to minimize the chance of heavy objects falling on it (or small objects into it). Not under the shelf where the cats like to walk, for instance. Cat hair, play toys, and inquisitive cat feet are emphatically not good for printers.

Don't plug a printer into an outlet that's already being used by electrical equipment that uses a lot of power—especially anything that heats, like a toaster, or that pulls power in surges, like an air conditioner. An overloaded circuit means low voltage, which shortens electronic component life. And too many devices on the same circuit can blow a fuse—which also blows documents off your screen and ruins print jobs.

Printers require very little maintenance beyond basic cleaning. Clean the outside surface periodically with a mild cleaning solution—mild dish detergent will do, or window cleaner. Don't use the industrial-strength stuff that dissolves plastic. Use a small plastic vacuum cleaner attachment to clear paper dust and other debris from the interior of the printer periodically. (There's no need to disassemble the printer to do this; simply clean what's exposed when you open the printer's cover—if it has one—and remove the ribbon.)

CHAPTER 5

Peripheral Vision: Mice, Modems, and More

OVERVIEW: THIS CHAPTER COVERS

1. What you can do with a mouse.

2. Telecommunications for writers; electronic mail; manuscript delivery by E-mail; online research.

3. Cables and extensions.

4. Cards for memory expansion; hard drives on cards; more.

5. Add-on disk drives.

6. CD ROM: tomorrow's technology today.

A PERIPHERAL IS ANY DEVICE you attach to your computer that's either controlled by the computer and/or exchanges information with it. Printers are peripherals, as are disk drives. But there are many more, including "mice," modems, and CD ROM devices. We'll discuss all of these—and more—in this chapter, focusing on what you can do with such devices and what they can do for you.

MORE ON MICE

As described in Chapter 1, a mouse is an input device that consists of a streamlined box with one to three buttons on its top, a roller ball built into its base, and a cable that connects it to a computer (the mouse's "tail").

As the mouse is rolled on a desktop, the ball in its base moves and sensors transmit this information to the computer. A special program translates this movement, as well as the signals sent when one of the buttons is pressed, into information that moves the cursor around the screen and selects items (just like pressing ENTER/RETURN). (A variation on this device is the "trackball," which features a roller mounted on top. The roller is turned to move the cursor, while the device remains stationary.)

The net effect is that the cursor moves smoothly about the screen in analog of the way you move the mouse across the desktop. The primary application of mice is with programs that make use of "pull-down" menus and prompts.

Mice are great for getting the cursor to a particular area on the screen fast, and for allowing you to do things like mark blocks, select menu items, etc., quickly, once the cursor is there.

With a little work, you can develop "mouse reflexes" to the point where it's significantly faster to use the mouse than the keyboard. However, the reflexes take time to develop (you have to move your hand from the keyboard, etc.). If you're used to

moving the cursor around the screen using cursor-movement keys, you may find that you have to unlearn your current cursor-movement habits.

Mice are available for a wide range of computers. They come as standard equipment with the Apple Macintosh, Atari ST, and Commodore Amiga, and can be purchased for use with IBM PC and PC clone computers, the Apple II series, Commodore, and most other brands.

TELECOMMUNICATIONS FOR WRITERS

Like many other professionals and businesspeople, writers and editors are discovering the easy availability and utility of microcomputer telecommunications (or, as we prefer to call it, telecomputing). Simply described, telecomputing is communication and information transfer via computers, the computers being linked by telephone lines and the connection facilitated by modems.

What we'll discuss here is really just the most basic information about telecommunications. For more in-depth information about how telecomputing works, how to select and use equipment and software, and what's out there in the form of electronic mail and other services, you may find *The Modem Reference*, by Michael A. Banks (Brady Books/Simon & Schuster, 1988) of help.

MODEMS

The first item you'll need to add to your computer system to telecompute is a modem. A modem is a device that "translates" computer data into a form that can be transmitted by telephone line and, on the other end of things, translates that data back into information that can be used by the computer.

Modems come in one of two forms: external and internal. An external modem, as shown in Figure 5.1, is a small box (with indicator lights) that connects to a computer via a cable. The part of a computer that a modem connects with is a special device called a "serial port" that usually takes the form of a card that plugs into the computer internally. (See the section on "Cards" later in this chapter for more information.)

An internal modem, like the one in Figure 5.2, doesn't require a serial port for connection, as it has a serial card built into it. Internal modems are more expensive than external modems, but provide several advantages, not the least of which is the fact that they don't take up desk space. (They do, however, take up expansion slot space *inside* your computer's housing.)

COMMUNICATIONS SOFTWARE

You'll also need communications software (aka "terminal" or "terminal emulation" software) to communicate via modem. A communications program makes your computer act like a communications terminal rather than a word processor and handles most of the chores of computer-to-computer data transfer. Like WP programs, communications programs may be menu-driven or command-driven; if you know little or nothing about computer communications, we suggest that you use a menu-driven program like ProComm for the IBM PC. Menu-driven programs offer more "hand-holding" and step-by-step guided procedures than do command-driven ones.

TELECOMPUTING CHANNELS

Once you have your computer set up with a modem and communications software, there are two major ways to communicate with others who have computers. The first consists of online services; the second is

Figure 5.1, External Modem

direct-dial, which is direct communication between two personal computers.

MAKING THE CONNECTION: ONLINE SERVICES

Online services are commercial operations that offer services to subscribers at a rate that typically ranges from twelve to fifty cents per minute. The services offered may include electronic mail (E-mail), research databases, news services, stock quotes, real-time conferencing capability (in effect, typing over the phone directly onto the screen of someone else's computer), special-interest groups, shopping, and more. Based on large mainframe and minicomputers, online services contain millions of bytes of data in the form of databases and private and public messages, and can host from a few dozen to several hundred users simultaneously.

Some services, like CompuServe and DELPHI, are general, and offer a full range of services. Others specialize. MCI Mail, for example, specializes in E-mail and associated services (including access to Telex and FAX). Dialog, Knowledge-Index, and NewsNet specialize in offering news and topical databases and newsletters, covering subjects ranging from chemical engineering to book reviews. A list of the major services, with contact information, is included as Appendix B.

Selecting an online service is a comparative proposition, meaning that you must take a look at what each has to offer, then decide whether it meets your needs. There is nothing to stop you from using more than one online service, of course. And because most are offered on a pay-as-you-go basis (you pay only when you use them), signing up for more than one service doesn't mean you'll be paying proportionally more.

Figure 5.2, Internal Modem

DIRECT-DIAL TELECOMPUTING

Only rarely will you have occasion to dial up another personal computer directly; not only is the cost of using an online service as an intermediary less than long-distance telephone calls, but it's also far easier to connect by means of an online service, for several reasons. Online services are always available, so you don't have to coordinate schedules with another person to exchange messages or send/receive a manuscript. Too, online services are designed to communicate with just about every kind of computer and modem combination currently in existence. This means that you'll find the processes of making connection and transferring files to be relatively trouble-free.

If you need to exchange files with a collaborator or an editor who's not on one of the online services, you'll have to dial that person's computer directly, but be prepared to do a little experimentation before you get the connection working properly.

WHY TELECOMPUTE? APPLICATIONS FOR WRITERS

Now that you have an idea of what's out there and what you need to access it, let's take a look at how you can use telecomputing to your advantage.

The major applications of telecomputing for writers are E-mail for contact with editors and manuscript delivery, online research, and special-interest groups.

ELECTRONIC MAIL

E-mail is one of the wonders of the computer world. Consider: It offers instant delivery, it's relatively cheap (have you checked the cost of overnight delivery services lately?), the "post office" is never closed, and you don't have to address envelopes or lick stamps. E-mail is private (only you and the addressee can read your messages) and—perhaps best of all—you don't have to leave your home or office to send an E-mail "letter" or other document.

E-mail has for several years been recognized as a powerful tool by business and, more recently, by professionals and the general public. (Over ten million electronic mail messages are delivered every day!) Almost every large publisher is tied into some electronic mail system or another nowadays. Even the least progressive of the larger publishers have Telex and/or FAX (facsimile transmission) equipment (which often consists of computers)—and the E-mail services on most online services can send text to Telex or FAX "addresses."

Writers who use E-mail to maintain contact with editors find its convenience without equal. E-mail is a convenient and economical substitute for expensive long-distance telephone calls, and answering an E-mail message is so simple and non-demanding that even the most dedicated procrastinator has a hard time not replying. It can be a real time-saver, too, when you need to get the same message to more than one person.

E-mail can help you meet manuscript delivery deadlines, too, as most online services can transfer at least a chapter's worth of text in one block.

The bottom line is this: If you have a computer and modem, you can use E-mail to send messages and manuscripts to perhaps 70% of the country's major publishers—as well as to hundreds more overseas. This is not to say that all editors accept E-mail submissions (and you certainly must have advance permission to transmit a manuscript this way), but it is a coming thing.

There are many more benefits to using E-mail, but the people with whom you need to communicate must be online, too. You don't necessarily have to use the same system as the person to whom you wish to send a message, though. There exist a number of inter-system links (CompuServe users can exchange E-mail with those who use MCI Mail), and at least one service that will carry E-mail between online services, called DASNET.

ONLINE RESEARCH

Talk with many business and professional modem users, and you'll come away convinced that the sum total of human knowledge can be found online.

That's almost true. Sophisticated services like Lockheed's Dialog Information Service provide access to a wealth of general and specialized information that is nothing short of staggering. Information utilities such as NewsNet and Dow Jones News/ Retrieval offer the latest information in a variety of special-interest areas, as well as updates on current and recent events, and business news. Business, economic, and general news from AP, Reuters, USA Today, and other sources is available on a variety of online services, and some magazines publish online versions.

Comprehensive encyclopedias with sophisticated search and cross-referencing capabilities can be found on several services, too.

Suffice it to say you'll be able to find information online on just about any topic, technical or non-technical, common or obscure. And finding the information is relatively easy; sophisticated searching capability allows you to find the smallest, most specialized reference to a topic, or to locate information by cross-reference. Once you've located the information you need, you can "capture" it on one of your disks for future reference.

Such services are often expensive; you must pay for the convenience of home access, as well as for the specialized knowledge you won't find elsewhere and for the rapid search capability that online databases offer. Online research charges can range from as low as twelve cents per minute to access general encyclopedias to as high as five dollars per minute to use specialized databases and newsletters. However, with most database and information

retrieval systems, you're likely to spend thirty to forty dollars at most (if that) to track down full background on a topic. (NOTE: A number of general online services offer what is called "gateway" access to database and information text retrieval services. This means you access other services without leaving the one you're on.)

Incidentally, a relatively recent development in information storage technology that may offer a viable alternative to online services is the CD ROM, discussed later in this chapter.

ONLINE SPECIAL-INTEREST GROUPS FOR WRITERS

A special-interest group (SIG) is, as the name implies, a group of people who gather to pool knowledge and resources and to share news and other information of common interest. Special interest groups on online services are likewise meeting-places and resource areas for people who share common interests—be they computer, professional, hobby, or personal.

SIGs are hosted on major online services, such as DELPHI, CompuServe, and GEnie, and are typically available at no cost beyond a host system's normal connect charges. On some systems, certain SIG services are offered at a discount.

It's easiest to think of a SIG as a club where you can meet other members in conference (if provided) or via private E-mail, post questions and comments on a bulletin board, and access vast libraries of information and software.

Examples of SIG services include shopping services, private areas for members of national organizations (as is the case with the Science Fiction Writers of America in DELPHI's Science Fiction/Fantasy Group), online newsletters, and more. SIGs also duplicate the services of their host systems with real-time conferences and access to E-mail. Many provide some unique services of their own.

Writers' SIGs typically offer a wealth of

downloadable material in databases, including programs of interest to writers. A typical SIG's databases are organized into such topics as are appropriate to its members' interests. For example, a SIG for writers might feature topics such as "Markets," "Fiction," "Nonfiction," "Magazine Writing," "Book-Length Works," "Critique Exchange," "Manuscripts Wanted," and "Professional Resumes," in addition to a "General Interest" topic.

SIGs also offer bulletin board areas where you can participate in ongoing conversations with other writers (and, in many cases, editors), and regularly-scheduled real-time conferences with editors and writers of note. Perhaps most important of all, they put you in touch with writers and editors from all parts of the country, with all sorts of interests. In this respect, SIGs function in the same way as conventional "networking" among writers via writers' club meetings, conferences, and correspondence.

SIGs catering to writers can be found on most of the commercial online services, including BIX, CompuServe, DELPHI, and GEnie.

CABLES

A computer must have a connecting cable to communicate with a printer, a modem, extra floppy disk drives and/or external hard drives, or other peripherals. A separate cable is required for each peripheral you use, and they're not interchangeable. Each peripheral's cable is wired differently and uses different kinds of connectors, which means that you can't use your printer's cable to connect your modem to the computer when you're not printing.

We won't get into how these cables are wired; we'll just say that if you don't have the right cable, your equipment will operate improperly or not at all. And there's a very good chance that the peripheral or computer will damaged by improper cable

wiring! Obviously, you want to be very careful about selecting cables.

You can make cables (it's really simple—but you have to know what you're doing), but when you buy a peripheral you should receive with it a cable that's appropriate for connecting that peripheral to your brand of computer. If you don't get a cable with a printer or modem, or whatever, ask for one (it should be included at no extra cost). If the establishment selling the peripheral can't provide a cable, or demands an exorbitant price, take your business elsewhere.

EXTENSIONS

OK, you have your printer set up and it's clicking merrily away—too merrily for your tastes. In fact, it's a bit loud in the rather confined space of your home office. And it takes up too much space on your desk. But you can't move it more than six feet from your computer because that's the length of your printer cable.

What do you do? Get another cable and plug the two together? Splice in a few feet? Well . . . maybe. The individual connections between pins must be duplicated exactly—if they're not, you're in for trouble. Unless you understand electricity and can solder or use solderless connectors, we don't recommend trying to modify or build your own cable. Instead, shop for a longer cable or ask someone who knows how to make one for you. Computer stores have them, as do the many catalogues of computer supplies you'll find advertised in computer magazines.

Incidentally, the maximum practical length for data-carrying cables is fifty feet; longer cables tend to "lose" information.

PICK A CARD . . . ANY CARD

Computer cards (sometimes called "boards") are printed-circuit boards on which are mounted integrated circuits and other devices; they are actually sub-computers in themselves, designed to perform specific jobs. (The internal modem in Figure 5.2 is one example of a card.) Cards typically plug into what are called expansion slots inside a computer. Not all computers have expansion slots, but for those that do, cards provide a way to expand and enhance a computer's power and capabilities. (Cards can usually be installed by the user, by the way. Full instructions are provided, and the most difficult aspect of installation is opening the computer's case. This is not to say that you can't or shouldn't get a computer technician to install a card for you; it all depends on how mechanically inclined you are.)

There are different cards for different jobs, some of which (parallel and serial ports) we've already introduced you to. Several are worth examining in more detail.

THANKS FOR THE MEMORY . . . MEMORY EXPANSION CARDS

Memory expansion cards add RAM (Random Access Memory) to a computer. Being able to add this kind of memory (not possible with all computers) is a desirable feature because RAM is where all the work is done by your computer. (Floppy and hard disks merely provide storage and a base of operations for programs.) The amount of RAM available dictates in part how large a document can be, how quickly you can move through it and perform various WP program operations, and even whether you can run certain programs. It's the "K" in a 640K computer—in effect, the computer's "waking consciousness" and usable capacity.

HARD CARDS

Simply put, a hard card is a hard disk on a card. Rather than putting data on rotating disks of magnetic media, however, a hard card stores information on a special kind of microchip that retains information even when a computer is turned off.

Hard cards provide faster access to data than conventional hard disks (there are no moving parts) and are less prone to "crashes" and other problems. (NOTE: We should add that there are many hard cards that actually contain a "conventional" hard disk.)

PORTS OF CALL AND OTHER CARDS

We mentioned earlier that your computer must have a parallel port to communicate with a typical printer and a serial port to communicate with a modem. These ports are sometimes used to communicate with other peripherals, like mice, as well. So it's worth having these kinds of cards installed in your computer when you first buy it.

Other kinds of cards include a clock/calendar, which keeps track of the date and time for systems that use such information; special video cards that enable a computer to display high-resolution colors and graphics; "speed-up" boards to make a computer run faster; emulation boards that allow a computer to act like another brand of computer (these are rare); boards that work with a special kind of disk drive to allow, say, an Apple computer to read an IBM disk; cards to control access to disk drives; and cards that provide FAX, modem, and other capabilities.

It's worth noting that many cards offer multiple functions. For example, a memory-expansion card may include a clock/calendar function; or a hard card may include RAM expansion. If you're going to add more than one function to your computer, look for a card that combines as many as possible.

ADD-ON DISK DRIVES

Add-on disk drives—either floppy or hard drives—are something that most computer owners will consider at one time or another. If, for instance, you buy a computer with only one floppy drive, you are going to want to add a second sooner or later (probably sooner, once you discover the limitations of a single-drive system). Or you might want to upgrade a computer that has 5-1/4″ drives by replacing the drives with 3-1/2″ drives—or adding a 3-1/2″ drive to enable you to use both types of disks. And whether you have a one- or two-floppy drive system, you'll eventually want to add a hard disk.

ADDING FLOPPY DRIVES

You have two choices when it comes to floppy disk drives of any size: buy equipment made by the manufacturer or buy from an aftermarket supplier. If you buy a drive made by the original manufacturer of your computer, it's a safe bet that the drive will work with the computer—but it will almost always cost more than an aftermarket supplier's drive. Aftermarket drives, on the other hand, must be selected carefully; it's best to find a dealer in your area who will install the drive and guarantee its operation.

The major technical consideration in buying a floppy drive is whether it will be able to communicate with the card that controls communication with disk drives. This is easily determined; simply plug the new drive in and see if it works, after checking with the person you're getting the drive from, to make sure it's intended for use with your computer.

ADDING A HARD DRIVE

The same cost considerations apply to hard drives, but you have more things to consider. First, you have to decide whether you want an external drive or an internal drive. An external drive offers a price advantage over an internal drive, but it will take up more desk space and, because it's more exposed to the usual variety of desktop hazards, is more prone to breakdowns. An internal drive is less likely to suffer mechanical failure (having no moving parts), but is more costly than an external drive.

That settled, you must select a hard-disk controller card (for external hard disks only; internals have their controllers built in), which requires some additional investigation.

Where controllers are concerned, there's the little-known fact that not all hard disk controllers designed for a particular type of computer (MS-DOS, for instance) will work with each model of computer. And, perverse as it is, the controller may well work initially, then start acting bizarre later—when the drive has a certain amount of information stored on it, or when you try a tricky formatting operation. Explaining why would be too complicated to be worth it; trust us. So as with floppy disk drives, look for a local dealer who can install and guarantee the operation of the controller and drive. Or, at the very least, buy the controller and drive as a package.

CD ROM: TOMORROW'S TECHNOLOGY TODAY

One of the most exciting technological innovations in recent years is the compact disk, or CD, which is fast replacing vinyl disks and cassette tapes as the medium for audio recordings. The capacity and recording quality of CDs far exceed those of any other medium, facts that won the CD almost instant acceptance in the marketplace.

Not surprisingly, this superior technology has been adapted for computer data storage in the form of "CD ROMs." A CD ROM (Compact Disk Read-Only Memory) is a compact disk—just like an audio CD—that contains information in a computer-readable format. Recent breakthroughs in CD ROM technology have enabled startling quantities of information to be stored on a CD ROM. Entire sets of reference works, such as encyclopedias and dictionaries, are already on the market—each on one CD ROM.

The implications of CD ROM technology

are wonderful. With a CD ROM, you can not only have an entire encyclopedia at your fingertips, but also the ability to search for data and cross-references at computer speeds. This may sound a lot like online research, but there are two differences: using a CD ROM is faster than dialing up an online database, and CD ROMs offer graphics capability—meaning you can view digitized pictures from a reference work on your computer screen. It's also cheaper to own the reference work in CD ROM form than to dial up an online service for the same information, if you use it a lot.

To use a CD ROM, you need a CD ROM "player" (an external device that attaches to your computer), as well as an interface/controller card to enable your computer to read information on the CD ROM. These can be expensive—as much as you paid for the computer itself in some cases—but worth it if you use certain reference works very often. The CD ROMs themselves are not inexpensive, either (the cost is on a par with the printed books they contain). As with other computer technology, however, costs will drop as technology advances and demand increases.

We feel that CD ROMs are the wave of the future. Within ten years, most computer users who need them will have several hundred reference tomes and an encyclopedia or two stacked in a couple of square feet on their desks, ready for instant access.

We do have one reservation about this marvelous technology (and this applies to online research, as well, by the way): The potential for plagiarism is enormous. It's all too easy to insert a paragraph—or an entire article—into a document from a CD ROM. However, as the technology becomes more common, safeguards against this will undoubtedly be developed.

PART TWO

Words on Screen: What Your Manual Won't Tell You and You Didn't Know Who to Ask

A Compendium of Time- and Keystroke-Savers, Tips on Troubleshooting and Avoiding Common Problems, and Writerly Shortcuts in Generating Text on Screen, on Disk, As Telecommunications Signals, and As Hard Copy Printouts.

CHAPTER 6

Are You Saved?

WHEN, WHEN NOT, AND HOW TO SAVE

OVERVIEW: THIS CHAPTER COVERS:

1. Establishing a sensible, comfortable, *effective* routine for saving both what's on screen and what's on disk.

2. Setting up and using the automatic save feature some WP programs offer; recovering backed-up data after a power failure or major mistake.

3. Keeping a disk's total contents and individual files within the maximum workable size.

4. Avoiding the mistake of thinking there's nothing onscreen when there *is*, even if you can't see it.

5. Optimizing disks.

6. Backing up and archiving disks.

7. Deleting wisely.

THIS CHAPTER DEALS WITH THE PRACTICALITIES and finesses of using one of the fundamental functions that make computers what they are—their capacity to store and retrieve data.

The primary consideration is simple survival: preventing your document from vanishing into the ether. But we'll also cover related considerations, like shifting your data from disk to disk and organizing the storage format of the disks themselves in a process called "optimizing" to help prevent data loss due to disk failure. You'll also learn about the need to make backup and archive disks to store both working documents and writing that's complete, in final form. Lastly, you'll learn how your WP program's save function can make your writing life simpler and easier and how to avoid the predictable crises of the WP writing life.

SAVE YOUR WORK!

Saving the work on your screen is absolutely vital. Until it's saved, your working document is only a bunch of electronic squiggles that vanish if you turn your computer off, or there's a power failure, or you unintentionally or thoughtlessly exit your WP program. When your screen goes blank, that unsaved document is gone, and there's absolutely no way to get it back. Therefore, it's important to get every working document into permanent storage (on a floppy or hard disk) frequently, saving the document at regular intervals as you change and expand it.

If you work more than ten minutes or so on a document, don't wait until you've finished working on it to save it. Save your work periodically as you write. That way, the most you will lose is a paragraph or two, should disaster strike. Your most recent changes will be lost, but the main document, up to the last save, will be on disk, safe and ready to use.

And with most systems, the version preceding *that* one will also be on disk, in the

form of a "backup" file (usually with the filename extension .BAK, or something similar). Programs of this type (i.e., programs that retain an earlier version of a file) normally keep only one previous version—the most recent one.

In short, any time you've made a significant number of changes in a document, save it.

DO YOU KNOW WHERE YOUR FILES ARE?

WP programs handle documents and saving two different ways.

Most programs scroll your document through memory a few pages at a time, returning to disk when you need to see a part that precedes or follows what's currently in memory. Such programs write a new file to disk as you go, too. This kind of program design is a holdover from the early days of personal computing, when computers typically had very little memory, and in fact is retained in many programs today because not every computer has a lot of free memory—either by design, owner's choice, or because the WP itself takes up so much memory. As you'll learn, this kind of program can make it difficult to save when you run into problems with, say, a full work disk.

Some few programs put the entire document in your computer's memory at one time. XyWrite III+ for MS-DOS computers is one example of such a program. This is a grand feature, because that way you can swap disks and save the document without worry. You aren't restricted to the original work disk because the program doesn't have to go back to the disk to find additional sections of the document.

BACKUPS

When you first create and save a new document, only one version of it exists on disk. However, when you recall that document for editing, almost every WP program can optionally retain the original version on disk, in case you decide to abandon the new version without saving it. (This applies to a new document that you've saved without exiting, as well. Once you've saved something, it's on your disk in one or more versions.)

A majority of WP programs—though by no means all of them—can optionally create what is called a "backup" copy of any document that already exists and is called up for editing. (Again, this includes new documents that you've saved without exiting.) A backup copy in this context is the most recent, or pre-edit, version of the document. It's the version you began with when you called the document onscreen.

When it saves the new version, the WP program renames the old version of the file—typically, the same filename, but with the filename extension .BAK. Under this system, a file named STORY.SRT would have a backup file called STORY.BAK. (.BAK isn't always used, but it's the most common backup-filename extension.)

(NOTE: Some programs allow you to "turn off" the feature that saves the previous version of a document as a .BAK file. We recommend against this, because you'll often find that you want to retain the preceding version for later comparison. Too, if you decide you've made the wrong kinds of changes—like a lot of wholesale deleting—in a file, then save it, you still have the old version for reference. The default for this feature is usually "on." Alternatively, if your WP program allows you to create filenames, you can rename the file you're working on with a temporary filename like NOW.)

Do You Have Enough Room for Your Backup File? If you're lucky, your WP program will offer a directory ("menu") of the files on your work disk that tells you how much free space is left to write on—or in this case, save on.

It's risky to use any disk—WP or data—whose available space is less than twice the size of the file you intend to edit. This al-lows room for the old .BAK file and for the (usually) expanded version of the file you'll save after editing.

If there isn't that much space left on your work disk, see if there are any files you can safely delete—old .BAK files, for instance. If there are no files you can do without, copy off some of the files to another disk before you begin editing or copy the file you want to work on to a new disk. Do this before you begin editing, from your computer's operating system, rather than from within WP, if your program doesn't let you delete files in WP. Otherwise, you could be stuck staring at the dreaded "disk full" warning with your document, unsaved, on your screen.

How Many Backup Files? You usually need only one backup copy of the document you're currently editing, and this is all most WP programs create. But even if the capability to create multiple automatic backups is there (and it rarely is), there's no need to have the program save each old version or "generation" of the document as a new file, unless you want to retain each and every generation. If you do, give them separate names—and delete them when the piece is in final form.

AUTOMATIC SAVES

Some systems have automatic save capability. Some WP programs, such as the MS-DOS program FinalWord II, has a pre-set timed backup every two minutes; MS-DOS WordPerfect, by way of comparison, doesn't do automatic backups until/unless you tell it to, but afterward will do them at whatever intervals you specify.

Incidentally, the reason the program can save at specified intervals is because computers keep their own internal time while they're turned on; some also have built-in, battery powered clocks that remember the time and date even when the computer is turned off. If you have an automatic save option (your software manual will say), your WP program watches the computer's internal clock to know when it's time to save the document being edited.

HOW SHOULD YOU TIME YOUR AUTOMATIC SAVES?

Saving a document takes a few seconds, during which you'll be essentially locked out of writing. You'll get a message on the screen asking you to wait, and nothing you type will show up (although on some machines, like IBM PCs and clones, you can continue typing a few dozen characters— that won't show up onscreen—during the save process, and it will all spill out on your screen when the save is completed). This interval of waiting can be distracting when you're in the throes of intense compositional excitement.

So you want to use a save interval that will be short enough to keep you from losing much work, but long enough to keep you from finding yourself staring in frustration at a "wait" message every few minutes.

If you're a slow, methodical writer who can spend ten minutes working over a single sentence, then a longer interval will probably be safe: 45 minutes or an hour. Supplement that with deliberate saves, using your SAVE command or key, each time you complete a paragraph. Hit the ENTER/ RETURN key, then hit the SAVE key. Make it a habit.

But if you're generally a fast writer, or if you often spin out quick rough drafts to polish at a more leisurely pace later, you still want to be sure those initial thoughts don't escape. In this case, a save interval of somewhere between 15-30 minutes should do. And supplement that with deliberate saves every time you come to the end of a thought, while you're concentrating on what should come next. You won't find the wait message so annoying while you're thinking, and the combination of automatic and deliberate saves ought to give you enough protection.

WHERE DO YOU SAVE, AND HOW MANY COPIES ARE ENOUGH?

Almost all programs save files to the drive you've specified as the work (or data) disk. The default for this is usually drive B: (or drive 2, depending on the kind of computer you're using) or the current directory, for you hard disk users. Drive A: or 1 is normally used for the program disk, as drive A: or 1 is where the computer looks for a program when it's first turned on. However, when you establish how often the onscreen document is to be saved, you may also need to tell the WP program on which drive it should save backup files. It's generally better to keep them in the same drive as your work (or data) disk, assuming you're careful to keep enough space on each data disk to accommodate multiple backups and versions of every individual file on it (at least twice the size any given file you might choose to edit).

If you have a hard disk, you may have to specify the subdirectory in which the document should be saved; this should normally be the same subdirectory in which your document resides, the active or "logged" directory, but there's no harm in specifying the directory where the WP system is: hard disk directories expand as needed. You can't "fill them up," short of exhausting the capacity of the whole hard disk. But if you're working with two floppy disks, saving to the program disk may be impossible: many WP programs take up an entire disk, or even two, inserted in sequence. The work disk may be your only practical choice for saving.

Not all programs will ask you to specify a drive to which files are saved; in fact, the majority of WP programs can't change from the specified ("logged") work disk drive because they have to return to there to read portions of a document even when saving. But since we recommend you save files there anyway, this really shouldn't be a problem.

Disk-Swapping Remember that some WP programs—most, actually—don't allow you to switch work disks while a document is on-screen, because they need to read portions before and after the part you're working on, the part actually in the sytem's memory and capable of being changed. The disk you began with as a work disk has to stay in its drive. Otherwise, the program will get confused or maybe crash and lock up your keyboard, and you'll lose your changes.

If you *can* change disks when saving a file that's outgrown its disk, but you don't have another work disk available, you can in an emergency specify that a file be saved to the disk containing your WP program. You may have to delete files on the WP program disk to make room for the saved file, however, and any such deletion must be done carefully. While you should be using a *copy* of your WP program disk and will be able to replace files, you can end up deleting a file that contains something the program needs to be able to save a file, thereby neatly shooting yourself in the foot.

In general, files with the filename extensions .CFG, .HLP, .LRN, .PRT, .PRN, .PRS, and .SYS can be "safely" deleted. (Just be sure to make a note of which ones you delete and copy them back from your original program disk later.) All of this, of course, assumes that you're using a program that allows you to issue delete and other operating system commands from within WP.

You can also use this trick with programs that don't allow you to swap disks or specify alternate disks on which to save a file. Simply use your program's block/save (export) function to mark the entire document, from beginning to end, and save the block to an alternate disk. (This may not work if you swap disks on a program that doesn't allow you to swap disks, so try saving the document on a disk or subdirectory already in place.)

BUT NOT ON YOUR RAMDISK!

If you're using an "imaginary" C: or D:

drive (a RAMdisk) *and* your WP program gives you a choice about where your document will be saved, DON'T, DON'T, DON'T EVER DESIGNATE THE RAMDISK AS THE DRIVE WHERE YOUR BACKUPS ARE TO BE STORED. If lightning strikes and the power goes off, your backup will be gone: the very thing you're making automatic backups to prevent!

If you have a hard disk, that will generally be C: and any RAMdisks will be D:, E:, and so on. If you have one or two floppy drives but no hard drive, your RAMdisk (if you've created one) will be C:.

Always save your work to a *real* drive, one with a real disk in it—floppy or hard. If your WP program doesn't allow you to specify a drive for saves other than the work disk (the RAMdisk, if it were your "logged" or working drive), then save the document, exit your WP program, and copy the RAMdisk file onto a real disk—frequently. *Especially* before you turn off your computer. That way, your backup won't vanish along with your temporary RAMdisk whenever the power goes off or a computer pfft strikes.

NO EXIT: SAVE BEFORE QUITTING!

More than a few writers have lost several hours' worth of work by not remembering to save a document before exiting their WP programs. Some WP programs are kind: they ask you whether you really want to exit without saving your work, or they're structured so that you *can't* exit the program completely without making a conscious decision about whether or not your work gets saved.

But until you know your program quite well, don't count on its doing the saving for you! And if your program does let you exit without prompting you to save your work, don't get in the habit of typing the commands that exit a document. You can easily wipe out your document before you stop to realize that you haven't saved it. The

TIP #5: HOW BIG SHOULD A FILE GET?

You can actually make a file so huge that it won't fit in your computer's memory, and you won't be able to save it, either. Some systems limit individual documents to a maximum size. This is sometimes inconvenient, but it can save you trouble. A well-thought-out program (like PC-Write for MS-DOS) will advise you when you're getting near the file-size limit. But don't count on this. If there are limits on your file size, be sure you know what they are and check the current size of your document every now and again to make sure you're not near the limit. If you're approaching the file-size limit, save the present document (perhaps with an extension like .1) and begin a new document as part two (FILENAME.2), rather than trying to stretch the present one to jam into it every single character you possibly can.

At the other end of the spectrum, if you have one of the more powerful WP systems that put no limit on file size, you have wonderful space to work in—and unparalleled opportunities for disaster.

One way to end up with a gigantic file is to innocently add on pieces by selecting additional documents from the directory and calling them into, before, or after what's already on your screen.

One of this book's authors actually wrote a novel by appending each additional chapter merrily to those before until the resulting single file wouldn't even fit into the computer's system memory. She (all right, I admit it: AD) found a friend whose computer had more than her system's 364K memory, and got the gigantic thing (well over 200,000 characters by then) onscreen at one time. Using the block and move function, she blocked it off chapter by chapter, saved each block, then deleted the block from the onscreen document. Eventually what was left onscreen was only the final chapter, which she saved, and then scuttled home with her disks in embarrassment and considerable relief.

However, a newer 640K machine happily accommodates *two* documents, *each* over 200,000 characters, one each on main and alternate screen. This entire book, available for editing on main screen and alternate screen, at the same time. It just goes to show how quickly and radically computer capacity has developed.

So the moral of the story is that you should learn what your system's capacities and limits are, and respect them scrupulously.

HORROR STORY: THE BLANK SCREEN BLUES

Another way to end up with a bloated document relates to what we've come to call the "blank screen blues." This is how it works.

You're writing away, and perhaps the phone rings, or it's time for lunch. Returning, you see a blank screen and call up your document from the directory, thinking you must already have exited and cleared your screen. But the screen *really isn't blank*: the cat walked by, perhaps, and stood for thirty seconds on the ENTER/RETURN key. Or you'd been expanding the document, unknowingly pushing a lengthening line of hard returns (codes that result from pressing ENTER/RETURN) ahead of the cursor. In either case, what you're *actually* looking at isn't a blank screen but, instead, a screenful of invisible hard return codes. The screen *looks* empty, but your whole document *is still there*. And so you've called a duplicate into the existing document, either at the end or right into the middle. And when you try to save it that way . . .

fingers are quicker than the mind: sometimes, disastrously so.

Instead, get in the habit of saving as a separate operation, something you do as soon as you even think about exiting. If your exit routine then prompts you to save, do it again, just in case. Murphy's law strikes those who neglect to use both belt and suspenders. Another save's not going to hurt anything, and spending a couple of seconds to save isn't going to interfere with the flow of your thought processes at that point—after all, you're exiting anyway.

RESCUING BACKUP FILES

If you follow the advice we've given you thus far and save your work early and often,

At the best, you've got a garbled document that could take you hours to disentangle. At the worst, you've got a huge monstrosity your system refuses to have anything further to do with and adamantly refuses to save.

A similar thing can happen if you're using one of those "screen-saver" utilities that blanks the screen if you don't type for a couple of minutes.

Make it a practice never to call up a file from your directory until you're absolutely sure you've cleared your screen. If your WP program indicates present (in memory) document size, look to see whether or not it's 0. If not, you have a document there, friend, whether you can see it or not.

If your directory doesn't tell you, look at the position guide, wherever that is on your regular WP screen, the screen you normally write on. If it doesn't tell you you're on document 1, page 1, line 1, there's something hidden away that you don't dare ignore. At the very least, type the command that moves the cursor to the beginning of the document and see what's there—something, or nothing.

Some of the newest WP programs courteously ask you if you're *sure* you want to call a new document into the one already onscreen, warning you that one is there. But even if your WP program doesn't do this, you can be aware of the problem and take appropriate steps to prevent the problem from arising in the first place.

Of course if you *want* to call one document into another—boilerplate paragraphs for submission letters, for instance—then go ahead and do it. The new material will come into your present (onscreen) document at the position of the cursor. But be sure that won't bulge your document out to the point of disaster.

In no-filesize-limit systems running on middle-power computers (364K), a file over 80,000 characters can become annoyingly unwieldy. It takes half of forever to move around in a file that big or make changes easily and simply. Spell-checking will be something you do over a weekend—*if* your spell-checker will accept a file that large.

In any event, *no* file that's a data (words) file should be over 100,000 characters unless you have a top-power (640K) computer. It's better to keep files to half that: 50,000 characters or less. We've found no meaningful difference in speed in working with a file that's 10,000 characters and one that's 50,000 characters. But after that, speed and handling ease drop severely, though using hard disks and/or RAMdisks can, to a degree, compensate for this.

Know your computer's and WP system's capacities; keep your files to a size your hardware and software can manage easily; and don't call a document from the directory until you're sure you *really* have a clean screen, not just a blank one full of invisible space, unless you're deliberately adding one document to, or within, another.

And if you find you've somehow assembled a monster document on screen, don't even *try* to save it (except as an experiment you can afford to have your system fail without losing data): you may not be able to get it onscreen again, once it's saved. Go to the document's beginning and chop it off by marking sections and saving them as individual files with the block/save (export) function, whittling away at it and saving each blocked piece individually under its own name and then deleting the marked block onscreen, until you have a document you and your system can again live with.

you'll have no problems if the power goes out, someone unplugs your computer, or another disaster strikes. In fact, you'll be congratulating yourself because your most recent save won't have been lost.

But what if disaster strikes and you haven't saved those changes? It's okay; your original work will still be on disk. Depending on the program you're using, it will be there under its original name or under a ".BAK"-type name.

Once you're out of the disaster and back into your WP program, all you have to do is locate the file and (if necessary) rename it.

If, however, you have a WP program that saves various temporary versions of your file as you go, you'll have to find, recover, rename, and save the temporary backup, especially if that's the only copy of your latest work on the document.

If you remember where your temporary backup files are stored, go to that directory as soon as you resume WP. Select the backup file (unless, of course, it was on your RAMdisk—in that case, begin your period of ritual mourning). When you locate your backup, get it on screen and save it with a name you give it: preferably a temporary name, so that if you have a version of that document already on disk, you'll have time to decide which one you really want to keep or whether you want to blend features of both documents before saving the result under the original filename. You might name the recovered backup file SAVED: easy to key, easy to locate on your directory tomorrow or next week.

If you don't remember where your backups are stored, check all your directories: A:, B:, and C: too, if you have a hard disk. Look for a document with either the filename or extension of BAK and get it on-screen to see if it's the right one.

Some small memory-resident utilities programs (Sidekick, for instance), which give you a notepad and a calculator, make backup files, too. Thus, when you go back to your note about Anthony's birthday, edit and save it, such utilities automatically create a backup of the original. If you're using one of these programs, you may find more than one file called BAK. If the rest of the file's name or extension doesn't tell you what it is, you'll need to call it onto the screen and look at it. When you find the right one, christen it SAVED and save it at once.

If your power goes out and you return to edit a file afterward, many systems will warn you a backup file already exists and give you the option of "overwriting" the file: that is, replacing that backup with a fresh copy of whatever's on your screen. Choose that option, provided that (1) you're sure you don't want the backup anyway or (2)

you immediately recover, rename, and save the existing backup. Depending on your system, you may need to delete the no-longer-needed backup from the directory before a new backup file can be created when the next automatic save happens.

SAVE YOURSELF

Of course you don't need the ability to schedule automatic saves to keep your document from vanishing forever from your screen. Merely forming good WP habits will be enough.

The save function locks in changes by recording them on your disk. So think of it this way: every time you've done something worth locking in, save your document.

Working on first draft material, you'll need to save fairly frequently, because everything you're keying is *new* and doesn't exist anyplace else. So tie your save routine to something that means you have a substantial chunk of new stuff.

As suggested a minute ago, one reasonable thing to tie your save routine to is finishing a paragraph: that is, hitting your ENTER/RETURN key since, with word wrap, the only time you do that is at the end of a paragraph rather than, as with a typewriter, at the end of each line. If that's too hard to remember, make a macro (more about macros in Chapter 9) to do the whole sequence for you. Then hitting CTRL-R (for instance) will end the paragraph and save the document (assuming you've already given it a name) all in one step.

Likewise, when you've made some major decision about the document—switching a couple of paragraphs, writing a new beginning, or even writing a sentence that perfectly pins down what you were trying to get at—save the document the minute that feeling of satisfaction hits. If you can do a spell-check while editing, save after the spell-check. After you type the title, save.

Tie your save routine to your own writing rhythms. Make it as automatic, as

TIP #6: RESET CAN RUIN EVERYTHING

Your computer's power can fail in a number of different ways. A fuse can blow; power can go out on your entire street; you can trip over the cord, thereby unplugging it; you may inadvertently hit the OFF switch. But there's one way you can completely ruin your work yourself, right from your keyboard. It's called "resetting" or "warm-booting" your computer. Resetting is the equivalent of hitting the panic button, to be used when absolutely nothing else will serve to free a locked keyboard or stop a berserk program.

And what about the result to your unsaved document when you reset your computer? It's just as dire as if you'd shut off your computer in any of the more conventional ways. It's gone.

Most computers have a reset button, usually located somewhere near the back, safely out of reach. It's there so that if something dreadful is happening on your screen and your keyboard freezes, you still have a way to stop things before they get completely out of hand. (Some few computers have the reset button in a stupid place, like near the number keys; consider carefully how likely you are to hit that button while typing before buying such a computer.)

Hitting the reset button isn't the only way to reset your computer. MS-DOS-based systems duplicate the reset function from the keyboard. If you press CONTROL, ALT, and DELETE at the same time, your screen will go blank and the computer will restart itself, (almost) as if you'd just turned it off and on. We say *almost* because using the reset causes what's called a "warm boot": the computer stays on, so there's no sudden power surge, as there is when you turn the computer on. (Most computers won't let you turn them off, then right back on again, anyway: there's a built-in delay which can be very frustrating if you don't know what's going on.) The same is true of the Apple IIe, which resets if you press CONTROL, "OPEN APPLE," and RESET at the same time, and there are similar key combinations for many other computers.

Therefore, don't hit ALT, CONTROL, and DELETE (or the equivalent on your computer) at the same time if you can help it. Looking at the keyboard, it would seem to take deliberate action to hit a multiple-key reset combination, but you'd be surprised at how often this is done by accident. So you have yet another reason to save your document at judicious intervals so that even if the worst happens, the most recent version of your file (and your friendly .BAK file) will still be there, only slightly stale and ready for retrieval.

much a natural part of writing, as you can, rather than considering it only as an afterthought: something you do when you're *done* with a document. If it's an afterthought, you can expect your documents to go to the neverland where lost socks reside on a regular basis.

If you have a power failure, all you'll have lost is the material that was added or changed since your last routine save. That's not perfect, but it's a whole lot better than nothing.

SAVE YOUR DISK!

Next to saving a document frequently as you work on it, the best thing you can do to prevent lost data is to keep extra, backup copies of all your work on separate disks. This is simply a matter of periodically copying all the files from all of your work disks to other disks that you'll store in a special place, away from the rest of your disks.

Making backup copies applies to hard disks as well as floppy disks. They have been known to fail and lose data with no warning. So you should make backup copies of everything on a hard disk frequently—using either your operating system's copy or backup utility to copy the hard disk's contents onto floppy disks, or special utilities to speed-copy and maybe compress the hard disk files.

As mentioned before, it's a good idea to keep important files in more than one

TIP #7: IF YOU PRINT FROM DISK, DON'T SAVE

Suppose you want to print out a document while continuing to work on it onscreen. If your WP system gives you the option of printing a document while you're editing it, keep in mind that when you save, you replace the file on disk. If you're printing a file from disk and save a document under the same name before the whole file has gone to the printer, everything goes haywire because the file will not only have changed, it will have *changed position on the disk*. Your print program will be looking for the file in its original place, and it will instead be spread in chunks all over the disk somewhere else.

This won't hurt the file, the disk, the computer, or the printer. But it will ruin your print job. You'll end up with snatches of other files all jumbled into what you meant to print out.

Most intelligent WP programs won't let you save a document while you're printing it. But to be safe, don't even try to save an open file under the same name until the print job is complete.

If you must save, either (1) give the file a new name first, before you start printing it (PRINT.1, for instance) and then print that from disk while continuing to work on the document and saving it under its original name; (2) save the onscreen document under a new name and continue saving it under that name until the print job's over; or (3) print "from screen" rather than from disk on documents you want to continue working on (if your WP program will let you—not all do).

If you can do it, printing from screen is the safest route, because the WP system creates a temporary print file with the whole document in it, and feeds it a piece at a time to the printer. The WP system, in this case, is neither reading your screen nor your data disk—only its own temporary print file. So when and how you save will then have no effect on the print job.

place and to copy them to both locations whenever the files change. There are several ways to do this, depending on what your system lets you do. If you can swap disks and save a document to more than one disk, then save the document twice— on two different disks—before exiting your WP program. Or you can copy the saved file from one disk to another either from inside your WP program or from your operating system.

Once you have the most recent files on two or more disks, store each disk in a different place, so that a physical disaster (fire, tornado, etc.) has less of a chance of wiping out all your backups.

KEEPING ARCHIVE DISKS

It's important to keep extra copies of the data on a given disk to make sure, if that disk gets coffee spilled all over it or suffers some other disaster, you still have a copy of your files.

We've called the duplicates of working disks "backup" disks. Backup disks are updated periodically. Disks that hold finished work that may not change for months or years, we'll call "archive" disks.

You can further embellish the backup process by archiving a disk's files using an archiving program, as described in Chapter 3. Archiving condenses files so that you can get more on a disk.

OPTIMIZING DISKS

As was mentioned in the tip about printing from disk, documents are saved, not all in a chunk, but in different locations of the disk. Generally, when you save a document, those locations change. The more frequently you edit, change, and save a document, the more fragmented the resulting file will be. The longer the document is, the more it sprawls. Multiply that by all the files on the disk, and it can end up being quite a mess.

BEWARE OF "DISKCOPY!"

Nearly all computers have a simple file-copy utility, either built into the operating system or provided on a separate disk. A file-copy utility merely copies specified files (or all files) from one disk to another. However, there's another kind of copy utility that copies an entire disk as a unit—creating a mirror copy of the original disk on a new disk.

In MS-DOS a utility called DISKCOPY performs this chore; for other kinds of computers there are similar utilities, often billed as "backup" utilities. No matter what such copy utilities are called, they can be extremely dangerous to data because they wipe out whatever's on the disk you are copying *to*. Diskcopy-type utilities copy not only visible files, but invisible files as well, indiscriminately overwriting everything on the destination disk. (File-copy utilities, on the other hand, leave what's on the destination disk intact and stop copying when the destination disk is full.)

Diskcopy-type utilities make it easy to destroy disks by erasing them, too! If you were to mistakenly tell your system to copy the contents from a blank disk to a backup or archive disk using a file-copy utility, the utility would look at the blank disk and report that there were no files to copy. However, a diskcopy utility would do exactly what it was told and copy the blank disk onto the data disk, thereby erasing all the files on the data disk. You'd end up with two blank disks.

This actually happened to one of us, destroying better than eight months' work on a novel. And to make disaster complete, the disk in question was the *only* one: it was in trying to make an archive disk that the disaster happened. Fortunately, a hard (paper) copy of much of the manuscript had been printed out, so not everything was lost. But the novel had to be completely re-keyboarded, and about 1/3 of it had to be reconstructed entirely from memory.

To avoid that kind of disaster, when copying ordinary data disks never use the diskcopy utility. The risks are simply too great, and a file-copy utility works just as reliably and more safely.

Eventually the files can become so severely scattered that the disk itself can fail.

There are various kinds of special "disk optimizing" programs for floppy disks that will organize a disk's files into more rational order and "clean up" bad sectors on the disk. But you don't really need those. It's just as easy to copy your files onto a new disk once a week or so and be done with it. However, it's a good idea to check your work disks and the backup disks periodically with your operating system's disk-checking utility (CHKDSK, for MS-DOS computers, for example). If your operating system doesn't offer such a utility, buy one as add-on software.

Hard disks are another matter entirely. You can, (and should, with care), optimize your hard disk. There are special disk-optimizing programs to do this: either commercial/shareware programs or operating system utilities, depending on what kind of computer you have. Such programs go through the disk and reorganize file storage to free wasted space, lock out bad sectors (and almost every hard disk has some of those—no matter what the salesperson told you), and generally set up your hard disk so that it's more efficient in how it stores and reads data.

Warning: Before you try to use this kind of program, copy everything on your hard disk to floppy disks, as insurance. It's all too easy to type the wrong operating system command or make the wrong program selection and wipe out everything on your disk.

Do save those completed projects on archive disks. The Banks half of this team has on disk everything he's ever written on computer and published, as well as unpublished material, and is in the process of having eight years' worth of published material, originally typewritten, keyboarded and stored on disk. Why? Longer material, when reprinted several years after it was written, often needs to be revised. Shorter works can often serve as source material for new work (block/save reusable segments). And you never know when the opportunity will arise to assemble a number of articles or short stories as a book.

DELETE WITHOUT TEARS

The opposite of save is delete. Delete is the data eater, whether you wipe a character, a paragraph, a file, or a whole disk. Delete is a little like death.

But without delete, as without death, overpopulation and chaos would result. The old has to be respectfully laid to rest, to make room for the new.

So make it a habit to delete whatever's really no longer being used. Put documents on backup disks while you're working on them and on archive disks when you're finished. Then delete all the preliminary stages, unless you're sure in fifty years your biographers will kill (or pay handsomely) to look at all your rough drafts. After a writing project is done, tidy up all the scraps and loose ends, to start the next project fresh.

But although delete is necessary, it's dangerous, and you need to know what delete functions are permanent and which are temporary: the data can still be recovered.

AMAZING RECOVERY

If you wipe out a disk by reformatting it, that can be final, although special "unformat" utilities may be able to recover at least scraps. If, however, you wipe out a disk with a command that deletes the individual files, all you've really done is wiped out the labels that told the computer where all the scattered parts of each file are on the disk. The files themselves are still there, untouched, and you can buy other utilities that will let you retrieve the data itself, relabel it by saving, and have everything back again. If you've had trouble unwisely reformatting or deleting whole disks, you might want to investigate data-retrieval utilities that can minimize the disaster (these are discussed in Chapter 3).

SAVE, SAVE, SAVE! (AND BACK UP!)

Finally, there's no protection from a mistaken delete better than making saving an absolute priority. Save often and regularly. Save documents and files. Save whole disks. Make backup and archive disks and keep them someplace where absolutely *nothing* can happen to them. We know a writer who goes so far as to keep his archive disks in a safety deposit box at a bank across town, so that not even a tornado which destroys his whole house is going to touch those archive disks.

You may not want to go that far, but think of it this way: if your backups and archives disappeared in some disaster right this very minute, what would you now be thinking you *should* have done? How upset would you be if all your work for two or three or five years were to vanish this minute in a flash of lightning? Imagine it happening—and it *can* happen—and start to do *now* what will make your saved data as safe and permanent as the public monument of your choice.

CHAPTER 7

Seek and You Shall Find

UNUSUAL USES FOR THE SEARCH/REPLACE AND GLOBAL SEARCH FUNCTIONS

OVERVIEW: THIS CHAPTER COVERS:

1. Marking your place in a manuscript.

2. Noting "to come's."

3. "Search and destroy": finding and deleting.

4. Splitting documents to work on them more easily.

5. Getting rid of "pet" or overused words.

6. Renaming people or places.

7. Replacing for ghastly long or hard to type titles, names, phrases.

8. Formatting and reformatting through search/replace.

9. Searching formatting codes.

10. Searching hideous mistakes.

THE SEARCH FUNCTION IS ONE OF THE REAL workhorses of any WP program. With it you can locate any sequence of letters and spaces or any string of numbers. With some programs, you can also find invisible formatting codes.

Add to that a search-and-replace (aka search/replace) function and you can do almost anything you want with the searched item. You can substitute something else for it or even remove it by replacing it with nothing at all, thereby deleting it.

The longer and more complex any document gets, the more uses you'll find for search and search/replace (also called, on some WP programs, "global search").

FINDING AND MARKING YOUR PLACE

In working on something as long as a chapter or an article, you'll often find yourself having thoughts about several parts of it at once. This often means flitting from one part of the document to another (right— you can make notes on paper, but we're talking *computerizing* your writing here).

There are two ways to move around to specified points in your document. The laborious way is to go to the beginning of the document and read down until you find the place you're thinking of revising or want to check. That's a perfect example of typewriter thinking: forgetting that to your WP system, the whole document is available to be searched at lightspeed.

Which brings us to the easy way: using your WP program's search function. Use search in combination with a marking system to set things up so you can quickly move anywhere in the document. Simply put an asterisk in the document where you're currently working. Then either search backwards (reverse search), or return to the beginning and search, for a word, part of a word, or a phrase you think is near the place you want to work on. When you find the place, put in an asterisk

there. Now you can zip back and forth between the two places, just by searching the two asterisks.

If you find that you need to move among several locations in the text, you can develop your own system of numbering. You might, for example, use *1 *2 *3, etc.

If you're using asterisks as a part of your document, you can, of course, use another symbol or symbols—a percent sign or a dollar sign, for instance. XXX is also handy. Whatever you choose, get into the habit of using the same marker symbol all the time, one you rarely need otherwise, to eliminate the possibility of confusion. These marker symbols can be saved with a work-in-progress, too.

If your manuscript is complex, you may want to use a variety of markers to designate different chores. If so, be sure to note at the beginning of the document what each marker stands for, so you won't find some forgotten marker printing out in the middle of your submission draft. (And don't forget to remove those notes and markers before you print your manuscript.)

(NOTE: Some programs, like WordStar, offer ready-made place markers, which are not printed and disappear when you save a file. These are useful, but you will probably want to use your own "saveable" marker symbols even if your WP program does offer place markers.)

SEARCH AND DESTROY

When you're finished with the markers, go back to the beginning of your document and use search/replace to delete them. That is, tell the search/replace function to find the marker symbol and replace it with nothing (this is usually accomplished either by pressing ENTER/RETURN when the program asks you what to replace the search string with, or by simply setting the search process going with the SEARCH key without filling in any replacement string). Tell the program to do this with or without

TIPPECANOE AND SPLIT SCREEN TOO

Using search/replace in a long, long document—40,000 characters or more—can turn into a tedious process when you're searching for text marker symbols, particularly if your computer doesn't have a hard disk. (Many low-memory WP programs that operate with limited memory load only a part of a file into memory, which means they must read a new part from the disk whenever you move a few pages forward or backward through the document. This slows things down considerably.)

If your WP program has split screen ("windowing") or double screen capabilities, divide the document into two parts by marking the first half of it as a block, then writing or saving that block under an appropriate name, like CH1.A (for "Chapter 1, Part A"). Then delete that block (the first half). Save the remaining half under a new name (CH1.B), or save it and rename it—whichever way your program can handle such chores.

If you need to, use block/move to transfer any needed format codes (margins, tabs, headers, and so forth) from the top of CH1.A to CH1.B. Then put each half of the document either in your split screen window or on your spare screen, and jump back and forth through it without long waits.

This is, incidentally, a real time-saver when it comes to spell-checking, which can tie up your computer for many minutes. (Some WP programs will let you spell-check one document while you're happily working away on the other—but not all do.) Breaking up a large document lets you break up the spell-checking process into manageable chunks (in terms of time), so you won't waste time watching the screen.

Many spell-checkers that check a file while it's open (i.e., on your screen, ready to edit) have the peculiarity that, if you tell the utility to check the whole document, it returns to the beginning and starts from there, no matter where in the document your cursor is. You can't check just from the cursor on, except by doing it page by page. However, with your document split in two parts, you can check one part that's ready, and start in the middle (where the document is broken) on the other part when that's in more or less final form, too.

Of course, if you want to, you can always start out by dividing documents into easily manageable chunks, giving the parts filenames with extensions like .A and .B. But many writers find it distracting to have one piece of writing—a chapter, or an article—divided into little snips. They like to be able to read it whole. If you're like that, maybe you'll decide to write it in pieces, then combine the pieces when the document is complete, so you can reread or print it as a unit. If you do that, though, be careful that the file doesn't exceed your computer's and WP system's capacities, as discussed in Chapter 6.

confirming every instance found, as you prefer.

MARKING ROUGH DRAFTS

Using a marker system can be especially useful when you're working on a rough draft. It's all too easy to bog down at some point when you need to check your research materials, or you aren't finding the words you want, or meet any of the thousand invitations for temporary writers' block to set in.

Don't let it.

Instead, mark the place with something like /TK/, which is publisher-speak for "to come"; the slash marks, or "virgules," are added to make it easy to identify later, in case a lot of words in your document have the sequence TK in them. (Or, if you don't like that, just throw in a series of question marks, thus: ?????.)

Skip over the bothersome place you've marked and keep right on writing what comes after. This will help you maintain your writing rhythm—so important in draft writing—and may even help you get through the draft in one sitting.

When you have the draft done, you'll be

able to see its scope, the relationship of its parts, and the amount and placement of its details, much better than you could when you first began to think about it. There's no better basis for effective rewriting than a solid, complete first draft.

Then, perhaps in a later writing session, you'll find it much easier to search each of the /TK/s and think about them individually, taking your time, without losing the forward dynamic of what you're trying to say. And, because they're part of a complete draft, you'll also find it easier to fill in the holes because they'll be holes in *something*, not holes in an even bigger hole: the unfinished manuscript itself.

ELIMINATING PETS

All of us have pet words and phrasings that we notice more quickly in speech than in writing. Have you ever had an attack of "you know's," or something like Valspeak's "to the max"? Remember "groovy"? Typically, you catch the phrase from somebody else, find yourself continually using it, then go crazy trying to *keep* yourself from using it. Eventually, everything goes back to normal, but it can get in the way of communication.

Pet words. Pet phrasings. They happen in writing, too, and are even harder to catch and root out than they are in speech. You even generate them yourself: a way of putting something that so exactly mirrors the way you think that you can't resist using it over and over. Push the same thought button and the same phrasing pops out, automatically and unnoticed. Instant personal cliché.

One of us recently had a terrible fit of "maybe's" and "almost's"—excess qualifiers—in a draft novel. Once a friendly reader pointed this out, each chapter was searched for *maybe* and *almost*, and 90% of them were replaced or eliminated. The remaining 10%, which were really needed, could then stay without achieving pethood.

A second pass eliminated about 50% of the "nearly's," that had gone completely unnoticed up to that point, as well. Another writer we know caught a terminal case of that monster word, "hopefully," and eradicated it with glee as soon as he became aware of it.

However you come to notice your unwanted pets—whether through past experience, your own reading, a friendly reader, or (horrors!) an editor—make a list. Perhaps (notice: not "maybe"!) you should make a file called PETS to keep them in and to remind yourself what they are from time to time. Otherwise you'll forget—it's inevitable. They wouldn't have become pets to begin with if each one didn't fit neatly into one of your personal verbal blind spots.

Make a point of searching out, replacing, or deleting those annoying pets from every document you work on thereafter. Don't just search/replace them automatically, though: if you consistently use one word to replace another, *the replacement word itself will turn into a pet!* Besides, no two words have exactly the same flavor: "perhaps" won't do for "maybe" in all circumstances—writing dialogue, for instance. "Perhaps" is too formal for some contexts. So replace judiciously, and check each instance to decide what to do about the offensive pet according to its immediate context.

A NAME IS A NAME IS A NAME

If you write fiction, especially long fiction with a cast of thousands, one of the problems you face is inventing appropriate and effective names for your characters. The resulting problem is keeping all those names consistent.

Mr. Reeder, back in Chapter 2 of your novel, can turn into Mr. Reader or Mr. Redder when you hit Chapter 18. He's only the grocer, and you've forgotten what you called him to begin with. You're not even sure what to search, to check up. You may not even notice until a perplexed editor points it out to you, typically in the most humiliating way possible, implying that if you can't keep your characters straight, she has the gravest doubts about the arrangement of your mental marbles, too.

The character might even turn into Mr. Rider or something else altogether. Ritter?

CAST AND GLOSSARY

Keeping a "cast list" can help. A file called CAST, or a filename ending in .CST (in a book called *Wonder Is Coming*, that file might be WONDER.CST, for instance), can remind you of the precise spelling of the names of all the characters you're working with. Some WP systems won't allow you to assign extensions, but most will, and you should take advantage of that freedom.

If you're working with nonfiction, you have even less option for variation. Names *must* be spelled right every time. Keeping an independent, easy-to-consult list then becomes an absolute necessity rather than an option.

Your CAST file might also include the names of places and objects ("The Arcturan picked up his *zzhlmmt* and walked away haughtily") you're going to need to know how to spell over and over. If you've got lots of invented words or special terminology, you may want to make up a file called .GLS containing your glossary.

You can consult this list in any of several ways. You might print it out, but if you're like one of us, you'll immediately lose the list, only to find it after you've completed your book. A better way is to keep the file on the same disk as your work files, then view it in one of these ways:

•Use your WP program's windowing or split-screen capability to view the file.

•Use a memory-resident "notepad" (like Sidekick for the IBM PC) to view the file.

•Or, if your program and/or computer allow neither of those options, merge the CAST file into the current document at the very end. To check the word list, all you have to do is mark where you're working, move to the end of the file, do your checking, then use search to move back to where you were.

ENFORCING THE ALIAS

It may also happen in fiction that you're not happy with a character's name or you're suddenly inspired with a better one. You want to change Joe Reeder to Hernando Jacobovski. Search/replace then becomes an invaluable tool.

If you search by eye, inevitably you'll miss one or two instances of the word or phrase to be replaced, and editors will either shake their heads or snicker. But search/replace can find them for you, with no exceptions. Search Reeder, replace with Jacobovski. Then search Joe, replace with Hernando. Easy as that.

THE MYSTERY CHARACTER

Of course, your character might *start out* as Hernando Jacobovski, and you soon get sick of keying in his wretched name. You have a choice: change the name, or do it the easy way: choose a specific marker (like %%%) that's used to represent only that name. Insert the marker wherever the name's going to appear. Then, when you finish a session or a section, search/replace to change %%% to Jacobovski from beginning to end. This way, you only have to type the name once.

We've heard of several authors who don't name their characters at all until they've finished the first draft. The characters' names are things like AAA, BBB, CCC and so forth until the author gets to know each well enough to have developed a feel for what each character's name ought to be.

Using three identical letters is better than using two. Very few words have a sequence of three, whereas many words may have a sequence of two. It makes finding them easier. And using letters (AAA and so on), rather than some other symbols, has the advantage of reminding you to avoid naming two characters too similarly and confusing the reader. AAA may become Al, BBB becomes Bert, and so on.

Of course you can always short-circuit this protection by naming two sisters Melanie and Helena, whom readers will never be able to tell apart anyway. Which goes to prove that word processing can save you only from the more obvious and mechanical kinds of mistakes. You're still free to make the really big and ingenious ones yourself.

THE ALBERMARLE MUNICIPAL WATER SYSTEM AND SEWAGE TREATMENT FACILITY

Just imagine a document in which you had to key "The Albermarle Municipal Water System and Sewage Treatment Facility" 26 times. Do we need to suggest search/replace is the answer? Wouldn't you prefer to type MMM than "The Albermarle Municipal Water System and Sewage Treatment Facility"? The authors did, and typed it only once: of the other two times, one was a block/move clone, upper-cased to make the head; the second one was done first, with search/replace simply for variety. That was the only time "The Albermarle Municipal Water System and Sewage Treatment Facility" was actually typed (another block/move clone here). You can do variations on this theme with block/move, too. (More about uses and dangers of the block/move function in Chapter 10.)

We're sure you'll think of other ghastly long titles, place names, and suchlike that could drive you crazy keyboarding. If you do it more than once, it's because you like to, not because you have to.

CHANGING FORMATS

Remember, some WP systems let you search formatting codes as well as alphanumeric characters and spaces. That can come in handy when your document suddenly goes strange on the screen, or in printout, or your carefully-aligned columns start wrapping when you don't want them to. It may be that the culprit is a buried formatting code, a key you hit by accident,

---

TIP #9: SEARCH AND SEARCH/ REPLACE LIMITATIONS

In the example of replacing "Joe Reeder" with "Hernando Jacobovski," you'll note that we recommend replacing the first name and the last name separately. This is because "Joe" may end one line and "Reeder" begin the next at various places in the document. Depending on how your WP program operates, it may not recognize strings that are split between lines, and thus miss them entirely. (And, perversely, most WP programs' manuals don't mention this fact.)

If you don't know if your WP program can find strings split between lines, use the one-word-at-a-time method to be safe. Or you can experiment by splitting a multiple-word search string between lines, then doing a search. If the search function finds it, you'll know you can do searches without regard to line breaks—a definite advantage.

Another limitation of search and search/replace in some programs is the inability to find certain formatting marks ("invisible" control characters and ESCAPE printer controls in particular). This is often accompanied by the inability to locate certain "special" characters, such as foreign-language characters.

(If you do find this limitation in your WP program, there *may* be a way around it if you can copy a block-marked or macro-generated string into the search field when the program asks you for the string to be searched.)

Then there are length limitations. Some programs allow you to search for only one or two characters, while others permit search strings up to 80 characters in length.

Such limitations are either negative or neutral, depending on how you work. In any case, you will have to make allowances for them in your work habits.

TIP #10: FORMAT FILES + MACROS

You can streamline format changes even further by combining format files and macros. When you've made the format adjustment the first time and gotten it just the way you want it, block/save it under a filename like FORMAT.1. (If your format codes are invisible, use the function that renders them visible so you can make sure you block only as much as you really want.)

And to make it simpler yet, you can create a macro or key definition that says, essentially, "When I press this particular key combination, retrieve the document FORMAT.1." Make another that says, "When I press *this* key

combination, retrieve FORMAT.2" (the regular format), and so on. So all you'd have to do, thereafter, to switch formats is hit the assigned key combinations whenever you wanted to change. The key combinations usually involve a CTRL key or (in the case of those computers that have them) an ALT key. Combine these macros with search for codes you no longer want and you have an easy and almost instantaneous way to reformat the document as many times, and as many different ways, as you choose. (More about making and using special writers' macros in Chapter 9.)

---

or a weird tab setup in a file you imported into a document onscreen which is proceeding to wreak havoc on everything that follows it.

You can search the offending format code and remove it much more easily than you can find it by eye, especially if it's invisible.

In addition, you can change formats in a document through search/replace. Once you've located either the format code or the marker standing for it, you can delete it and replace it manually with the format code you really want.

Search/replace won't replace with a detailed format code: your machine will probably beep at you if you try. (But you can do it with a macro, as we've described above. However, you can save sets of format codes as separate files: nothing in the file but a set of codes, no text at all. You can merge that file into a document at the position of the cursor. This is an important tool for working on documents that have frequent changes of format—before and after tables or lists, or switches between columns and full text, for instance. Making up the format codes once, then saving them as separate files, can save you enormous headaches.

THE WRONG STUFF

If search is handy for finding the place to insert things you actually want in the final manuscript, it's also useful for getting rid of what you *don't* want.

If you do something inadvertent, like tell your spell-checker to temporarily accept "mezzannine" as a word, you can go back and find it with search. If you're sure that somewhere you put $1,000.03 instead of $1.03 (computers do that all the time on phone bills, don't they?) and want to catch it before you print the document, search the dollar sign. For any ghastly mistake you suspect but can't seem to find (or don't want to try to find) by eye, laboriously scrolling through, search is your shortcut.

If it's a consistent error—a name spelled wrong, for example—search/replace it.

And if it's something you simply want gone, search and destroy it with search/replace, as described earlier in the chapter.

YOU AIN'T SEEN NOTHING YET

Besides its use in locating strings of characters in text on screen, search is also the typical first step in creating repeating ("chained") macros, which we'll discuss in

Chapter 9. It's also useful in locating items in databases of publishers, used in conjunction with a WP sorting utility: the subject of the next chapter.

There are programs for many computers that will search and search/replace all of the files on a disk for you. In the case of character name changes in a novel, such utilities are a real godsend! All you have to do is make sure that all of your working chapter files are on the same disk (or in the same hard-disk subdirectory), and turn the program loose on the files. This can save up to an hour of ducking in and out of files with your word processor. And the best thing about these programs is that most of them are free or nearly so, since they are "shareware" or "public domain" programs. (Flip back to Chapter 3 for a discussion of these programs.)

CHAPTER 8

Merge Right

SPECIAL APPLICATIONS OF MERGE FILES AND DATABASE GENERATION

OVERVIEW: THIS CHAPTER COVERS:

1. Database fundamentals.

2. What information to keep in your marketing database.

3. Creative sorting.

4. Creating macros to sort databases.

5. Multiple-query shortcuts and dangers.

6. Keeping LOG and LEDGER files.

7. Reslanting material for special markets.

8. Merging shortcuts and tips.

9. From salutation to envelope from one database.

WHAT'S A DATABASE? In the simplest terms, it's an organized collection of related information. The information is organized into *records*, which in turn are composed of individual *fields*, where the information is actually entered.

A stack of employment applications is a good analogy of this kind of organization. The stack of applications itself is the database. Each application is one record. The "Name," "Address," "City," etc. headings on each application are the fields, and the information written under those headings by applicants is the actual data stored in the database.

In terms of many of the better WP programs, a database is a secondary merge file: a list of names and addresses (and/or other information) you can feed into, "merge with," a single document (*primary merge file*)—a letter template, say—to fill in different names and addresses and the like to make *a series* of letters, all different from one another. Some WP programs call this utility "mail merge," which we'll nickname simply "merge." These top-of-the-line WP programs come with merge capability built in.

Of course there are also database programs you can buy. Although many of these, like Reflex, are aimed at number-crunchers and folk who do a lot of spreadsheets and pie charts, there are others aimed at wordcrafters.

STAND ALONE VS. BUILT-IN DATABASES

Stand alone database programs, like dBase III, Reflex, Lattice, *et numerous al*, let you add database-generating and -manipulating ability if your WP program doesn't offer a complete set of merge, sort, and macro functions built in. Stand alone database programs, because they're usually designed to do just one thing, have all these capabilities, though they're naturally confined to working on the database

from the operating system, not with WP text onscreen. Too, some of these stand alone programs are balky and don't work, or don't work easily, with files from all WP programs. Although you'll find some multiple-application programs, like Q & A for the IBM, which offer WP *and* database functions, it's far simpler in the long run to buy a WP program with merge and sort utilities built in, complemented with macro capability.

Whether you manipulate your data (once it's entered) with a combination of high-powered WP utilities or by putting it into a special database program and later extracting the data for use with WP, the effect is much the same.

If you have one of the more feature-filled and powerful WP systems, you'll probably be able to duplicate the effects achieved by add-on database software, with the added flexibility of having your other WP functions available at the same time. A built-in merge utility and a sort utility—*not* the sort utility available on DOS operating systems, but one that functions *within* the WP program—are all you'll need to really streamline and simplify the dullest, most tedious part of writing: identifying potential markets, writing queries and cover letters, and submitting your material. Macros can complete the job of generating and altering your database to keep it updated and useful.

If you've used the merge feature at all, probably it was for the obvious chore of making lists of names and addresses to combine with some sort of form letter to produce multiple mailings. Or perhaps you've used a secondary merge file—the part with the variable entries in it, as opposed to the primary file, the part that doesn't change—just to make the envelopes. If so, good for you: it's a beginning, one you can build on and develop. Easy, wasn't it? Making a database can be just as easy and much more profitable.

STANDING OUT IN THE FIELD

In merge files that serve these basic purposes—generating personalized letters or envelopes—you may have treated each entry as one item, nameaddress, a single unit. If you were generating salutations at the same time, however, you already know the most interesting thing about secondary merge files: their records can be divided into parts, or "fields." If the addressee's name is the first field (Field 1 or F1), and the address is the second field (F2), you can have F1 repeated in your form letter as the salutation by inserting the appropriate merge codes (which, in WordPerfect, for instance, would be a series of "F codes": ^F1^, ^F2^, ^F3^, and so on) more than once, to call the F1 information—that is, the information in field one—into the primary document (the template letter) in two different places.

You can also call the information from your secondary merge file into your primary document in any order whatsoever, *regardless of what order the fields fall into in the secondary merge file.* That is, your primary document (the boilerplate letter) may call for F3 first, then F5, then F1. Some fields you may not call into the document at all. So what are they good for, these extra fields?

It's those extra fields—what you put in F4 or F9—that can turn your secondary merge file into a true database, making it a wonderful timesaving tool to serve your writing.

WHAT SHOULD YOU PLANT IN YOUR FIELDS?

Assuming you already have or could begin a secondary merge file of publishers, what extra information, besides basic name and address, might you keep in separate fields for each record?

Ask yourself what different ways you might want to retrieve or use this information, then set up your fields accordingly.

Here are some suggestions:

1. Editor's full name
2. Editor's first name, or appropriate form for salutation
3. Editor's title
4. Publication name
5. Publication's street address, city, and state (usually two or three separate lines but *one* field)
6. Publication's zip code
7. Publication's phone number
8. Publication's interests (children's, mystery, fantasy, romance, whatever)
9. Length
10. Publication's percentage of freelance work accepted
11. Publication's pay scale
12. What kind of submission publication wants
13. Publication's policy on simultaneous submissions: Yes or No
14. Computer submissions acceptable: Yes or No
15. Publication's typical response time
16. Your work previously accepted by publication: Yes or No
17. Details of work previously accepted: Editor's name, title of work, date accepted/published (all previously accepted work in this one field)
18. Details of work submitted to this publication, but rejected: Editor's name, title of work, date submitted/date rejected (all previously rejected work in this one field)
19. Miscellany: friendly comments by editor? form letter rejection? any writing friends who know editor you might mention? Any recent publications in related subject area you should mention to editor, or send clips of?

It's absolutely vital you have exactly the same number of fields, in the same order, for every record, even if some fields end up being empty: that is, with no data in them. If you set up your records that way, it will enable you to sort and retrieve the whole record *according to the data in any one field* provided the fields are in the same order. That is, F13 (for example) *always* contains Y/N information on whether simultaneous submissions are accepted; F15 is *always* response time; F8 is *always* a publication's areas of interest, and so on.

It doesn't matter a bit whether you have all the categories we've suggested above or only six or seven. Nor does it matter whether you have them in that order or some other order, provided you're *consistent* from record to record.

One way to achieve that consistency is to make up a template document (call it DATA?) you call up, and then fill in, for every record you're going to add to your database. It should have the right number of fields, and all the information you'll never be calling into a primary document—that is, everything but name, address, and salutation—can begin with a heading to remind you of what goes where.

This might serve as a sample blank, as generated by WordPerfect:

^R
^R
^R
^R
^R
^R
7. Phone: ^R
8. Interests: ^R
9. Length: ^R
10. Percent Freelance: ^R
11. Pay: ^R
12. Wants: ^R
13. Printouts: ^R
14. Simultaneous: ^R
15. Response: ^R
16. Accepted: ^R
17. Details: ^R
18. Rejected: ^R
19. Miscellaneous: ^R
^E

Here's the same blank filled in with appropriate information about the magazine *Gentleman's Quarterly*:

Eliot Kaplan ^R
Mr. Kaplan ^R
Managing Editor ^R
Gentleman's Quarterly ^R
350 Madison Ave.
New York, NY ^R
10017 ^R
7. Phone: No phone given but *GQ* is a division of Conde Nast Inc. ^R
8. Interests: Nonfiction: politics, personality profiles, lifestyles, trends, grooming, nutrition, health & fitness, sports, travel, money, investment/business. Depts. include—Body & Soul (fitness, nutrition and grooming); Money (investments); Going in Style (travel); Health; Music; Tech (consumer electronics); Dining In (food); Wine & Spirits; Humor; Fiction; Games (sports); Books; The Male Animal (essays by men on life); and All About Adam (nonfiction by women about men). ^R
9. Length: 1,000-2,500 words. ^R
10. Percent Freelance: 60%. ^R
11. Pay: A $750-$3,000 nonfiction articles; $750-$2,000 departments/columns; pays on acceptance. ^R
12. Wants: query first with clips for articles, same or can submit complete ms. for depts. & columns. ^R
13. Simultaneous: Not stated. ^R
14. Printouts: Yes (prefers letter quality). ^R
15. Response: 1 month. ^R
16. Accepted: Nothing submitted. ^R
17. Details: ^R
18. Rejected: ^R
19. Miscellaneous: Aims at upscale male 25-45. ^R
^E

Your WP program may use a slightly different format, but it won't be unrecognizable when compared with this one. There will be some sort of end-field code (in this case, ^R) and some kind of end-record code (in this case, ^E).

The basic idea is the same: create a file in which each record has numbered fields whose contents are merged into a document or documents at the point(s) the corresponding F codes are inserted.

CHECK MARKET GUIDES, BOOKSTORES, MAGAZINES

Where'd we get all this information? From the *Gentleman's Quarterly* listing in *Writer's Market*. Once you have the basic information all entered in your MARKETS database, you can easily update it based on your own experience with a given editor or with the magazine, or on fresh information from *Writer's Digest*, your writers' grapevine, or any other source of information that would help you target this publication more precisely.

We'll call your attention to a few additional elements in the filled-out sample above. The information about pay, in F11, is preceded by an *A* because this publication pays pretty well and, moreover, is more than half freelanced material. So it would be an "A" market for most writers. Giving a publication a single letter, coming first in a field, would enable you to generate an *A* list, a *B* list, and so on. We'll explain how in a minute.

Also notice that F17 and F18 are blank, because there's no data to put in them. We haven't sold to *GQ*. Just the same, the fields are left there so the same information will always come in the same order, field by field, in every record. Finally, the numbers are there just to help you when you're filling in the fields, so it's easier to keep track of what the field numbers are in a record as long as this one. It doesn't matter if these headings are there, since you wouldn't be using this information as part of the text of a letter. These extra fields just present a useful, concise overview of a given writer's knowledge about and past experience with a given publication.

EXPANDING YOUR DATABASE, ONE RECORD AT A TIME

You'll first put into your database those publications you usually submit to. Then you'll add, to these initial records, magazines or publishers you'd *like* to submit to: potential markets that at least seem appropriate to the kind of thing you're writing.

You might make a point of doing a little market research: going to a bookstore and looking at jackets or magazines at least once a week; looking into a market guide like *Writer's Market, Novel and Short Story Writer's Market,* or *Poet's Market* every day. Then add at least one appropriate record to your database every day you write, for a couple of months. Then you'll have a base of, say, 30 or 40 records to build on.

What you'll end up with is a completely personalized, current, and *cross-indexed* market guide targeted specifically on the kind of material you write.

SORTING YOUR WAY TO SUCCESS

How is it cross-indexed, you ask? We hoped you would. Because that's where the second part of the wonderfulness of databases comes into play.

You can sort the records in terms of any field the whole record contains.

In other words, with your sort utility, you can pull out all records you've coded with an "A" or "B" or "C" as the first item in F11. Those complete records, and those only. Or, for instance, if you're a regional writer or want to submit to newspapers and magazines in a given area, you can sort your database just in terms of zip codes, grouping together publications in the same geographical area.

You can sort in terms of F9, length, matching the rough word count of a piece to the publications that will accept that length.

Sorting your master list, your database will generate a separate list containing only those records with the characteristics you've selected for, by whatever criterion you pick out on a particular occasion.

The more powerful sorting programs allow you to sort your database in terms of

TIP #11: DITCH TEMPORARY LISTS

When you've sorted your master list (which we'll call MARKETS) and retrieved and used the records you wanted, scrap the list of selections as soon as you're done with it. Otherwise, you'll end up with a bunch of lists with different and possibly conflicting information in them.

For instance, if you sort MARKETS and produce KIDS, a list of magazines which publish short stories for children 8-10, you're going to want to note which magazines you submitted to that time, and you're going to want to note the result: acceptance or rejection. If you note that information on the record in your mini-database KIDS, the changes won't have been made in MARKETS unless you go back to MARKETS and enter the data there, too. This can get to be a real nuisance, and you can end up with important data scattered across several lists, none of which is really complete or reliable.

Make all changes on MARKETS itself. Then, if you need to recreate KIDS again, do another sort of MARKETS. The new sort will only take you maybe a minute, and you'll be sure all the data is current and there.

---

several criteria, not just one. So you could sort in terms of high pay and previous sales and publications that accept simultaneous submissions, for instance. Or you could sort in terms of high percentage of freelance work but not located in New York.

Check your manual for the methods of using the sort utility available in your WP system. If your WP system won't sort for you, start thinking about trading up to more powerful software. The sort utility is absolutely worth having, as an aid to database management.

SEARCH YOUR MARKETS

If you're a nonfiction writer specializing in personality pieces, for instance, you could easily generate a database with hundreds of records, each containing increasing amounts of information as you submit and resubmit to the publications listed and come to know more and more about them. But if you're a novelist or write book-length nonfiction, chances are that your MARKETS file will contain only a dozen or two records, since book publishers are far less numerous than magazine publishers and you're more likely to be submitting only once or twice a year rather than week by week. What use is a database to you?

For one thing, editors change. You'll need a place to note new editorial names where you won't forget them (*Publisher's Weekly* is a good source of this kind of news). Moreover, publications move or are taken over by ENGULF & DEVOUR conglomerates; you need a place to note that if it happens. Finally, sources like *Writer's Market*, *Writer's Digest*, and trade magazines like *Publisher's Weekly* (and specialized writers' newsletters: for instance, *LOCUS* in the science fiction field) offer updated information about existing and new publications. Once your database is established, it will be easy for you to update, too, for those publications you're especially interested in.

If you do no more than search the record each time, that alone will save you thumbing through the pages of your market guide to locate mailing information. You'll also avoid the chance of typing the editor's name or the publication's address wrong, helping to prevent an editorial wince or a manuscript that's either lost or returned undelivered.

You'll find the work of querying and producing cover letters much simplified too: the minimal, routine work that secondary merge files are designed to do.

You're going to type those names and addresses anyway: why not keep them in a form so they'll do you some extra good?

SORTING WITH A MACRO

In Chapter 9, we'll be talking about macros. But a little discussion of how they can help you, in this present context, is needed.

We've already explained that it's crucial, in making a database, that the same *categories* of information come in the same order, from one record to another. You may already have noticed that in our sample field 8 (F8), there's a whole hodgepodge of information about what kind of things *Gentleman's Quarterly* is interested in. That information isn't in any particular order. You therefore couldn't simply sort to compile a list of magazines for seniors, for instance, unless you created separate fields for each possible interest—and that would get very tedious very quickly.

Yet you might very well want to sort just that way. So how can you do it?

With a macro.

You could make, with a macro, your own personalized sorting utility. It would go a little slower than a WP system's sort utility, but it would work perfectly well.

This is how you'd make a sorting macro:

With MARKETS onscreen, you'd begin by opening a window or making sure your second screen was available for use. Then you'd begin defining the macro and give it a name: say, SENIORS. You'd first tell the macro to search a keyword: *seniors*. (As mentioned in the last chapter, macros often begin with search.) Once the key word was found, you'd tell the macro to search backwards for the ^E or whatever character marked the end of the previous record (an end-record code). Move down one line, to the very beginning of the record you want, making sure you're at the left margin. Then tell the macro to begin a block at that point. Tell the macro next to search ahead for the same end-record code, to include the whole record you're interested in within the block. Now the whole record concerning a magazine that is interested in material for seniors is defined, beginning to end. You'd then tell the macro to *copy* that block (not *cut*!), switch the cursor to the window or the second screen, retrieve the block there and go to the very end of it, creating an additional line if need be. Then tell the macro to jump back to the main document, MARKETS.

At that point you can finish defining the macro if you want. When you wanted to use it, you'd just tell the WP system to do the macro

SENIORS 300 (or so) times to be sure you've caught all the possible records.

Or if you want to "chain" the macro and make it repeat itself as many times as necessary to catch every record with seniors in it, you'd have as the final step of the macro, invoking itself: invoke macro SENIORS. Then you'd finish the definition at that point. You'd then have a chained macro.

So the progression would go like this: (Have MARKETS onscreen)

1. Define a macro
2. Name the macro SENIORS
3. Search the word seniors
4. Search backward for end-record code of previous record
5. Put block ON
6. Search ahead for same end-record code of record you want (thereby marking the block you want to move)
7. Copy the block
8. Move cursor to second screen or window
9. Retrieve the block in the screen/ window
10. Move cursor to the end of retrieved block, adding an extra line if needed
11. Return to main document (MARKETS)
12. End defining macro

or

12. Invoke macro SENIORS
13. End defining macro

Some WP systems require you to define the macro in words. The friendlier WP systems do it by having you enter the actual keystrokes of the mac (search, block, and so forth) directly with the appropriate function, cursor, and alphanumeric keys, recording what you did and repeating the whole sequence whenever the mac is invoked. Whichever way your WP system wants you to do it (check your manual), the progression we've described will yield a mac that will serve to sort your database *no matter where the wanted information is located in the record*.

You could make a macro for KIDS, OUTDOORS, or whatever key interest word you wanted to sort in terms of.

Making such a macro may sound cumbersome, but if you do it just once, you can use it 10,000 times at the touch of three or four keys. Wouldn't that be worth it?

ADDING FIELDS

Suppose you initially set up your database with 7 fields and later decide you want a total of 10, or 13, or 20 fields. You certainly don't need to add all the extra fields by hand, record by record.

Instead, do it with a simple search/replace. Key global search/replace without confirmation. Then tell the system to search the end-record code, and replace it with 3, or 6, or 13 additional end-field codes plus the end-record code. Zip, it's done, just like that.

AVOIDING MERGE LETTER BLUES

NO LETTER BOMBS!

The most common hitch in sending multiple query or cover letters is getting the wrong letter into the wrong envelope: you have a letter to Publisher B that starts out saying, Greetings, Publisher A!

Editors see this basic dunderheadedness more often than you'd easily believe, and it always makes them wince. If you're doing a simultaneous submission to several markets at once, this mistake gives your letter slightly less impact than something you find stuffed under your door addressed to DEAR OCCUPANT. Any chance your letter had can die, right at this point, for no other reason than failing to check that the right letter got into the right envelope before licking the glue and sealing in your mistake like a ticking time bomb.

NO NINETY-SIX-PAGE CORRECTIONS

One of us recently ran into a classic example of typewriter thinking that's worth passing on, to keep it from happening to you.

A primary merge document (form letter) had been combined with a secondary merge file (names, addresses, and variable data) to produce a complete merge file of 96 letters, ready to print. Only it wasn't. It looked awful. Lines carefully aligned and tabbed to the proper position had magically wrapped, ruining the spacing and each letter's appearance.

What had gone wrong?

Well, the data from one field of the secondary merge file was of variable length. It varied between about 10 and 20 characters. But on the original primary document, the code defining where that particular field's worth of data should come in—the ^F3^ code—was only four characters long. And in tabbing over from there to continue the letter's text, no allowance had been made for data *that was sometimes longer* coming in when the two documents were merged. Naturally, all the subsequent tabs were bumped rightward by the longer incoming data, and each copy of the letter therefore went haywire.

If you're making a merged document with text of varying length coming into it, either: set tabs wide enough to accommodate the incoming data so it won't bump everything to its right off kilter; give the incoming data a line or a paragraph to itself; or have text that doesn't need to be tabbed but can wrap at will, regardless of the length of what comes in.

Now, though, comes the interesting part, the part that probably will have the most direct relevance to you. The person staring at that monster document was proposing to correct it. By hand. Page by page.

It would have taken hours!

Typewriter thinking: if the page is wrong, you have to correct it, don't you?

Well, yes and no.

If you have a merged document that's gone wrong in this or any other way, scrap it immediately. Abandon it and go back to your original primary document, the basic form letter, and fix that. Then do the merge again. Maybe three minutes for the correction, another minute or so for the merge. Perfect merged document, all ready to print, in five minutes or less, instead of three or four hours.

Likewise, if you notice a wrong address or some other glitch in your secondary merge file, scrap the merged document (assuming you haven't already started to print it), fix the problem in the secondary merge file, then re-merge. Unless all the other letters (or whatever) in the merged document have already been printed (in which case you'd correct the one offending part and print that separately), it's not worth hunting through the pages for an error. Scrap the existing merge, make the correction, then do the merge again. It can save you worlds of headaches.

DEAR EDITOR&*@$%#!!!

Glance over your merged letters after they're printed. You'll need to do that anyway, to make sure the inside address matches the address on the label or envelope, as recommended above. But you also should do it to be certain you said what you thought you said.

Sometimes, for instance, you'll be inserting a personalized paragraph explaining how you've been an avid reader of that magazine for years and routinely camp out at the newsstand in subzero weather to get the new copy. Except that you forgot to put an end-field code at the end of the paragraph in that record in your secondary merge file. So the merge utility didn't know where the field ought to end and picked up the next field as well. The result is a paragraph that ends with the next field in the wrong place, and a blank where that next item should have gone.

Alternatively, you added, in one record, an extra end-field code at the end of the editor's name. Thus your merge left a blank as the address and your salutation now consists of your submission's title: *Dear "Wandering the Winter Woodlands"*:

Same result: bad, strange letter.

Take enough time to check one printed letter in detail, every word, and to check all subsequent letters where merged text or data was imported, to see that a mistake in your secondary merge file hasn't rendered some of your letters really weird and embarrassing.

Don't take your merge on trust. You'll spot things in printout that completely escaped you on screen. Make sure your cover or query letter presents you as a thoughtful, good writer, not a slapdash sort of person who relies on a computer to catch the kind of errors no WP program can protect you from. You have to do it for yourself.

BEYOND NAME/ADDRESS

As we just pointed out, you can add special, personalized information to your merge/cover letter, in addition to the name and address in your database. You can add a magazine's name strategically at several points, while you try to impress the editor what a fan you are, how well you know the magazine's reader, blah, blah, blah. If it's done subtly enough, or if you really are a fan of the magazine and have some familiarity with its editorial stance and readership, it still can work. The editor may even form the impression that you're a discerning sort of person.

You also might want to add a paragraph or so about yourself, tailored to a specific market. For instance, to query educational markets or magazines for children, you might want to stress your familiarity with children and your previous publications related to your present subject. In querying a magazine aimed at leisure and "lifestyle" activities, you might choose different things about yourself to emphasize and a different selection of publications. You can add a paragraph like this as one field of your database, if you want to, or make a file of self-profile paragraphs and add them manually by calling each into the appropriate query.

Once you start selling, you might want to remind the editor of specific articles you've sold him or her, or make some

TIP #12: SPECIAL FILES TO TRACK SUBMISSIONS AND TO RECORD INCOME AND EXPENSES: LOG & LEDGER

We've already suggested a number of special files you might consider establishing: CAST, GLOSSARY, and MARKETS. Two others can make any writer's life much easier and more organized: LOG and LEDGER. Since this chapter is essentially about selecting markets and submitting, this seems an appropriate place to explain them.

LOG ROLLING

In addition to keeping and updating market listings, or perhaps instead of a MARKETS database if you're a writer who submits to a very limited number of markets—if you're a novelist, for instance—you'll want to keep track of the queries and manuscripts themselves: where they went, when, to whom, and when and how they were contracted or rejected. The easiest way to do this is by establishing a LOG file. It needn't be in database mode, set up as a secondary merge file, unless you think you may want to sort it later according to some criteria, like work sold in the last calendar year, for example. You can simply establish a form, a template that you call up and fill in each time you're ready to submit. It might look something like this:

TITLE:
DESCRIPTION:
WORD COUNT:

SUBMITTED TO:
    DATE:
CHECK ON IT WHEN?   CHECKED?
letter/phone
RESULT?
ACCEPTED/REJECTED
    DATE:
PAYMENT:
    DUE:
COMMENTS:

SUBMITTED TO:
    DATE:
CHECK ON IT WHEN?   CHECKED?
letter/phone
RESULT?
ACCEPTED/REJECTED
    DATE:
PAYMENT:
    DUE:
COMMENTS:

SUBMITTED TO:
    DATE:
CHECK ON IT WHEN?   CHECKED?
letter/phone
RESULT?
ACCEPTED/REJECTED
    DATE:
PAYMENT:
    DUE:
COMMENTS:
        Three tries is enough to start with, don't you think? And the last one you can always keep blank as a mini-template to dupli-

friendly personal comment based on your acquaintanceship. This also could be added by means of merge.

Any information specific to the particular market, whether it's as short as a magazine's title or as long as a whole paragraph of personal chat, can become part of your database. What goes in is limited only by your needs and your imagination.

TARGETING LOCAL READERS

Using the merge utility, you can add all kinds of information, not only to your query/cover letter, but to the article itself. Here's how you might do it.

Suppose you've written a general article on pet care that you're trying to sell to Sunday supplement sections or "lifestyle" sections of newspapers in different geographical areas. You're more likely to sell if you can make the information pertinent to a local readership: that is, introduce and conclude this general article with some details appropriate to the region. Since newspa-

cate with block/copy to make the form longer, if a given piece goes the rounds to twenty or thirty potential markets before it's placed or retired.

In the example above, you'll want to check the publication's average response time as stated in your market guide, add about half again as long, and note the date when, if you haven't heard anything yet, it will be time to check by letter or phone on the manuscript's status. You may even want to keep a separate file of these dates (named CALLBACK?) or use an onscreen calendar that lets you flag special days with messages, if you have a calendar like that. The latter method would let you check the date and see what manuscripts have been out long enough to need checking on. You can also check on payments due, of course, using this kind of onscreen reminder or "tickler" file or calendar, as they're sometimes called in the business world. Call it TICKLER, maybe?

Keeping a LOG file, whether it's set up in database fields or not, will give you a complete history of everything you've written and submitted, and whether and where it was sold.

LEDGER DOMAIN
Speaking of selling. Even if you're not a full-time writer, you may be claiming writing-related income and expenses on your income tax. You may have home office deductions you want to claim. If you do, it will take a lot of the headaches out of tax time if you list appropriate income and expenses *as they happen*, with date and full identification of each expense (was it repair? outright purchase? supplies or equipment? postage? phone calls to editors?) and each payment to you (publication name, material bought, etc.).

Several writers we know keep such LEDGER files, called up and added to throughout the year, totaled at tax time, then saved, both as printout and on an archive disk, to compare against following years. They put a copy of the printout right along with the duplicate tax forms and the manila envelopes of receipts and cancelled checks in the bottom of their closets.

You can invest in some household-expense/budgeting software to serve this purpose if you want to, but a LEDGER file can really do all you'll need, provided you remember to enter each new writing-related purchase/expense and income on the file right away, when the transaction happens, in a readable and relatively painless fashion.

---

pers typically require exclusivity only in the area where the paper's read, you can sell this article, legitimately, a zillion times if you can make it sound fresh and specific to each separate readership.

So you write a general first and last paragraph with specific "holes" left where you'll later plug in the city's name, the name of a local park, the kind of animal a reader's likely to encounter while walking a dog in that area, a local pet sales chain, and so forth. You draw the information from your imagination and the Yellow Pages of a phone book for that locale, which you consult at the library.

Then you make a database that, field by field, supplies this information. Voila: you've got at least a half zillion articles specifically tailored to that many local markets, from Los Angeles to Kalamazoo. And if you're lucky, and if the material in the rest of the article is well written, accurate, and lively, your chances of selling it—and selling it repeatedly—have just risen enormously.

It will take work to target each individual market, but your submission rate will take a leap skyward. Your acceptance rate has a good chance of going way down, but you *want* that to happen, provided it reflects an increased rate of submission. If you send out only two copies of an article and get one acceptance, that's a 50% acceptance rate. But if you send out forty, and sell only a quarter of them . . .

You get the idea.

READY, SET, MERGE!
The basic use of merge is to increase your submission rate by allowing you to query more potential markets with more specific, personalized queries, in less time, with

much less work than grinding out each letter individually. The more frequently you submit, the higher your chances of acceptance. This use alone is worth the time of learning how to create merge files and combine them into finished letters.

Every secondary merge file is an embryonic database in which all kinds of information can be kept, sorted, retrieved, and used. This database, especially if you're writing articles and submitting often to a variety of different markets, can become invaluable as the data grows. Onscreen, it's easy to consult; kept in notebooks or paper files, it would quickly become so hard to locate and look up that you'd soon abandon any attempt to keep the information current.

Your markets are your livelihood; your understanding of potential markets is the mark of your experience as a professional writer. Establishing and maintaining a database may become the step that enables you truly to turn professional.

However, don't get overambitious or let yourself become a data freak. If you establish database records with 25 fields in them, you're apt to leave half of them un-filled because it will be so much work to add a new record or update an existing one. Or, worse, you could find it so much fun to sort, resort, and change records that you mistake this activity for writing. Some people sharpen about 2,000 pencils, or sally forth in search of tons of yellow pads, and tell themselves that this means they're "really" writers. Databases have that potential too, and can be addicting.

Don't treat your database like a more exciting video game. Start out with only the number of fields you really need and will use. As we discussed, you can add extra fields later, as your information and your need for them grows.

A good database is a tool to help you with the secretarial side of writing: querying and submitting. Kept clean, uncluttered, and up to date, your database will be an invaluable resource geared specifically to your needs and interests and reflecting the contacts and editorial acquaintanceships you'll make as your reputation and experience increase. If you do get hooked on databases and/or find you really need to accumulate and manipulate lots of data, get a real database program and go to town!

CHAPTER 9

Macwonderful!

USES OF MACROS

OVERVIEW: THIS CHAPTER COVERS:

1. What macros are, and are for.

2. Built-in and add-on macros.

3. Keystroke-recording and word-based macros.

4. Making repeated punctuation and text easier with macros.

5. Using macros with windows and second screens.

6. Indexing with macros.

7. Macros and search.

8. Chaining macros.

9. Customizing your keyboard with macros.

ANYTHING—ANY SEQUENCE OF KEY-STROKES—you do more than twice, you probably should make a macro to do for you.

Macros are the workhorses of word processing. As discussed briefly, earlier, a macro records any sequence of keystrokes (including function keys and control-key commands, as well as regular text!) no matter how complex, and then replays the whole sequence either at the touch of two keys or when you "call its name" by *invoking* it.

For instance, both of us are working on several projects at the same time. With a single macro, we can save a present document from project 1, clear the screen, switch to another directory, and call the part of project 2 (or 3, 4, etc.) we're working on onto the screen, with the cursor right at the point where we left off—all of this by hitting ALT+C or ALT+S (the keys we've designated on our IBM clones as invoking the appropriate macro). The whole process takes about six seconds.

(Incidentally, although newer keyboards have both Control and ALT keys, older ones may have only Control. For the purposes of macros, though, the two keys are generally interchangeable.)

The more powerful WP programs (like WordPerfect for IBM and the Atari ST and Word for IBM and Macintosh) have macro capability built in; and some of the more basic systems can make simple macs with what's called a "glossary" function: they "paste" a word or a function to a given keyboard key and type that word, or do that function, when the key (plus a glossary function key) is struck. If you're shopping for WP system software, whether or not a given WP system provides mac-making capability is a factor worth taking into consideration, as we discussed in Chapter 2. But if you're happy and comfortable with your present WP system, you can still get mac-making capability as an add-on.

Stand-alone macro software includes such programs as Smartkey and Newkey for MS-DOS computers. These programs are typically memory-resident programs that you load before your WP program.

KEYSTROKE-RECORDING VS. PROGRAMMED MACS

There's one major difference between the various kinds of macro programs, whether built-in or add-on: some *record the actual keystrokes*—that is, you simply *do* once what you want the macro to do over and over—whereas others require you to *write out the steps of the macro in words*—in effect, writing a mini-program.

There are advantages to both kinds.

The keystroke-recording macs are easier to make, because you're doing the actual procedure just as you want it repeated; but once made, they're harder to change or "edit" because each mac is a solid unit of codes—you can't alter one step of the sequence without going back and doing the whole mac over from the beginning, unless you've *also* bought a special add-on macro editing program. But with such a program, you can edit keystroke-recording macs, changing the individual steps as though it were a written-out mac. And you can always turn off your computer and start over with many such programs, as some allow you to make temporary macro assignments to keys.

We should note, too, that you must be very careful when setting up a keystroke-recording macro. It's easy to accidentally assign the macro to the wrong keys or key. For instance, if you call up the macro program intending to create a macro assigned to the Control-0 key combination, but miss pressing the Control key when you enter the key assignment, you'll find your macro (maybe "Sincerely yours," or your WP program's SAVE command) popping onto the screen every time you want to type a zero!

The written-out, "programmed" macs

are harder to create, since you're writing steps on the screen rather than *doing* the procedure; but, with written steps, the completed mac is easy to edit, since you can just call it onto the screen like a document and change its written instructions. No additional software is needed.

Whether you opt for a keystroke-recording mac *plus* a mac editing utility, or choose a written-out macro system that makes mac-creation a little more cumbersome but allows editing without additional software, macro-making capability is well worth having. Choose a programming macro program if you expect to be defining long, complex macs with fifteen or more steps: such long macros can be a nuisance to recreate. But if you're chiefly using simple five- or six-step macros, you may find a keystroke-recording program is all you'll need, without any editing capability at all, since it's no great chore to recreate the mac from scratch if you want to change it.

With macs you can customize the whole writing process all the way from making small punctuation marks easier to key in, to making major alterations throughout several documents in succession, creating templates, sorting databases, and opening windows to let a little green-screen sunshine in.

PUNCTUATION AND WORDS

Remember "The Albermarle Municipal Water System and Sewage Treatment Facility," the ghastly long name we mentioned two chapters ago? Putting that phrase—or *any* preexisting text—into your onscreen document could be done with a macro. (Sure, it could also be done by retrieving from disk the file with the added text, going to your directory and selecting that file, or by search/replace. But the other methods would require anywhere between three and sixty-seven keystrokes, not even counting the quote marks or moving the cursor to the right file on the directory. And the beauty of WP systems is that there are about three ways to do anything you want to do.)

Using a mac, all you'd do is define the mac to pull that file (the one whose text reads *The Albermarle Municipal Water System and Sewage Treatment Facility*) off the directory and insert it at the position of the cursor. You could either give the macro a name, or assign it to ALT or CTRL plus a letter key: for instance, CTRL-A. Hit two keys, and that ghastly phrase is there. Or, if you're using a keystroke-recording mac, you can simply assign the phrase to a keystroke combination.

You can save *any* text, and any *amount* of text, as a separate file, then call it into your current document with as few as two keystrokes. How about letterheads? Sure! How about the "sincerely" part of letters? You bet!

Any text that you use over and over in the same form should be saved as "boilerplate," then called up as needed. A macro can do it for you. Create a file with the text, then create a macro to call up the file. It's that simple.

MANAGING PUNCTUATION

As with long, cumbersome words or phrases, any sequence of keystrokes you find awkward you can replace with a macro. For instance, on her keyboard, Ansen has two kinds of hyphens: ordinary hyphens and *required* hyphens that lock the hyphenated words together so that they won't break apart when the phrase wraps at the end of a line. That's important for writing dialogue that ends with a dash: two hyphens. Ordinary hyphens could leave the dash orphaned, on a line all by itself, or, worse, split into two single hyphens. Ugly. Embarrassing. Unfortunately, making two required hyphens is an awkward stretch of fingers, requiring the use of two right-hand keys; half the time she found herself hitting the wrong keys. So she made a

TIP #13: ALT/CTRL MACS VS. NAMED MACS

The ALT/CTRL keys (if your keyboard has both), plus the letter keys, give you a total of 52 potential two-keystroke macros. You'd think that would be enough for anybody. But there's a drawback you should be aware of.

Some WP systems save all macs to your WP disk or directory and therefore won't let you create two macs with the same name. But some save them directly on your current data disk or directory; and that can cause problems.

If on one floppy disk or in one directory you've made a mac called ALT-M which changes your margins, and on another disk or directory you have another ALT-M mac that calls up a memo template and fills in the date, the two macs aren't going to like one another. If you try invoking the second after having used the first in the same session, a "ghost" of the first use will remain in the system memory; your WP system will neither recognize nor perform the second ALT-M mac and is apt to flash you some weird error message instead, such as "Unknown display state," or "Recursion detected."

There's a way around this, though.

You can rename the macro on your directory. In our example, if you renamed the second ALTM.MAC to be MEMO.MAC, you could then invoke it by its name and use it even though you'd previously used the other ALT-M macro.

If a mac that previously performed just fine for you starts acting up or refusing to work, check to see whether you've made, and have used, a different macro "pasted" to the same ALT or CTRL plus letter sequence. Try renaming the mac, and that may solve the problem.

This problem seldom arises with named macs, since it's less likely you'll create two macros with identical names. (And if your WP system saves macs to the WP disk or directory, it won't occur at all: your system will alert you that another mac by that name already exists.) However, if you find the minor inconvenience of adding the extra name keystrokes, when invoking a macro, worth not risking having conflicting, identically-named macros that refuse to work, you can name all your macs if you want to. But it's hard to beat two-keystroke macs for convenience, even if once in a while you have to sort out which ALTM.MAC is which and rename one of them.

Also note that besides renaming macros, you can copy them from one disk or directory to another, just as you'd copy a file, if your WP system saves them to your data disk. If it does, changing disks or directories can make a macro unavailable for use unless you copy it to other disks or directories where you may want to use it.

---

macro, ALT-D (for dash) which inserts two required hyphens just like that. Problem solved.

If there's some key combination you find annoying, you can likewise program it into a mac and do it with ease and convenience.

WINDOWS AND MACROS

You'd probably make more use of alternate screens and windows if they were easier to use. With a macro, they can be.

For instance, in creating a window, most WP systems ask you how big the window ought to be—12 lines, or more, or less: how much of the screen the window ought to take up. Several keystrokes, to describe the

window you want, are needed before the WP system will set the window up for you. But if you almost always find a half-screen window a good size—12 lines—then you can make a simple mac to create one for you.

We're describing the macro in words, because it's easier to read that way. With your own WP system, you'd be either using words or doing the procedure, according to what kind of macro program you're using.

It would go like this:

1. Start defining macro

2. Name the macro or give it an ALT or CTRL plus letter designation

3. Do whatever your system requires to create a window

4. Select a window 12 lines long
5. Create the window
6. End macro definition

There'd be no point in making a macro to take you to your second screen, because on most WP systems, that's *already* accomplished by just two keystrokes. In that case, a macro wouldn't have saved you any trouble and would only complicate the procedure to no purpose.

If you're frequently adding cut text to a SCRAPS file, you can add an extra wrinkle to the macro definition above. First, block, then cut the text you're taking away (with your block/move function key(s)), so that the WP system is holding it in its memory. Then do the macro definition above through step 5. Then continue:

6. Move cursor into the window
7. Call SCRAPS onto the screen, in the window
8. Go to the end of SCRAPS, adding a fresh line if necessary
9. Retrieve the cut text (into the window)
10. Go to the end of that text and add a line
11. Save SCRAPS file
12. Exit SCRAPS file (clearing your window's portion of the screen)
13. Move cursor back to main screen (out of window)
14. Redefine window as 24 lines long: that is, remove the window
15. End macro definition

You can, of course, do the same with a second screen rather than a window, if you find that more convenient.

The result will be that when you cut a piece and then invoke this macro, the cut portion will be almost instantaneously added to the end of SCRAPS, SCRAPS will be saved with the new material in it, and you'll be back to the document you're working on in a matter of a second or two. Easy, right?

Some of the newest WP systems accomplish the same thing by offering, as a possible choice on the block/move menu, the command *append*, which adds the cut block to a given file on disk. If you have that capability, great: you don't need this particular mac. But if you don't, you can do it anyway, and that's the beautiful thing: macro generation and use allows you to, in effect, *define your own function keys* to do what you want done, independent of the functions that come built-in on your WP program. Not surprisingly, WP software developers and publishers notice what blind corners macs are being made to get around, and in their new products, offer these procedures *as options right on the function keys*.

So the mac of today is the function key of tomorrow.

INDEXING

A variation on this technique can greatly simplify the process of compiling an index—whether for one of your own manuscripts, a manuscript on disk you're indexing as a freelancer, a list of the magazines you subscribe to, or whatever.

When you hit something you want to add to the index, type an asterisk *before* the item, add the page number and another asterisk *after* the item. Then define a mac to block from one asterisk to the next (by searching asterisks, first backward—block on—then forward), copy the block, transfer the block to your second screen or window, where you're keeping the document INDEX, go to the end of INDEX and retrieve the copied text, delete both asterisks (by searching back, delete, then searching forward, delete), add an extra line at the end of INDEX, return to your main document and end macro definition.

You can do this individually, with each item as you encounter it, or globally, tagging the items with sets of asterisks and adding page numbers, then having your mac do the job all at once when you've finished tagging one whole section or chapter.

This assumes you're not using any asterisks in your document; if you are, use some other marker. If you want to do it all in one fell swoop, you'd either tell the mac to do itself 1,000 times (it will quit when it finds no more asterisks) or *chaining* the mac to repeat as long as it finds asterisks. The result will be the same either way. We'll explain how to chain a mac, or several macs, in a minute.

If you're keeping INDEX on screen (on the second screen or in a window) as you work, you won't need to be constantly calling it up, saving it, and exiting it unless you want to for some reason.

When all the entries are in INDEX with the right page numbers, *sort* the index to put all the entries in proper alphabetical order. This saves hours of searching through to put each new item where it belongs *while* you're making the initial list. Let the sort utility do it for you!

The ability that some WP programs have to alphabetize through sorting can take much of the pain out of indexing even if you have to work from a hard copy, rather than a file on disk. Just make the notations randomly on your screen as you encounter items in the manuscript that need to be indexed. Note the item and page number, then alphabetize afterward. Then combine duplicate notations, now conveniently grouped together through having been sorted, so that all an item's page numbers are together, in sequence, and attached to a single index item rather than several individual duplicates. Then check whether any items should be sublistings of another item—*WP software* as a sublisting of the major listing, *software*, for instance. You can do these minor adjustments much more easily with the block/move function than you can by fiddling around with little 3 x 5 cards.

(NOTE: If your WP program doesn't have sort/alphabetize capability, there are utilities—usually named something like SORT—for almost every computer to do this job for you. There are also indexing programs, either as built-ins with some WP programs or as add-ons. If you're doing a lot of indexing, you might investigate these. However, a full-featured WP program *with macro capability* will let you do it anyway, without buying additional—and possibly noncompatible—software specially made for the purpose.)

MACROS AND SEARCH

You may have noticed that several of the more complex macros we've described begin with search. There's a reason. If you're asking a macro to go through a whole document and do something to it, the macro has to know, somehow, when it's at the right place to do the thing you want it to. That involves searching for and finding something—a string of characters, a marker, or a format code—that's repeated within the document, then stopping there and doing the macro function at that point.

As discussed in the previous chapter, that's why it's important to keep database entries in precisely the same form, whether or not you put your database in the form of an actual merge file with end-field and end-record codes. If each whole record has an extra line before it, and has no completely blank lines within it, a macro can search the two "hard returns" (ENTER/RETURN, ENTER/RETURN) and know where each record starts. It can then search for the next double hard return and know where the record ends. The consistent format of the information allows you to make macros to sort, add, delete, or otherwise change the information in your database (for instance, adding extra fields to each record) all at one time. A macro can, as we explained in Chapter 8, even copy any record that has the word "mystery" or "romance" *anywhere* in it, deposit the record in a separate document, and thereby compile a personalized submission list from a miscellaneous database of markets.

Similarly, if you're working through a document and want a macro to do something—change a formatting code, for instance, to change margins or tabs—you have three choices. You can scroll through the document, screen by screen, until you find the place where you want the macro to do its stuff; you can *tag* the place with some consistent marker (an asterisk, for instance) while you're working and later set the macro to search the marker and make the change; or you can set the macro, as the first step of its definition, to search a particular character, set of characters, or code that already exists within the document.

Thus, the macro can serve as a kind of super search/replace. It can search an item and not merely replace it with another but *do* something at that position—change tabs or margins, cut a paragraph and put it someplace else (for instance, into a SCRAPS file), add a subheading, or anything else you choose.

The basic way to think about it, when you're defining a macro, is that you need to be able to tell it "When you find THIS, do THAT." Then, as one of the macro's final steps, make sure you have the macro move the cursor *beyond* the character string, marker, or code being searched, so it can find the *next* place to go to work, rather than do the same operation over and over at the *same* position.

By having something consistent to look for, the macro can do as many procedures on a document as you want—all at the touch of two keys.

CHAINING MACROS

If the final step of a macro is to invoke itself, that macro is said to be "chained." It will, when invoked, continue to operate until the initial search string (characters, marker, or code) is no longer found.

You could accomplish the same thing, with an individual macro, by telling it to perform itself X times: 1,000, 2,000, whatever you feel like keying in (usually done with the Escape key). It will still stop whenever it can't find any more examples of the designated search string.

But the really interesting thing is that one mac can be set up, at its conclusion, to *invoke another, different mac.* Those *two* macs are then chained together.

For instance, suppose you want not only to copy an entry from a database, but to make a notation on the master database that you've used the entry in a targeted market list. That way, you could go back after six months or a year and purge the master list of any entries you've ended up not using (by sorting and selecting the ones you *have* used). That second procedure, making the notation, could be a second macro, invoked when the first macro has copied the entry and returned the cursor to the master database.

If you wanted to do two procedures like this, you'd make the second macro, the one for the second procedure, *first*, then make the primary macro afterward.

It would work something like this: Have your database on screen, and your second screen or window ready to use.

1. Start defining macro
2. Name macro TWO
3. Search end-entry or end-record code or marker
4. Cursor up one line, go to the end of the line, add a hard return (ENTER/RETURN) to begin a new line, or an end-field code, if you're using designated fields
5. Key phrase "Used (date)"
6. Invoke macro ONE
7. End macro definition

Then define the primary macro:
1. Start defining macro
2. Name macro ONE
3. Search (keyword)—for instance, *mystery*
4. Search backward to start-entry marker or end-entry marker of previous item, whichever is easier

5. Block on

6. Search forward to end-entry marker

7. Copy block

8. Switch cursor to window or second screen

9. Retrieve copied entry on window/second screen

10. Move cursor to end of entry, make sure there's an added line

11. Return to main screen

12. Search backward to start-entry code or end-entry code for previous item

13. Invoke macro TWO

14. End macro definition

This macro would copy the entry, move it to another list, return to the main document and make the notation that it had been used on that date. The two chained macros would continue, in alternation, until macro ONE no longer found the keyword it was searching for.

Two, three, or even more macros can be chained in this way in a complex system of "IF YES" and "IF NO" alternatives—that is, do one thing if the search string is found, and another if it isn't. Here, we're bordering on outright programming and advanced database management that we assume most writers will neither need nor want to know about.

If you do want to know more about chained macros, your manual (either your WP manual or the manual that came with your separate macro utility) will describe how to make macros to perform these sophisticated functions.

Macros can, as we hope we've shown, be as easy or as complex as you want to make them. A mac is good if it makes *the kind of thing you're already doing* easier, simpler, and faster. If constructing a mac becomes more complicated than the job you're asking the mac to do, it's a waste of time.

For instance, we recently saw a freeware disk that purported to offer special macros for writers using WordPerfect. In practice, though, all it did was enable the user to do with five or six keystrokes (all the macros were named) what *already could be done with two, or sometimes even one*—jump to the second screen, for example. The freeware was worth every cent of its price, but not a penny more.

MACROS AND YOUR KEYBOARD

A macro can repeat, endless times, anything you can do on your keyboard.

That includes using function keys.

As discussed earlier, function keys are just permanent, built-in macros tagged to specific keys to the side of, or above, your alphanumeric keyboard. If you find any function key hard to use because of its position, or find any function key chore that takes three or more keystrokes, but which you find yourself doing often, you can make a mac to do the whole sequence for you.

You can use a mac *instead* of a function key sequence.

For instance, creating a header containing automatic page numbering, to appear on every page except the first, can take twenty or more keystrokes. Although some WP systems will allow you to save the whole header as a separate file you can call into the top of each new document, some won't. But you still may be able to do it through a macro. The macro's definition would be the process of setting up the complete header—either in keystrokes or in words—and afterward, all you'd have to do would be invoke that mac, two keystrokes, to have the complete header on your new document.

Macros can do the work of any and all function keys on your keyboard. We've already explained how they can serve as a slower, but more flexible, form of the sort function. They can also change tabs and margins, change pitch and point size, change spacing, delete or add bold codes, save your document, and so forth—whatever you want them to do.

The result of this is that you can customize your keyboard and, to a large degree, compensate for whatever limitations you find your WP system has.

If you're used to using PC-Write and are switching over to XyWrite III, for instance, you can ease the transition by creating macros to duplicate the familiar PC-Write formatting codes as you work on the document in XyWrite, then replace them with XyWrite codes when you're ready to save or print.

If your WP program doesn't come with an automatic date function, you can make one with a macro. If your WP system will search/replace only forward, not in reverse, you can fool your system with a mac and make it search/replace backward anyway.

If you have a very basic WP system and are essentially happy with it and dread learning a new set of keyboard commands, it may be that what you really need is not a new computer and a new WP program but a flexible, powerful macro utility that will let you customize and compensate for the lacks of your dear, familiar (if somewhat clunky and outdated) system for years to come. A writer/editor of our acquaintance has done just that with XyWrite's macro capability; he's set up his copy of XyWrite so that he can issue WordStar commands to it for saving, marking and moving blocks, etc.

Macros are exactly what you want them to be and do exactly what you want them to do. They can be programming without the pain, or a simple dash inserted where you want it. Once you start using macros, you'll wonder how you ever managed to struggle along without them.

And remember: anything you do more than twice the same way, you can do with two keystrokes—with a mac.

CHAPTER 10

Revision Without Tears . . . or Seams

EDITING TIPS AND SHORTCUTS

OVERVIEW: THIS CHAPTER COVERS:

1. The advantages and drawbacks of editing on a computer.

2. Blocking text; how it works and what it can do for you.

3. Uses of the block/move function and "parking" text.

4. Copying text and preventing repeated text.

5. Block saves.

6. Block deletes; deleting disasters and how to recover from them; undelete.

7. Alternatives to deleting; moving and saving blocks; SCRAPS files; practical and creative benefits of saving rather than deleting.

8. Preventing seams and holes when data has been cut or added.

9. Writing notes to yourself: with footnotes, markers, strikeout, or files called AFTER or ASIDES.

10. Practical advice on saving multiple versions of a document; creating and using temporary filenames like NOW and FRED.

11. Saving drafts: how, when, and how many; keeping disk files in order.

12. Keeping superseded drafts on an ATTIC disk.

13. Allotting one disk or directory to each project you're working on.

14. Keeping track of revisions.

ONE OF THE UNIQUE AND SPECIAL THINGS about word processing is how easy it makes review, revision, and editing. Almost painless, really.

The beginning and ending of the writing process differ little whether you're using a typewriter or a computer. Typing is pretty much the same whether you're using a computer keyboard or a typewriter keyboard. The pages end up looking pretty much the same, too (provided you have a "letter quality" printer). You could accumulate paper files and probably even find them, instead of storing them on disk. But the difference WP makes to the editing process is what word processing is really all about, for any writer. Ask Stephen King, Jerry Pournelle, or your humble authors, all of whom rave about what switching to word processing has done for their ease in revision and their satisfaction with the finished manuscripts.

First of all, a WP document expands as you work on it, leaving room for endless notes to yourself, inserted text, and extra pages, instead of marginal arrows pointing in seventeen directions, pages numbered 188q, and trailing scraps of alterations stapled all over your draft copy to the point that you have to peek carefully under them to read the text.

WP documents shrink, too. If you cut a paragraph or a page and what remains makes an awkward join, you're less likely to miss that fact because it's all there before you in final form, just as if it had been retyped. So it's a lot easier to follow the continuity of a piece of writing—whether pace, logic, or coherence—with what is, in essence, always clean copy. Achieving the same result on a typewriter would mean retyping the whole thing every time you made a substantial change. With WP, though, the whole document is reformatted and adjusted as you work, growing and shrinking, changing under your typing fingers.

But as with all wonderful things, there are drawbacks. The errors permitted by and common in word-processed manuscripts are of the bizarre kind no typist in his/her right mind would ever make. For example, you can change "for" to "because," forget to delete "for," and leave both words sitting there. If you use wide margins and a program that doesn't force-wrap every line, text can disappear off the right hand side of the screen. You can forget it's there, because you can't see it without making a deliberate effort. The result can look excruciatingly dumb in printout. As the saying goes, "To err is human, but to really screw things up, it takes a computer." Truer words, alas, have seldom been spoken.

Or instead of having wrong words repeated, the right ones may simply vanish. Many things in WP can be frighteningly permanent because the data is in many ways fragile. Until you save your work, any changes you've made are so many electrical states on silicon chips. After you save your document, it's just a bunch of electromagnetic charges on a disk. When something is gone, it can be gone beyond recovery and beyond reconstruction. So your primary effort, in editing, has to be directed toward giving yourself almost unlimited opportunities to change your mind—the one way, or the other—before anything becomes permanent. Your secondary effort, a result of the first, is to avoid multiplying alternative versions of a given document to the point that you completely lose track of what in the world you meant to say or in which draft you came closest to saying it.

Successful editing is a judicious balancing act between taking full advantage of the ease of editing WP allows without falling into any of the dozen or so pitfalls yawning to swallow up the unwary. We'll try to guide you in doing both.

BLOCKING TEXT

Virtually all WP systems allow you to mark a

certain section of text, from a single character to pages at a time, and then *do* something to it: move it, delete it, save it, or any of about five other things. This function is generally called BLOCK and involves marking a section of text to identify it to the WP program as the piece you're going to do something to. Hit a key or two to mark the beginning and ending of the block, and it's yours to do with as you will. Block is a powerful tool—with several "attachments," to continue the analogy—and one of the most distinguishing features of word processing.

MAKING YOUR MARK

The first step in using block is marking a block (i.e., designating the text to be manipulated). WP programs use two basic methods of marking blocks. The first is to give a command to mark a block's beginning location, move the cursor, then mark the block's ending location. This is best for scrappy blocks: a phrase, 1-1/2 paragraphs—things like that. The other way designates *units*: a sentence (what ends with a period, question mark, or other terminal punctuation); a paragraph (what ends with a "hard" return rather than ordinary word wrap); or a page (what ends with a hard or soft end-page code) with a single command.

Whichever way you designate a block, the block is normally identified onscreen by highlighting or a similar alteration of its onscreen appearance.

A POCKETFUL OF TEXT

In addition to making blocked text recognizable as a block by highlighting it, coloring it, or at least placing markers at the beginning and end of a block, most WP programs make a temporary invisible copy of the block. The copy is stored in what's called a "buffer," analogous to an invisible pocket.

Once the text is in this block storage

pocket, the WP program draws on it to perform certain functions, such as move or copy a block. But beware! This block/move pocket can hold only one piece of text at a time; the size can vary up to a set limit (the pocket can "stretch"), but if you mark a new block, the old block disappears from the pocket. You therefore need to work on your blocks one at a time.

Incidentally, some WP systems kindly prevent you from blocking a new piece when something (a block or a unit—sentence/paragraph/page) is already in the block/move pocket waiting for relocation. Such systems may *force* you to recover the data in the pocket before they'll allow you to do anything else. Software designers know that one of the chief aims of WP software is to cut to the absolute minimum the chances of your losing data. So newer, more sophisticated (read: expensive) programs have fail-safes the older and cheaper ones don't.

BLOCK/MOVE

The major function associated with blocking is MOVE. You take either a marked block or a designated unit (sentence, paragraph, or page), zip it out of its original location and move it anywhere in the document.

This process of blocking and moving, sometimes called the "cut and paste" function (because it's like cutting and pasting a typewritten manuscript), involves several steps that may vary from one WP system to another. But we're going to talk about it as though it were one process: block/move— the capability to zip out text and put it elsewhere (or, with some systems, put it nowhere, thereby deleting it).

The block/move function is the safest in editing. You can always return a block of text to its original position, or to yet another place in the manuscript, if you don't like the new lineup.

BLOCK/COPY

Perhaps the second most-frequently used block function is copying text—that is, putting a duplicate in the WP system's block/move pocket but leaving the original in place, right where it was. Suppose you need to repeat a sentence or paragraph in a novel, for whatever artistic reasons. Rather than retype it, you can block and copy it. Ditto for repeating sentences or paragraphs in non-fiction work or submission letters. (See how word processing eliminates the drudgery?)

A ROSE IS A ROSE IS A ROSE UNTIL YOU'RE SICK OF THE WHOLE THING

It may have occurred to you that since you can copy rather than move a block of text, you can compare how the block reads in its new location with its effect in its old location. But doing this creates an opportunity for something less than disaster, but more than a mistake: you can inadvertently repeat the same block/sentence/paragraph/page twice or more, in exactly the same form, in different parts of your document.

If you copy and relocate a block, it appears on screen in both places (as well as being held in the block/move pocket, until you bump it out by blocking something else). If the original block isn't removed later, it will still be in both places; and in reading over the manuscript, you may not notice the repeat if the instances are far enough apart.

So choose *move* over *copy* if you're trying out material in different order. If it's gone from one location, you can always get it back by block/moving it again. And it won't still be sitting there, a ticking time bomb of potential duplication waiting to go off and make you look (and feel) like an utter fool, in the way that only overlooked computer errors can.

The only time block/copy is a good idea is if you know you're going to use that piece several times: remember "The Albermarle Municipal Water System and Sewage Treat-

ment Facility" in Chapter 7? You want the original there, and you also want the repeats. You can call a given block out of the block/copy pocket as many times as you want, as long as you haven't blocked something else in the meantime.

Some WP systems that don't use pockets will nevertheless obediently copy the block you've marked as long as you leave it marked—one time, or twenty. So un-mark that block, as soon as you've copied it, and delete the repeated text in the location where you don't want it, right away. (NOTE: Be sure to mark both locations with a marker like "%%%" so you can move between them, as described in Chapter 7.)

To be really safe, if you're going to repeat a certain stretch of text, *save* the block under an easy filename (ABC?), delete it from the onscreen document, then retrieve it from disk whenever you want it; or set up a simple macro to do the retrieving for you. (More on saving blocks as files in a second.) That way, you'll have it when you want it, but only when you want it. It will be safe on disk in the meantime, not in a sometimes unreliable electronic pocket. And when you're done with it, it's easy enough to delete the file off the disk (and any no-longer-needed macros, too).

You'll also realize the benefit of not having to go back and re-mark a frequently-copied block after you've marked a different block for another reason, bumping the earlier block out of the pocket and into the never-never.

BLOCK/SAVE

Most WP programs will save a block to disk. This operation (sometimes called "writing to disk") creates a new file on disk and copies the block into it. The saved block is now, itself, a file that can then be edited or called into another document. (Note that we said the block is *copied* into the new file; it's not moved, copied to another location in the document, or otherwise altered, and remains marked for further operations.)

This operation has a number of applications. For example, if you decide that the chase scene in Chapter 2 of your novel really belongs in Chapter 4, it's easy enough to transfer the scene. Simply mark the entire scene as a block, save it to disk, then delete the block from the current document (one of the many other things you can do to a block, beside move or copy it, is *delete* it). When you go to work on Chapter 4, the scene will be waiting for you on disk, ready to be called in at the appropriate spot. Or you may find, in writing an article, that a long, bulleted list should really be a sidebar. Again, block, save, and delete.

Block/save has some saving graces of its own, too. For instance, if you have a book chapter that's really too long to be manageable, you can use block/save to cut it in half, as we described in Chapter 6. And as we'll discuss presently, doing a block/save is often preferable to straight deleting.

BLOCK/DELETE (WITH DISCRETION)

Besides block/move and block/copy, you can, as just mentioned, delete large or small chunks of your document. In the process of making changes, you put something in and as a result you'll often need to take something out.

The deleting process can be accomplished in a number of ways: with "search-and-destroy," as discussed in Chapter 7; with either the delete or backspace keys; with the "delete to end of line" or "delete to end of page" key-combinations some WP systems offer; by changing your keyboard from "insert" to "overwrite" or "typeover" mode, so all characters (although not codes, generally) vanish as you type over them; by blocking text, cutting it, and then not putting it anywhere (unless your WP system insists you recall it, as mentioned above); or by just telling your WP system to delete the block outright.

With all of these convenient ways to eliminate data, it's important to know all the ways you can get it back if you delete too much, or unwisely, or if you simply change your mind.

Deleting a block is a useful function; marking and deleting a large block of text with two or three commands is a lot easier (and less time-consuming) than deleting it one character at a time. And you'll often have occasion to delete large blocks of text—experiments that don't work, dead-end scenes that bog down a story, whatever.

But use discretion in deletion! Before you start thinking of block/delete as a good way to "clean up" a cluttered manuscript, read on . . .

DELETING DISASTERS

Being able to delete a block can be a potentially disastrous capability. You can accidentally or thoughtlessly enter your program's block/delete command rather than, say, block/move. Or when you forget (some WP programs won't let you) that you have text in the block/move pocket waiting for relocation and reblock and thereby lose the text (and it does happen—count on it!), you can wipe out a lot of work.

Or you could change your mind after deleting a large block of text and want it back. What do you do then?

Recovering Deleted Text Whether you lost the text through bumping it out of the block/move pocket or through deleting it, you may still be able to get it back.

If the lost text was part of your original document, you're all right. (If it wasn't, and what you did was delete it, you may be all right if you can undelete, as we'll explain in a minute. If it was new stuff, unsaved, and you can't undelete or you emptied and re-filled the block/move pocket, we're afraid you're out of luck.)

You could junk your present onscreen document—and all your recent, unsaved changes—and go back to your original version to block/move that lost text. But junking your document this way is rarely a good idea. If you made a lot of intermediate changes before the delete disaster struck, you could be sacrificing a lot more than you'd gain.

There are better, simpler, and more effective ways.

1. Rename the onscreen file, save it, exit it, and recall the original document onto your screen to recover the lost piece. *Do NOT save the onscreen document without renaming it: you'll lose the original!* (If your WP system automatically makes a .BAK-type file of any original you call onto the screen, however, no harm will be done even if you *do* save it under its original name.) Once you have the original document, block the piece, save *that* under some simple name, exit the old document, recall the version you were working on, and insert the lost material (whew!).

2. If you have second-screen or windowing capability, or if you use a notepad that desktop utilities like Sidekick offer, leave the working document onscreen. Switch to your other screen or notepad and call up the original document there, find the lost piece, and block/move it over to your working version (also whew!).

Although these methods work, they're fairly cumbersome and disrupt the flow of your writing/editing. Undelete is better; that's why, as you may recall, we listed this as a major consideration when discussing WP software features in Chapter 2.

Undelete The delete function, with many WP systems, keeps its own buffer or "pocket" which is *separate* from the block/move pocket, a fact for which all writers who have such fail-safes are humbly grateful, grateful, grateful. Unlike block/move pockets, delete pockets often are several levels deep: that is, they'll keep and hold the text removed in up to three total deleting sessions—periods in which you hit only the delete (or backspace) key,

regardless of how many total characters you deleted.

Here's how undelete works: whenever you delete something— be it a letter, line, paragraph, or marked block of text of any size—the deleted text goes into the delete pocket, whether you used the delete key, the backspace key, or did a block/delete. (It won't help with overwritten text if you switched from *insert* to *overwrite* mode, though—sorry. So stay out of overwrite mode next time!) All you need to do is tell the WP program to undelete and—voila!— the deleted text is restored.

If your WP system has this capability, it's worth noting that each *session* of deleting counts as *one* delete, no matter how much or little text is involved and no matter how often you hit the delete key (or backspace) during that session—a single character, or whole pages, cut before you struck some other key. As long as you do nothing but delete, ten individual deleted letters will show up as one (or more) deleted word(s), not as ten separate deletes, even though you did the deletion character by character.

DON'T DELETE IT—PARK IT!

It's important to remember that, once text has been blocked, you can lose it forever if you don't immediately save it or put it elsewhere. (As we said above, some of the newer systems *insist* you recover or save the blocked text immediately; but *most* systems won't offer this safeguard.)

If you mark a block, fail to relocate or save it, and then mark a new block, the first block is really, absolutely gone. And because the contents of undelete pockets are replaced by subsequent deletions, unrestored text is eventually lost for good, depending on how many sessions of deleting your WP system is able to store—generally, between one and three.

You might fall back on one of the more cumbersome text-recovery methods described earlier: calling up old copies, block/

moving or block/saving the lost text, then reinserting it. But not all programs have the features that make those methods possible. And if your WP system really makes deleted text vanish utterly and forever, as some do, you're going to need to be *very* careful about what you delete.

So, you're thinking, Is there any foolproof method to protect myself against deletion disasters? Or am I condemned to lose my work by accident or design, no matter what?

Well, now that we have you thoroughly suspicious of using block/delete, we'll suggest two alternatives to deleting: moving and saving blocks. One is the equivalent of long-term parking for anything you may want to use later, or may decide to bring back into the present document at another location. (This, of course, includes any large block of text you want to delete, too.) The other is, in effect, a handy electronic garbage can which you can, figuratively, paw through to recover the junked text (if you decide you really need it after all) and can easily empty at any time.

"MOVE IT OVER HERE, MAC!"

OK, so you got in over your head on that biography of Paul McCartney and wandered too far afield in discussing the Beatles' breakup. So you decide to take out eight paragraphs to save space and avoid boring your reader. Fine, just block and delete—but, wait! What if it later turns out that the chapter you're writing needs all or some of the material you're about to delete? You never know if a book chapter is going to change drastically before you're done with it (and chapters have a tendency to do that). So rather than delete the material, why not move it safely out of the way, so you can see how the chapter goes without it, and get it back quickly if you need it?

And where might you move it? Why, to the end of the chapter. Block the text, move your cursor to the end of the document, type *** to separate the addition from the "main" text, and move the block (and unmark the block, if your WP system needs it). Then if you find you later want the text or some portion of it, it's where you can get at it. And of course you can move more than one block of text to the end of the file.

This works best for shorter files and with small bits of text. Saving potentially disposable text with a file tends to make it unwieldy by increasing its size. For larger files—ten pages or more—we recommend that you use block/save instead.

FILE IT AWAY

So there you are, in the middle of a 34-page chapter chock-full of heart-stopping action and stunning suspense, when you come to something that doesn't belong there—a three-page flashback in which the viewpoint character recalls a quiet interlude with a friend in London. Certainly, that quiet flashback doesn't belong in the middle of an action sequence. But what if you're just being overly self-critical, and things look different later? What if you want to relocate the flashback to another section without losing your concentration on the present scene? You may want that scene back, but at the moment you need to see the entire action sequence "in the clear," and you don't want to make the present document any larger than necessary.

The smart thing is to get that scene out of the document completely, but *in a way that lets you get it back later*, no matter how many other blocks you mark or deletes you do. Just as you can block/delete as a more cautious substitute for block/copy, as discussed above, you can remove and then recover text with block/save followed by block/delete, founding the file that can serve as the "electronic garbage can" we mentioned earlier.

Mark the flashback as a block, use your program's block/save function to save it to disk as its own file, then delete the block from the document. You've lost nothing and gained a lot. You can delete the file later, if necessary, after you're sure you won't need that flashback.

Saving the Scraps If you edit heavily (or have a bad day and have to cut a lot later), you may end up with a lot of little (and not-so-little) scenes and paragraphs and miscellaneous chunks of text as you edit. You can save these trimmings in a SCRAPS file: a combination filing cabinet and garbage can containing all the flotsam and jetsam that writing generates and then leaves stranded on the electronic margins of things.

If you can switch from one screen to another, or if you have windowing capability, with two separate documents on the same screen at the same time, block/move the pieces you want to delete to that other screen (or portion of screen) with a little space between each block, so you can tell where one piece ends and the next begins. Then save the resulting document as SCRAPS.

Each project ought to have its own SCRAPS file, one per disk or directory that project occupies. (In fact, when you're writing a novel, you probably should save all the material you park at the end of each chapter in a SCRAPS file. As each chapter is completed, block the parked material at the end, add it to the SCRAPS file and save SCRAPS, then delete the block from the present document.)

A warning: if you block and then save the block, under the name SCRAPS, that new section of text will replace your entire SCRAPS file if one already exists. So be sure to add the new cut pieces to the file. If your WP system allows, you can "append" the block rather than save it, thereby tacking it onto the end of SCRAPS, on disk. Or you can accomplish the same thing by calling the whole file onscreen (either on your "spare" second screen or windowed) and adding the fresh material at the end of what's already there. Then, when you save, the whole SCRAPS file will be safe on disk,

old pieces as well as new. (You can, incidentally, make a macro to do the whole process for you, as discussed in the preceding chapter.)

If necessary, you can create a series of SCRAPS files (SCRAPS.1, SCRAPS.2, etc.), as you write, and periodically combine them into one general SCRAPS file. Each segment can be suitably annotated as to source and purpose, as you wish.

SAVER'S BONUSES

An interesting benefit of saving text you would otherwise delete, whether you do it via a SCRAPS or other disk file, or by dumping it at the end of the document, is that you can keep all the castoff material in one place. And as all writers know (or should know), scenes, descriptions, and even paragraphs are potentially valuable, to use in other work or contemplate as sources of inspiration. Memorabilia, we might say. What castoff treasures are hiding in *your* attic or hibernating at the bottom of *your* closets? And, unlike dejunking attics or closets, disks are a positive delight to clean out if you decide those half-forgotten treasures are really only junk, after all.

Too, knowing that you can make changes with so little effort (compared to writing on a typewriter), you're free to write "with the flow" as sloppily as you please, then clean up later without fear that your changes have to be permanent. It's easy enough to replace something you've deleted without having to type the manuscript for the third or fourth time.

Like love, parking your copy rather than deleting it outright means never having to say you're sorry. And like the truth, it can make you free.

MAKING SURE YOUR SEAMS DON'T SHOW

Writers who edit and rewrite heavily share a common problem: smoothing out the seams (or hiding the rivets) where they've dropped in or cut out a large chunk of text.

Because WP makes revising so easy, writers who use it tend to edit and rewrite more easily, enthusiastically, and heavily than do those who use typewriters; so their problem of handling the joins is proportionately more severe.

Fortunately, and by way of compensation, WP also makes it easy to smooth those seams and cover those rivets. Combine your program's search function with the ease of rewriting (ah—a problem that is its own solution!), and you have the tools to cover your tracks.

If you move a block of text into a different position in your document, you'll have disrupted the original flow of your thoughts in two places: where the material came from, and where it is now. Making a point to do a special check for continuity can save you from embarrassing goofs.

Mark the original location (with something like *** or %%%) before blocking the passage, so you can find that spot again. Then, when the passage has been moved into its new place, check to make sure that what comes before and after it still makes sense. Expect to write new, stronger transitions; check that you're not taking for granted some information you explained later in the document, at a position that now follows the passage you've moved. Maybe the definition or explanation now needs to come earlier, to make the relocated section clear in its present context.

Once you've done that, zip back to where you left the markers and do the same at the former position of what you moved. See that no hole or gap has been left—either in the wording or in the thought.

One of us failed to do that in an intermediate draft of a novel, moving a paragraph to about a page earlier than it originally had been. Although the bulk of the paragraph made better sense there, an unnoticed result was that the character put on his coat before he'd put on shirt or pants, which he then proceeded to add to his attire. A reader would have blinked hard, hitting that passage, if it hadn't been noticed and corrected in a later draft.

Block and move. Then check. You'll need to do a final hard-copy readthrough before final printout, as well, to check that all seams are straight, all holes properly filled in. We'll discuss that in Chapter 11.

ASIDES & AFTERTHOUGHTS

As you work on one document, you may come up with ideas for another. Or you may want to make a list of things you want to do, later, to the section you're working on. There are four basic ways to write notes to yourself, either in the present document, at its top, or in a separate file which you may want to call ASIDES or AFTER.

If you want to write reminders to yourself (something like "Move cut material from Chapter 7, on SCRAPS files, here"), some of the newer WP programs allow you to add that comment in a non-printing code. That is, the whole comment is there, but none of it prints out. Onscreen, it looks like this:

> COMMENT: This is a display of a comment as it would appear onscreen.

You can search the comment code and locate it anytime you're ready to review a given document. That's the easiest way, if your WP system allows it. But as with so much in WP, there are ways to do it anyway, even if your WP program doesn't have all the latest frills and furbelows.

For instance, you can type a remark right into your document, then tag it with some particular marker (***, $$$, %%% or whatever marker you're not otherwise using in the document) that you note at the beginning of the document as a reminder. When you've thought about or done what the remark noted, cut it and the marker code.

Or if your WP system can handle footnotes, you can note your remarks in footnote form. To check what notes you've left yourself, you'd simply search them. With some WP systems, footnotes stay invisible on the normal screen, so you don't even have to look at them unless you want to. Just remember to cut them when you're through with them.

A special feature the more powerful WP systems offer is "strikeout": putting a special mark, that shows up during printout, on a section of text. This is what it looks like:

[STKOUT]~~This text is what strikeout mode looks like, except that the codes would be invisible.~~[stkout]

The text so designated can be deleted in one sweep before you're ready to print out. That text can be your remarks—there when you want to refer to them, gone when you're done with them. And the strikeout code, like a footnote, can be searched. If you have text that a number of people are going to contribute to—this collaborative book, for instance—each writer or reviewer can, on screen, make comments on the document that will be easy to identify (with initials?) and yet be easy to remove.

If you use any of these systems of making notes in the document itself, whether through a comment function, in footnote form, using a marker, or with strikeout capability, be sure you use some consistent, searchable marker (or code), then make a point of finding and eliminating such working notes before your final printout. It would be embarrassing to have them show up ("REWORK THIS") on something you're submitting. Even the non-printing comments would show up on a disk submission. Tidy up after yourself.

A less high-tech solution anybody can use is simply to set up a file called AFTER or ASIDES, which you keep for thinking on screen about the project and writing notes to yourself about things to consider, things

to do. Write all your comments in the same place (at the beginning or end of the document), or mark them all and collect them in the same place with block moves, then block/save them in the AFTER/ASIDES file. (Since, as we advise below, you'll have a separate disk or directory for each project, there won't be any confusion about which project the notes in your AFTER file refer to. This comparatively low-tech procedure has the advantage that it sets up separate files, so you won't have to sleuth down and eliminate notes from your actual document.) Or you could use the notepad of a desktop utility like Sidekick for the same purpose.

TEMPORARY FILE NAMES: NOW & FRED

Suppose you want to tinker around with an existing document, trying it different ways, editing for pace or for clarity in the way WP makes so attractive and painless. But you don't want to do anything permanent to your rough draft file on disk until you've made up your mind what changes really work and which ones you don't want to make after all.

How can you have your cake and yet eat it: locking in changes while keeping the original file intact?

Easy. Give any file you're working on a temporary name, and save it under that name until you're satisfied what version of the changed document you want to substitute for the original. Then, when you're sure you want to keep the changes, save the revised document back under its original name. Or if your WP program doesn't accommodate saving a file under different names, block the entire file and save the block under a different name each time you've generated a version worth saving. Or take advantage of some WP systems' readiness to rename the original file something like .BAK when it's retrieved, freeing the regular filename for the version of the file on your screen.

Using temporary names also prevents that frequent goof, thoughtlessly saving a wretched mistake (a screen that has only the word *the* on it, for instance) in place of your whole original file. That's happened, believe us, and it can be a real heart-breaker.

For instance, suppose you're writing a document that, so far, hasn't been given a name because you haven't yet saved it. You *should* have saved it (as we advised way back in Chapter 6), but say you haven't. While working on it, you call into it another file that *does* have a name. Your computer will now think that name is the name of the whole file, having no other name to go by. And if you save it at that point, your on-screen document will replace the existing file that went by that filename. Several of the more powerful and popular WP programs—including WordPerfect for MS-DOS computers, the Atari ST, and the Apple Macintosh—are so structured that this can happen, even though most of them require you to confirm you *really, really* want to replace the file on disk. The fingers can be a lot quicker than the eye, and they sometimes go on automatic while the mind's occupied elsewhere.

One of us kept cut material from a novel in a huge file called SCRAPS. The file SCRAPS was called into a version of chapter 12 because the writer thought, "Aha! This is the place that cut piece from chapter 4 really belongs." So the portion of chapter 4 was inserted (from the SCRAPS file) and the rest of the material deleted. But when the onscreen document was saved without having been renamed, the writer stared in horror at the prompt announcing that the system was obediently saving a document called SCRAPS. It was too late: the original SCRAPS file, with cut material from several chapters, was gone forever. (The author hadn't made a backup disk at that point, either. Most of us learn to avoid disasters the hard way. But you don't have to.)

NOW/FRED FILES

And what temporary filename might you use in these instances? One writer we know uses NOW as the filename (or sometimes the extension) of any working document onscreen that began as a file on disk. So she's always sure that any document called NOW in the directory of a data disk can be replaced without harm, because that was just an onscreen alias used in the previous WP session. The result is that there's never more than one NOW document on any data disk. If she's trying out a different version of chapter one (which has the filename 1. on disk), it becomes 1.NOW or NOW.1 while she's working on it. When revision is complete, the onscreen document is saved under the filename 1. again.

If you don't think NOW is an aesthetically pleasing word, pick one of your own. A three-character name gives you the flexibility of using it as either a filename or an extension. How about your initials? Or WRK for "working document?" Or, if you're content to use it only as a filename, how about VERSION? (Avoid using TEMP, though: several WP programs use that as a file name for "printing preview" of documents.) Another writer we know prefers, for reasons that are still murky to us, to call her temporary documents FRED. And if she generates further intermediate documents while wanting to keep FRED itself intact, she calls the versions FRED.1, FRED.2, and so on.

What three- or four-character name appeals to you? You can choose a filename up to 8 characters, with most WP systems, and an extension up to 3, if you're willing to put up with the nuisance of typing a filename that long. Be creative! As long as you're consistent about what name you use, the only limit is your imagination.

SAVING DRAFTS

Using temporary filenames too liberally, however, can lead to your having 15 different versions of chapter 1 on disk with no idea which one you actually want to keep.

One way to distinguish among them is to note, on the directory, the date and time each of the temporary files was created. That's one very good reason for using the boring system of military time many computers require, and for not ENTERing quickly through the boot-up prompts for DATE and TIME, if your computer provides them, without filling them in. With most WP systems, if your computer knows the date and time, it will label your files with the time they were last saved. So you'll be able to tell, thereafter, which one is the newest, check it briefly onscreen to make sure that's the version you want, and then delete the others to tidy the disk directory.

You can also, if you wish, add an explanatory note to each version of a file you save—at its beginning or end, so it will be easy to find.

ENOUGH, ALREADY!

Nobody likes a confused, cluttered disk any better than they do a desk piled high with papers and scribbled notes, old sandwiches, and so forth. But somehow such disks, and desks, do manage to exist. Are yours like that—what's sometimes rationalized as a "well-organized mess?"

Maybe you're like the lady in the story who, when asked if she liked waffles, responded, "Oh, yes—I have trunks full of them!" Or maybe you save string.

Before you run out of patience, or your disk out of space, set yourself a maximum number of versions you'll save before scrapping (at least) the first in the sequence. If you're a really dedicated reviser and saver, you could easily accumulate a dozen or more drafts of a single document, perhaps differing from one another by only a single word, a change in margins, or a deleted comma.

Five is a good number for a single document you're working on intensively. But you can choose three, or whatever number you find comfortable and appropriate for the way you write.

If you absolutely can't resist saving every one of the two hundred drafts of your article on the dangers of fluorescent lighting, then have one special disk for keeping superseded drafts. Your ATTIC disk, where all the junk gets stored until you can bear to part with it and toss it out. On your ATTIC disk might be files called LIGHT1.DFT, LIGHT2.DFT, and so on, DFT standing for "draft." Then, when your article has appeared in print or whenever you're ready to part with all the temporary thoughts, blank its ATTIC disk. Keep, of course, the final version of the article (named LIGHT) on your data disk, and/or on an archive disk reserved just for the final forms of finished work. (Or if you expect to be venerated later in your career, save everything on archive disks for the future delight of your many biographers.)

If you're using floppy disks, be careful to delete or copy off to another disk earlier versions of your document as you go, lest you be rudely surprised by a "disk full" message when you attempt to edit or save a document.

ONE DISK PER PROJECT

In the process of deleting or adding material to an existing document, you're obviously changing it—a little or a lot—when the final document is compared to first draft. But saving the intermediate versions can let you lock in the changes in a form that prevents them from being lost if you have a sudden computer pfft, while allowing you to refer back to each important stage in a project's development, whether the text involved is sections of an article or a report, a short story or poem, or chapters of a book.

Don't cheap out on disks: it's worth having one each for every individual project you're working on (two for a long book).

When several projects are complete, you can always consolidate them onto an archive disk, perhaps even in compressed format. But start out with enough prepared (formatted) disks that you can grab one easily to begin something new. It may mean a little more disk swapping, if you don't have a hard disk, but there are advantages. You're less likely to lose everything you're working on if a single disk fails; you won't encounter the dreaded "disk full" message so often; and you'll know what's where with a fair amount of clarity. And after all, how many total projects do you tend to work on in a single sitting anyway? Two? Three? Is that much disk swapping really going to impede the flow of your creative juices that se-

verely? Give each project its own disk, or its own subdirectory, if you have a hard disk.

If you allot nothing less than a whole floppy disk to each project, you'll have lots of space for alternate files. Suppose your first draft copy is in a file you've named SUPER.1. Well, you don't really need the SUPER, do you? Because SUPER is all that's on the disk: the whole disk is devoted to your developing book, *Super Nature Photography for the Timid*, or your article, "50 Super Ways to Beat the Arbor Day Blahs." This frees you to call the individual files jazzy things like 1 and 2—simple and direct. That, in turn, frees you to subdivide the nomenclature of files that record a major alternative version of the developing text.

TIP #14: MAKE YOUR FILES MEAN SOMETHING

Each file should be some recognizable unit of the whole. If you break a work into several chunks for artistic, personal, or practical reasons, you might want to call each chunk's file BEG (beginning) MID, and END.

If you're writing longer works, then chapters or other similar divisions (providing that the resulting files don't become so huge as to be unwieldy) are usually a good place to break the text from one file to the next. Names like CHAPTER.1, CH1 (which accommodates multiple versions by leaving the filename extension available), or NOVEL.1 are clear and descriptive.

If you're obliged to divide a file simply because it's becoming huge, don't get your 1A's mixed up with your ONE.A's. Give such divided files special but simple names that let you know, at a glance, what each is a part of and which version it is. Keep your version designations for extensions, perhaps, and your divisions as part of the filenames, yielding things like 1A.MON, which can be easily distinguished from both 1B.MON and 1A.FRI.

Make your filenames mean something, keep them simple and clear, and use them consistently. This will do wonders in solving disk clutter and confusion about what's what.

If you can, given the capabilities and quirks of your particular WP system, don't save anything less than a specific unit as a single file. You'll find it easier to manage your original files and all their revised cousins and generations that way.

VISIONS AND REVISIONS

Paraphrasing J. Alfred Prufrock, WP offers time (and space) for almost infinite "visions and revisions" and opportunities to "murder and create." If you set up some consistent way of keeping track of intermediate versions, do much more parking than deletion, prevent seams and fill holes, and

tidily empty your electronic "garbage can" at the completion of every project, you'll find revision can become almost as creative an activity as typing your first words on screen.

Or, to put it Murphy's way (as in the Law), uncontrolled revision will multiply to fill available disk space.

CHAPTER 11

Printout at High Noon

GETTING YOUR MANUSCRIPT READY TO PRINT, MAIL ON DISK, OR TRANSMIT BY MODEM

OVERVIEW: THIS CHAPTER COVERS:

1. Drafts and final printouts: why you need a hard-copy readthrough *before* final printout.

2. What defaults are and why they're worth changing.

3. Justification vs. ragged right.

4. Creating and using heads and subheads.

5. Taking it from the top: setting and maintaining a consistent typographical style throughout a document.

6. Headers and footers.

7. Troubleshooting hard page codes and other problems when a document is prepared for printout; shoving in whatever sticks out.

8. Why a computer word count is misleading and how to do an *accurate* one.

9. Automatic page numbering—what can go wrong and how to make it go right.

10. Translating to ASCII characters, why and how, and how to save a whole lot of time taking out the extra hard returns; what ASCII does to your wonderful indents, hanging paragraphs, centers, and other format flourishes.

11. Translating between incompatible systems—how to do it, where to do it, and what it costs.

12. Final readthrough and getting rid of tear strips.

13. Protecting a disk in transit from magnets, heat, and other disk-eaters.

14. Electronic publishing: the final secret.

PRINTING YOUR DOCUMENT OUT or preparing it for mailing on disk or for transmission on telephone lines is the final step of every project. That's the point where what's been private, for your eyes alone, goes public, to be seen and judged by others. Therefore, it's vital to end up with something worth looking at. You'll probably have printed out intermediate drafts—one or several—to look at and perhaps pass around to trusted readers for their comments and suggestions. Whether you have or not, though, you'll need to do so now because some things only show up on paper and tend to be completely overlooked on the screen.

HARD-COPY READTHROUGH

One drawback of WP is that most (not all) programs allow you to read through the document only a screen at a time. Comparing one page with another, one file with another, is difficult and cumbersome if not impossible, whereas with the text on paper, it's relatively easy: lay the two sheets side by side and look back and forth between them. Or lay them all out on the floor to get an overview. You can't do that with all WP programs. As a result, you can easily overlook mistakes on the screen that absolutely yell at you from the printed page.

For instance, on screen, what will be printed as a blank page may be indicated by only two horizontal lines, one right after the other. If, reading through, you happen to hit one line at the bottom and the other at the top of the screen, you well may not notice. But the result can create absolute havoc in the automatic page numbering of a long document—a book manuscript, for instance. One of us virtually *never* does a printout of a whole novel without finding *something* has knocked the page numbering off—typically, about page 70, so that the following 400 or so pages are all wrong. The blank page is glaringly visible as a solidly white piece of paper with nothing but a

page number on it, but onscreen, it's two harmless-looking (and overlooked) horizontal lines.

Other problems are just as easy to miss. Maybe you inserted a boldfacing code when you didn't mean to, and three words on the page scream at you in printout, whereas the contrast wasn't enough to make them stand out on screen. Or Mr. Gershom, on p. 12, has transmuted to Mr. Gresham on p. 80. Looking at a manuscript only a screen at a time without doing a hard-copy readthrough opens the way to all kinds of failures of consistency—of content and of format.

Trust us. You absolutely *must* check what your manuscript looks like *on paper* before doing your final printout.

DRAFT COPIES

As discussed in Chapter 4, most dot-matrix printers offer what's called "draft mode": fewer dots to the inch, less distinct characters, more speed. If your printer offers draft mode, take advantage of it. Any fault will show up as well in draft as in letter-quality printing and costs less—if not in paper, then in ribbons and in the time the printout takes in draft mode.

If you hit an indent when you meant to hit a tab, and the whole following paragraph is skewed, if you forgot to change a tab definition and your carefully tabbed columns are wrapping and throwing the whole page off, you'll notice. If your chapter openers look squashed or your C heads look more important than your A heads, it will show up on the page. If a lonely subhead lands at the bottom of the page with no text following it, you'll spot it.

Mark up the draft copy with corrections and ideas for better format. But don't try to make the draft copy do double duty as your submission copy. Your final version should be as nearly perfect as you can make it: each letter crisp and distinct, the paragraphs comely, the pages inviting and easy to read. Letter quality all the way.

Even if your printer offers only letter-quality print, plan to do a draft copy anyway. You'll always, always find something you didn't expect when your words go from the screen to the printed page. There'll always be something else you can do to make your manuscript visually more appealing and effective than you thought of when you were concentrating on getting the ideas straight, rather than on how they'd look.

FORMAT BY DEFAULT

The margins you set, the tab settings, the indents and columns, the hyphenation style, the use or non-use of such things as literal italics, justification, bolding, heads and subheads, headers and/or footers—all add up to a manuscript's total appearance, its format. It's vital that the format be maintained consistently and that it be appropriate to the content: that, without being a distraction, the way each page looks helps the reader to follow your printed thought.

Those involved in desktop publishing can go a step further: into actual page layout, position of illustrations or photos, variations in type style and size. But such considerations are worth a book in themselves; many fine books are available to help guide you in using the newest in graphics and desktop publishing software. And such techniques aren't appropriate for producing manuscripts for submission anyway: publishers insist on imposing their own design on what they print and don't welcome writers trying to dictate such matters in advance.

We'll concentrate on producing submission-quality manuscripts, in either pica (preferred) or elite (less preferred) type, on ordinary 8-1/2″ x 11″ 20 lb. bond paper, either in tractor-fed fanfold or single sheets.

Such things as margin set (top/bottom and left/right), tab set, how many lines to the page, and justification (or non-justification) can be set, individually, document by document. They can, however, also be set up as the WP system's norms by so designating them in the system's *defaults*. Check your manual to see if your WP system allows you to set and alter the existing defaults . . . and if it *does*, do it.

The defaults, set "at the factory," were intended to suit the WP system to business use, not for manuscript preparation. If you've found yourself changing margins and other format factors on virtually every document you write, probably it's time to reset the system defaults to reflect what you *really* need, the style *you* prefer. That can save you a great deal of trouble and also help to preserve a consistent format on chapters of a novel or nonfiction book without going through about twenty steps to set the format of each one individually.

FORMATTING FOR THE EYE

Whatever format you choose, either section by section or by adjusting the defaults, has the purpose of making your manuscript easier to read.

Your manuscript should have adequate margins—at least an inch all around. We also strongly advise against right justification because most editors actively loathe it, as we said in Chapter 4. Leave the right ragged. It will be even more ragged if you follow our further advice: don't hyphenate. That will mean some lines will be visibly longer than others, but the individual words will be easier to read if they're not broken by hyphenation. And readability, rather than trying to make a manuscript look like a poor imitation of typeset copy, must be any writer's first priority.

Don't multiply typefaces: your manuscript will end up looking like a ransom note. Keep to one, or two at the most, even though you may have a dozen to choose from. (The editor or designer will specify the actual typefaces to be used in printing your work anyway; you have no real say in that.)

Keep things as simple as you can. Don't junk up your manuscript with unwelcome (and less readable) justification, literal italics, or special graphic doodles in the margins.

TAKING IT FROM THE TOP

Whatever format you choose for your manuscript, what's important is that it's simple, clear, readable, and consistent. There are various ways to achieve this consistency. One of the best ways, available on a few of the most powerful WP programs, is document formatting or "style sheets." Such programs enable you to set up the defaults *just for that document* (even if it's in several individual files: chapters, for instance) and impose that format on every part of it with a single command. It's like having special-chore formatting defaults.

Other WP programs allow you to *save* the format as an individual file, then call it into each new section at the top (Ansen, who uses this system, calls such files TOP). Then all you need to do is add the appropriate new page number.

HEADERS AND FOOTERS

Typing at the top of every page, *Annual Report of the Albermarle Sewage and Waste Water Treatment Facility* would be an immense pain. But by adding a single header at the top of the first page (and then, if your system allows it, replicating it as part of the basic format in a TOP file) of each part of your total manuscript, your WP program can do it for you.

Even though the header (and/or footer) may not physically appear on the screen, it will be there, in the proper position at the top (or the bottom) of the page, when your document is printed out.

If your manuscript is nonfiction—a discussion or a report—you may want to get even fancier: repeating, as a header, the A head designating what that part of the discussion/report is about. This kind of head-er has to change as the topic changes, and adds one more thing to go wrong or to distract a reader. You have to decide if such a changing header would be an aid to readability or just format clutter.

If you're writing fiction, it's customary to have, as a header, either your last name or part of the title, to identify the pages in case your manuscript falls off the top of the editor's eighteen-foot pile of submissions and the editor's assistant has to play fifty-two-pickup with an assortment of loose sheets. In this case, the header doesn't change: it's part of your basic format, the same throughout your manuscript except for the changing page number (of which more in a minute).

FINAL TROUBLESHOOTING

On your draft copy, look for anything that sticks out.

We earlier recommended that you disable any automatic hyphenation and justification features your WP system has, so that all words are left whole and normally spaced. They're more readable that way. But the result is inevitably that some long words don't wrap and are left, because of surrounding short lines, sticking out like the proverbial sore thumb. Any single letter—an *A* or an *I*—looks strange sticking out there, all by itself near the right margin.

So does half a dash: the end of one line ends in - and the start of the next line follows with the other half of it, beginning -. Ditto for the hyphens used in hyphenated words, like Control-I; if your WP program ignores hyphens that you purposefully insert and breaks a word at the hyphen, your editor may think the word was intentionally hyphenated over the two lines and rejoin it, thus giving you ControlI rather than Control-I. (You can, instead of using a hyphen to make a dash, use something called a *required* or *hard* hyphen that locks the word before, the hyphen, and the word after together as one unit, as long as you leave no space between words and hyphen. This works for dashes—double hyphens—too. Check your manual to see if your WP system can make required hyphens.)

Other things can go wrong. The first line or last line of a paragraph can be left lonely at the very top, or very bottom, of a page. (These are called widows and orphans, and some WP systems eliminate them automatically, provided paragraphs are more than three lines long; unfortunately, that's not always the case with dialogue, for instance, in fiction.) Or your wonderful bar graph is split between pages. Or end-quotes can get a line all to themselves in lonely, peculiar isolation, like this:
."

There's nothing grammatically wrong with any of this; it just looks odd. And who wants odd, sticky-out things cluttering their manuscript?

You can simply add hard returns (with the ENTER/RETURN key) to force the offensive protrusion to wrap and force page breaks to make sure your graphs (and paragraphs) are reasonably intact. (Some WP systems allow you to surround a given block with codes, requiring the page to break either *before* or *after* it—not *during*. But you wouldn't want to handle *every* paragraph that way!) You can change margins for just one line, to get those end-quotes up where they belong, not sitting on a line all by themselves. (Or you can even do a little editing and add or delete a word or two in a line to get things looking normal again.)

Changing margins or inserting codes, however, can cause problems later on, because those altered margins, those extra hard returns and end-page codes, are all *strictly cosmetic*: they don't really *belong* in the document. Some features—that which protects against "widows" and "orphans," for instance—are dependent on recognizing where paragraphs begin and

end. Reformatted by you or by a publisher, your cosmetic hard return may give you a paragraph break where you didn't want one.

If there's any possibility you may end up sending the disk itself to a publisher, transmitting the document electronically, or merely changing the document before a future printout, those cosmetic codes could become a real headache to locate and remove: just *try* to search a document for hard returns! You'd have to check every single paragraph!

MAKE PRINT FILES

We mentioned earlier that, if your WP system offers the option, it's better to print from screen, or from a RAMdisk file, than from the file as it's stored on a floppy disk. That way, there's no chance of your lousing things up by saving what's on screen and thereby changing the file your WP system is trying to transmit, a piece at a time, to the printer. But there's another good reason to make separate print files, one way or another—whether as separate files on a floppy disk, copied to a RAMdisk, or through printing from screen. You can make these needed final adjustments *to the print file(s) only and leave your original intact*, without intrusive hard returns or end-page codes that are there merely to alter how your manuscript looks on the page.

All simple mistakes you find, like spelling mistakes, should be changed on your master files, early in the getting-ready process. But make it part of your final check—after you've done a readthrough for content, spelling, grammar, and punctuation—to spot typographical oddities on your draft printout, then correct them on special print files without altering your master copy. You *can* have it both ways!

PAGE NUMBERING

Fooling around with page breaks is likely, in a long manuscript, to change how many

TIP #15: A WARNING ABOUT COMPUTER WORD COUNTS

Many spell-check programs can, as one of their features, do a word count for you. Or it can be done by dividing the total number of characters in a document by 6. And these word counts are accurate—*too* accurate.

No account is taken of extra lines, short lines, pages that break early, or any other substantial white space. Only the actual *words* (or total characters) are counted.

Yet in the printed version, all this white space is going to matter. The printed version won't be solid text, margin to margin, any more than your onscreen version is. But the word-counter or division of characters takes no account of this very vital factor.

So the manuscript you deliver is liable to be, in actuality and in practical terms, as much as 20% *longer* than a programmed word count or the figure arrived at by a division of the total characters *claims* it is. And the longer the manuscript, the more pages that 20% will add up to. Editors all across the country are tearing their hair and muttering in their paper cups of coffee over manuscripts that are *technically* the contracted length but in fact will require a substantial number of extra pages to print, and over authors who, innocently and self-righteously, can't see what all the fuss is about since the computer count is absolutely accurate and computers don't lie—do they?

In this case, they do. Instead of relying on the computer word count for anything beyond the roughest approximation of the total length of a piece, *divide the total characters by 5 rather than 6*. The result will be a *much more accurate* reflection of how long the piece actually is, including its miscellaneous white space that doesn't get counted but *does* affect how long the piece will be to print.

Or supplement your computer word count with one done the old-fashioned way: count the number of lines on an average page. Then count the number of actual words (not the total characters) per line. Multiply the two figures to get the total words per page. Multiply that figure by the total number of pages in the piece, *including lines wholly or partly blank as with left/right indented blocks of quoted excerpts: count the short lines as though they were full lines of text*. Compared to your computer figure, the result will be significantly higher—but in fact *much* more realistic. And you'll stay friends with your editor.

---

pages are in each file. That, in turn, can play hob with correct sequential page numbering.

Many people, when first trying out word processing, do something very understandable but totally useless, something that in fact *causes* them problems: they type in page numbers wherever a page breaks, just the way they would on a typewriter.

That's fine as long as the page breaks stay the same. But the minute you add or delete something, change margins, or enforce a page break where there was none before, all the page numbers have to be laboriously relocated, one at a time. Ever done that? *We* have. But not lately.

Virtually all WP systems offer automatic page numbering. That way, only the first page needs to be specified—whether that page is 6 or 299; then, all the rest of that file is numbered sequentially, no matter how it shrinks or bulges in the editing process. If you haven't already, adopt automatic page numbering in all your documents *immediately*.

But there are dangers.

If you have a long project in multiple files (as with a book), and if an early section or chapter changes size, although the rest of that file will adjust automatically, the starting page number for any additional *files* in your total manuscript will need to be readjusted. At least that's not as bad as changing them page by page: you only have to do it file by file.

Be sure to institute, and then to *check*, automatic page numbering as the very last thing you do before preparing to print your final draft. If you don't do it last, you're sure to change something and have the subsequent numbers print wrong. Check the end of every file, and the beginning of the next, right through to the last file. Note what number each file begins and ends with and make sure the sequence is right. *Write it down*, or you'll lose count. Believe us, it happens.

ASCII, TRANSLATION, AND YOU

We just mentioned the possibility of submitting either on disk or on phone lines, via modem. That's becoming daily a more likely occurrence for all writers, regardless of their interests or specialty, because more and more publishers are equipped to handle accepted, and contracted-for, manuscripts in this form.

It's easy to see why publishers like it: retaining the author's keystrokes means that the publisher doesn't have to have the whole manuscript keyboarded all over again, even though certain typesetting and format codes may need to be inserted and copyediting changes will need to be added. Because there are fewer keyboarding errors, less intensive proofreading is required. In other words, the publisher saves time and money. Naturally, publishers *like* that.

Some publishers can even be persuaded to add to the contracted price for the material if the writer can supply the manuscript in electronic form. After all, the writers are giving the publisher what is, in essence, something for nothing. However, other publishers are beginning to *require* electronic submission in addition to hard copy—for no extra pay. It's assumed that preparing the manuscript however the publisher wants it is the author's job. That's the same logic whereby publishers

will no longer accept handwritten manuscripts: they've *required* that you know how to type and don't pay extra for it. Very shortly, we predict, publishers are going to likewise require that all authors know how to use a word processor, or that *the author* pay for having the manuscript prepared in that form. Them's the rules, folks. We just tell it like it is—or soon will be. But what the heck—we're all using word processors anyway, right?

Before this Scrooge-like authoritarian thrift becomes universal among publishers, however, see if there's something in it for you: extra money or even a new computer if you can wangle that as part of the deal, as we discussed back in Chapter 1. Get as much as you possibly can before you sign on the bottom line.

We don't suggest this out of vicarious greed, by the way (although we like to see good writers get more money for *anything*). It's just that you'll probably have to do some extra work to get the manuscript ready for disk submission—changing margins, inserting codes, and conforming to other specifications from the publisher. And, if you're required, or if you volunteer, to submit electronically, either on disk or via modem, you'll need to know how to transform your files, which may have been produced with any of a score of WP systems, into something the publisher can use.

"NO SPEAKA DA LINGO!"—WHAT TO DO WHEN YOU FIND OUT YOU'RE USING THE WRONG WP PROGRAM

A publisher may specify that the manuscript be submitted in whatever WP program the editors there use—anything from XyWrite III to WordStar to WordPerfect. But you *wrote* it in, say, Microsoft Word. What do you do?

Not to worry.

Dozens of programs can translate one program's storage format and formatting codes into another's. Most of them are PD software or shareware. Ask around, look in a few computer magazines, and you'll find some. Boot one up, tell it to change *this* WordStar document into one written in WordPerfect, and two seconds later it's done. No problem. Just make sure that the translation program does indeed translate formatting codes (such as underline and boldface), and that it preserves "tab characters" (which are what some WP programs insert instead of spaces when you press the TAB key. (The universal tab character is Control-I.)

Alternatively, you may find that your WP software provides a utility for translating its files into the format of another program (as is the case with the CONVERT utility provided with the MS-DOS version of WordPerfect).

WRONG FORMAT: INTO ASCII

If you have the basic Brand X WP program, or your software or hardware uses a data format incompatible with anything your publisher can use, or if your WP program's storage format is so alien that none of the translation programs accommodate it, you may have to take another route: a detour through ASCII (pronounced "ASK-ee").

ASCII (more precisely, 7-bit ASCII) is a text-file storage format that all personal computers speak. It's basically a code in which binary numbers represent letters and other characters, a code that all modern personal computers recognize. Get a file into ASCII format and virtually any WP program that operates on the same kind of computer as yours can handle it. Or at the very least, you can use the ASCII format as an intermediary step in translating from one WP program to another using one of the translation utilities mentioned above.

ASCII format, by the way, is necessary when you transmit text to computers other than the type you're using. You can transmit, say, an MS-DOS WordStar file as a WordStar file to another MS-DOS computer, but not to a computer that uses anything other than MS-DOS. You'll have to convert it to ASCII first. Overall—even if you're using the same kind of computer and WP software—it's safest to convert the file to ASCII format before transmitting it. (Look back at Chapter 5 for more information about this.)

ASCII-BOARDING YOUR DOCUMENT

There are three ways to translate your WP file into ASCII. The first two are built into some WP programs.

1. Many WP programs have ASCII conversion as a built-in utility, either saving or converting already-saved files into ASCII format (sometimes terming the results "text files," "DOS files," "7-bit," or something similar).

2. Some programs provide a "print to disk" menu selection or print command option. This creates an ASCII file on disk. (All versions of WordStar for all computers offer this.)

3. You can use one of the file-translation programs previously mentioned; virtually all provide the option of converting a file to ASCII, in addition to cross-conversion among various WP formats.

If you don't have any of the above available, or can't or don't want to handle the conversion yourself, you can pay to have it done—but it won't be cheap. Figure $10.00 to $25.00 per disk. Check with your local computer store for information on this kind of service; if the store doesn't handle disk conversions, the salespeople will probably know someone who does.

GETTING RID OF THE FLOURISHES

ASCII isn't quite magic. It's a system of substitution. It is, in a way, an exact photograph of your document as it appears on the screen, with nearly all the formatting codes wiped out.

Unless the translation program or WP utility retains the tab character (assuming you're using that rather than five

TIP #16: GETTING RID OF THE HARD RETURNS

If you are, as we are, preparing a manuscript for direct typeset, you may have to go through two stages: through ASCII, and then into some WP system the publisher's typesetting computer likes. For instance, ours likes XyWrite, although neither of us happens to be working in it. So we detour through ASCII, then drag each document into XyWrite and make the needed final adjustments—specifically, taking out the excess hard returns, because ASCII conversion turns the end of *every* line into a hard return!

One way to save headaches is to add one step just before doing the conversion: give the document the absolutely widest margins your WP system will allow. We can get margins of 0-250. Each file gets very short and *very*

wide. But the result is that, with fewer lines, fewer hard returns remain to be deleted when the file is dragged into, and through, the second WP program before submission.

As with paired codes, though, the newest version of the top WP programs address this problem and add conversion into something called "generic WP" (*instead* of into ASCII) as one of the conversion options. Only actual hard returns are retained, and the result is just as generally readable by the whole array of computers as is ASCII. Using this option eliminates the second stage of getting rid of a lot of excess hard returns. Again, if you're going to be doing a lot of conversion, this capability is worth checking on.

---

spaces), a tab becomes five spaces. A centering code becomes however many spaces are required to push your text to *that* position on the page. Underlining codes and bold codes disappear, unless they're designated by you in the text according to codes the publisher's typesetting computer can read. (For instance, ours designates underlining like this: [[A4]] *This line would be printed in italics— that is, underlined.*[[A3]].) Codes would differ from one typesetting program to another, though. Might the publisher *pay* you to put in all the right codes before submitting? Check it out!

What's left is, in essence, the naked words and a bunch of spaces.

All your fancy format flourishes vanish. That's why you need to submit a hard copy, as well, so that the typesetter can key the needed codes back in, assuming you haven't already done it *in a form the ASCII conversion won't strip out.* As an aid to the typesetter, you might convert your formatting codes to symbols that won't be stripped out by ASCII conversion. For example, you could use search/replace to change your WP program's underline code

to ^^^, so that an underlined word would come through like this: ^^^underlined^^^.

On older WP systems, there used to be a problem with "paired codes" like underlining: codes that have an ON code where underlining is to begin, and an OFF code that follows the underlined text. The problem was that the OFF code couldn't be searched separately. That meant changing each instance of underlined text manually, one by one, locating by eye where the OFF code should be put. Either through intelligence or chance, though, some of the newer WP programs recognize that problem and now allow you to search ON and OFF codes independently, allowing substitution of characters like [A3] or ^^^ to replace the appropriate ON *and* OFF codes, either with search/replace or by means of a macro. If you expect to be doing a lot of conversion, this capability is worth checking on if you're shopping for a new WP system.

FINAL READTHROUGH AND WHAT ABOUT THOSE TEAR STRIPS?

Once you've done your final printout, take a few hours and read through it again, from beginning to end—or, if you want to follow good proofreading practice, from end to beginning. Going a page at a time from back to front, you won't be as apt to get so caught up in the wonderfulness of your prose and wit that you overlook something that would be glaringly obvious if you were reading in reverse. (Not everyone has an impartial proofreader in-house, as Mike does—his wife is a professional proofreader. If you can, however, get someone else to look over your work, it helps; writers all too often see what they *intended* to write on the page, whether it's there or not.)

This is the final chance you have to correct any errors or have any last-minute changes of mind. Take full advantage of it, even if you're itching to get the hard-copy into the mail and/or the disk version zipped off into the ether via modem. No publisher likes afterthoughts that tag along behind after they've received what's purported to be the final manuscript. They have this prejudice that *authors* should make the final corrections and not leave it for editors or typesetters to do for them (even though they do reserve the final say). It looks careless and unprofessional. So sit down with your manuscript. Check page number sequence. Check everything. Don't send it out, in any form, until it's absolutely as perfect and error-free as you can possibly make it. Ask yourself, If it were published tomorrow, exactly as I have it here, would I be proud or embarrassed? Only when you can say, with conviction, *proud*, is it ready to leave your hands.

And by the way, remember to take off the tear strips and separate the pages, if you're using fanfold paper. The only reason to fail to do this is laziness, which is exactly what it looks like. You want your manuscript to make its very best impression: your care in preparing your manuscript is one of the main ways by which publishers, and later readers, will judge you. To paraphrase a

greeting-card company's slogan, CARE ENOUGH TO SEND THE VERY BEST.

SPECIAL HANDLING

You probably take great care when packing a manuscript for shipment to a publisher. You have to take even greater care with disks. Disks bend easily, and computers can't read bent disks, so you must take measures to protect the disk from being bent or warped. It can happen—think of all the people who will be handling/dropping your package along the way, and about the heavy sacks of mail it will undoubtedly be residing under during part of its journey.

"DO NOT BEND"

The simplest way to protect your disk is to use one of the light cardboard "disk mailers" to mail it. Better still, put the disk in a disk mailer and put *that* in an envelope. And mark the envelope "Do Not Bend!"

If you want to save money, use sheets of cardboard cut from a box that's going to be thrown out. Tape the disk's paper envelope to the cardboard, slip the disk in the envelope, and place another piece of cardboard over the first. Then secure the two pieces of cardboard with masking tape or rubber bands. *Then* slide the whole thing into a 9" x 12" envelope and mail that.

If you're mailing a disk with a manuscript, don't just drop the disk in on top of the manuscript. Use a disk mailer or cardboard sandwich to protect it.

MAGNETS, RADIATION, AND HEAT

As you probably know, exposure to magnetism can scramble or wipe out a disk's contents. X-rays and heat can do the same. So you should label the disk mailer or envelope or box containing your disk(s) accordingly. Most people use something like, "Magnetic media: do not X-ray; keep away from heat and magnetism." Similarly-worded warning labels and rubber stamps

TIP #17: DISK SUBMISSIONS: USE CHAPTER-SIZED FILES

We earlier warned you against assembling monstrously big files your WP system may not be able to handle. The same goes double for blithely presenting a monster file to your publisher to show off what high-powered hardware you have or in simple thoughtlessness. That you can *write* it doesn't mean your editor will be able to *read* it or use it. If, as is likely, your editor's equipment can't handle a humongous file, the result is needless delay and irritation for your editor, and embarrass-

ment (not to mention extra work and postage) for you.

If you're submitting a long manuscript on disk, divide the files into reasonable segments—50,000 characters or less apiece. Chapter breaks are usually good points to end one file and begin a new one. But to be really sure, check with your editor, before you submit, on what will be a convenient file size for his or her equipment to handle comfortably and then follow those guidelines.

---

are available wherever you buy disk mailers.

If you're shipping via a courier service, ask whether they have suitable labels available. (Mike, who ships a lot of disks to publishers via Federal Express, is particularly fond of their fluorescent green label that, among other things, boldly warns those handling his packages against exposing them to radioactive materials. The labels are intended for use with packages containing unexposed photographic film, but the idea is the same.)

MODEM MANAGEMENT

If you've never used a modem or haven't used one for very long, the idea of sending a manuscript over telephone lines may be a bit scary. Don't worry: in learning how to use your modem, you will (or should) learn a lot about *how it works*, and thus be prepared to handle trouble.

The best thing you can do to ensure trouble-free file transmission is to practice. The ideal venue is a local bulletin board and/or a local friend's computer. Practice transferring test files both to and from the other computer—it will cost you nothing but time and a tied-up phone line.

When you do get to the real thing, translating a manuscript to a publisher's computer or via an intermediary online service,

we recommend that you use a common error-checking protocol like Xmodem. (Here again we refer you to *The Modem Reference*, by Michael A. Banks and published by Brady Books/Simon & Schuster, for additional guidance.)

OFF THE SCREEN AND ONTO THE PAGE—OR MAYBE BACK ONTO THE SCREEN AGAIN

There's an irony to meticulously preparing your manuscript for submission: if all goes well, it will end up as printed pages, just as though you'd typed it . . . just as though no such thing as word processing existed.

But an interesting thing is happening. All kinds of software, programs, and even *text* (E-mail, generally) is being downloaded from computer networks of one sort or another. Whole encyclopedias are soon going to be available on CD ROM disks. Can true electronic publishing be far behind?

We predict that it won't be long before fiction, nonfiction, and poetry—all *kinds* of stuff!—will be commonly available *in electronic media* as the primary form of publication. You'll be able to read Arthur Author's newest novel by requesting it direct from the publisher's online ordering service and, in seconds, be reading it off your own screen at home. If you want to, you'll be able to print it out. But as screens continue to get bigger and better, it will be no trouble to read a whole novel directly off your screen without suffering terminal (pun intended) eyestrain.

At first, hard copy (books, magazines) will remain the primary format. But that will change. It won't be long before electronic media become the main—perhaps the *sole*—format of publication.

As a writer using word-processing, you're already part of this development: the nearly instantaneous transfer of creative work to anyone, virtually anywhere in the world, who wants it and has equipment capable of receiving it. And as you've already realized, you don't have to "talk" computer to read words on screen or to create words other people will enjoy, be informed by, and savor with the lasting fondness that's today accorded to a favorite, much-read, maybe dog-eared copy of a beloved book.

True electronic publishing is coming. And that's perhaps the most exciting "secret" of word processing for writers.

Appendix A

WORD PROCESSING SOFTWARE GUIDE

For those of you unfamiliar with what flavors of WP software are out there, we've compiled a summary guide to the more popular WP programs on the market.

The list is by no means comprehensive: many WP programs, although adequate for other uses, aren't worth writers' consideration; and we can't list everything—that would take another book. Our apologies if we haven't included your favorite program or computer.

We're not recommending any particular WP program over another. A WP program that offers graphics capabilities and a hundred typefaces may be exactly what one writer's been dreaming about, but won't even *run* on another's beloved 364K floppy-drive hardware, and will be a nuisance of wasted frills to a third who aches for a simple, inexpensive system with a really fine, fuss-free online dictionary.

We intend this as a representative overview of what's available for a range of popular computers—just enough to get you started in your own evaluation. We urge you to investigate further the features of any program that looks good to you at first glance. For more information, write the program's publisher at the address given. Try out the program, either at a computer store or with a good-natured friend who doesn't mind you camping out at his/her keyboard for an hour or two. Talk to people who have it, maybe through one of the various "user's groups" that often advertise their meetings in the "Community Bulletin Board" section of your local pa-

per. Use the guidelines in Chapter 2 to see how a given system measures up to your needs and budget.

APPLE II + /IIe/IIc

APPLEWORKS

Appleworks, offering integrated word processing, database, spreadsheet, and other functions, is the word processor of choice of most Apple IIe users. Limits on the lengths of individual files make it restrictive for authors of book-length work, however.
Information: Apple Computer, Inc., 20525 Mariana Avenue, Cupertino, CA 95014.

APPLEWRITER

Applewriter is an old "standard," liked by many because it can be specially programmed to suit one's tastes. In its raw form, however, before you succeed in customizing it, it can be difficult to use.
Information: Apple Computer, Inc., 20525 Mariana Avenue, Cupertino, CA 95014.

BANK STREET WRITER

An inexpensive, basic word processor that offers most necessary features, although page formatting is somewhat complicated. Bank Street Writer is easy to learn and use, but it's better suited to the needs of article and short story authors than to book authors. Menu- or command-driven, with an optional spell-checker available.
Information: Broderbund Software, 17 Paul Drive, San Rafael, CA 94903.

SCREENWRITER IIe

Powerful, flexible program for working on anything from fillers to novels. Provides all important WP features for writers, including word- and character-count, special macro capability, block moves, and more. The program is command-driven and easy to learn and use. Online help and a spell-checker are included.
Information: Sierra Online, Inc., Coarsegold, CA 93614.

WORDPERFECT

WordPerfect for the Apple IIe/IIc offers nearly all the WP features of interest to writers, and more. (This version of WordPerfect isn't as feature-rich as versions for more powerful computers such as the IBM PC and Atari ST, however.)
Information: WordPerfect Corporation, 288 West Center St., Orem, UT 84057.

APPLE II GS

MULTISCRIBE

Multiscribe is a full-featured WP program with a graphic-based orientation (this takes advantage of the II GS's excellent graphics capability). Best for those who want to combine writing with desktop publishing, where fancy fonts are required. (Also available for IIe/IIc.)
Information: Claris Corp., 440 Clyde Avenue, Mountain View, CA 94043.

WORDPERFECT

More powerful than the Apple IIe/IIc version, the Apple GS version of WordPerfect offers virtually all of the features of the MS-DOS version (check that listing, below).
Information: WordPerfect Corporation, 288 West Center St., Orem, UT 84057.

ATARI ST

ST WRITER

ST Writer is a no-frills public domain program. It doesn't accommodate the ST's mouse, windows, or menus. All commands are via control-key combinations, and there is no WYSIWYG. Automatic reformatting and all standard WP features are included, however, and the manual is included on disk for printout. ST Writer is particularly popular because of its speed in document handling and its price.
Information: ST Writer can be downloaded from many BBSs and most online services, or ordered for a nominal disk-handling fee from PD software distributors (check any ST magazine for ads from such companies).

WORD WRITER

Word Writer offers multiple resizable windows and can edit four documents simultaneously. Commands are issued via pull-down menus and key + function-key combinations. Manual reformatting is required when adding text or changing line spacing. A thesaurus, spell-checker, and a simple outliner are included.
Information: Timeworks, 444 Lake County Road, Deerfield, IL 60015

1st WORD PLUS

1st Word Plus is an upgraded version of 1st Word, which many people received free when they purchased their ST. It's a full-featured program that offers multiple resizable windows and the ability to edit four documents at once. Command input is via pull-down menus and function keys, and there is particular emphasis on graphic display of WYSIWYG. Changing text style is difficult, and manual reformatting is required when you add to existing text.

Page layout/printing features include a full range of type style and sizes (as supported by your printer), headers and footers, and graphics support. Text markers, word count, merge, and a spell-checker round out the features.
Information: GST Software, Electric Distri-

bution, 8 Green Street, Willingham, Cambridge, England CB4 5JA.

WORDPERFECT

As in other computer versions, WordPerfect for the Atari ST is an especially powerful program. It makes full use of the ST's graphics and operating system capabilities.
Information: WordPerfect Corporation, 288 West Center St., Orem, UT 84057.

WORDUP

A WP program that's particularly strong in terms of onscreen graphics and printer output. Full range of WP features. A "Glossary" function allows the user to create word-based macros which store large blocks of text for automatic insertion into a document. Print formatting is based on a master page design that can be varied within a document. Keyboard or mouse command input.
Information: Neocept Corporation, 908 Camino Dos Rios, Thousand Oaks, CA 91630.

COMMODORE AMIGA

DYNAMIC WORD

This is a fairly advanced WP program that takes full advantage of the graphics capability of the Amiga with its WYSIWYG display. All major WP features are included. The program Dynamic Word comes with a spell-checker and thesaurus, and is moderately easy to use.
Information: MicroIllusions, 17408 Chatsworth St., Granada Hills, CA 91344

PROWRITE WORD PROCESSOR

ProWrite is a full-featured word processor that emphasizes document appearance—onscreen and off. Given matching printer capabilities, ProWrite can print a large va-

riety of fonts and type sizes, and can include pictures in text. Full WYSIWYG. Command input is via keyboard or mouse, and utilizes pull-down menus. Up to eight documents can be edited (and text swapped between them) at one time via a windowing system.
Information: New Horizons Software, Inc., P.O. Box 43167, Austin, TX 78745

WORDPERFECT

WordPerfect is among the most highly regarded WP programs for the Amiga. It's full-featured and desktop-publishing oriented. (See the WordPerfect summary under the "MS-DOS" heading for an overview of WordPerfect's features.)
Information: WordPerfect Corporation, 288 West Center St., Orem, UT 84057.

COMMODORE 64/128

EASY SCRIPT (COMMODORE 64)

A basic, no-frills program that's easy to learn. Good for beginners, but lacking in advanced features.
Information: Precision Software, Inc., 464 Kalmath, Denver, CO 80204.

SUPERSCRIPT (64 OR 128)

Essentially an advanced, full-power version of Easy Script. Powerful, with all the basic features a writer needs, as well as many advanced ones. Highly recommended by writers who use it.
Information: Progressive Peripherals and Software, 464 Kalmath Street, Denver, CO 80204.

PAPERCLIP

Another highly regarded, full-featured WP program that's well suited to the Commodore 128's capabilities.
Information: Electronic Arts, 1820 Gateway Drive, San Mateo, CA 94404.

MACINTOSH

FULLWRITE PROFESSIONAL
Although FullWrite Professional is aimed at the desktop publishing market, it's quite serviceable as a word processor. Lots of bells and whistles. Computer hobbyists love it.
Information: Ashton-Tate, 20101 Hamilton Avenue, Torrance, CA 90502.

MACWRITE
Macwrite is the original "standard" WP program (it was bundled with all Macintosh computers). Light on features and best suited to working with small documents.
Information: Claris Corp., 440 Clyde Avenue, Mountain View, CA 94043.

MICROSOFT WORD
Microsoft Word has been called "the word processor for hard core word hackers." Users love its many features but aren't as enthused about its complexity. Loaded with almost every WP feature imaginable.
Information: Microsoft Corp., 10611 NE 36th Street, Redmond, WA 98073.

MICROSOFT WRITE
Essentially a lower-cost, cut-down version of Microsoft Word.
Information: Microsoft Corp., 10611 NE 36th Street, Redmond, WA 98073.

WORDPERFECT
WordPerfect scores high among Macintosh users with its many features and relative ease of use.
Information: WordPerfect Corporation, 288 West Center St., Orem, UT 84057.

WRITENOW
WriteNow is generally the best-liked WP program among Macintosh users. It has more features than MacWrite but fewer than Microsoft Word or WordPerfect. A good program for beginners without being too limited.
Information: T/Maker Co., 1973 Landings Drive, Mountain View, CA 94043.

MS-DOS (IBM & COMPATIBLES)

MICROSOFT WORD
Microsoft Word is loaded with all the WP features you can imagine—and many that you probably never thought of. It comes with a tutorial (needed), and sports full block operation, macro, and outlining capability. Other features include "redlining" for tracking edits, an enhanced "Glossary" feature for storing large blocks of text in a macro, indexing, and more. Word can be customized. A spell-checker and thesaurus are included.
Information: Microsoft Corp., 10611 NE 36th Street, Redmond, WA 98073.

PC-WRITE
The epitome of the "shareware" concept, PC-Write boasts over 100,000 users. The program itself can be obtained legitimately—at no cost—from anyone who has a copy. Documentation and online help are included on the program disks, but if you register as a user, you'll receive a complete, professionally-printed manual and continuing information on updates. The program offers all standard and most advanced WP features, along with a number of desktop publishing features. The command structure can be customized to the user's requirements (it can even be made to operate like any of several other programs). PC-Write is command-driven, and a spell-checker is included.
Information: Quicksoft, Inc., 219 First N., #244, Seattle, WA 98109.

SPRINT
Sprint is a full-featured WP program designed to balance ease of use with docu-

ment-handling power. The program offers virtually all the features of high-power programs such as WordPerfect and XyWrite, and more—including multi-document editing. A particularly interesting feature is the fact that, when started, Sprint picks up where you left off, with all documents that were displayed in various windows put back in place, ready to edit. Sprint is command-driven, with optional menus.
Information: Borland International, 4585 Scotts Valley Drive, Scotts Valley, CA 95066.

VARSITY SCRIPSIT
Varsity Scripsit is Tandy's MS-DOS version of the original Scripsit, which introduced thousands of computer users to word processing on the Radio Shack TRS-80 Model I, II, III, etc. Full-featured and easy to use.
Information: Tandy Corporation, 100 Two Tandy Center, Fort Worth, TX 76102.

WORDPERFECT
WordPerfect is one of the top three—if not the top—bestselling WP programs of all time. It has the full range of standard and enhanced features desired by "power users," but a beginner can pick up the basic document-creating and -handling functions in about an hour. A partial list of its features includes: user-definable function keys, mouse or keyboard command input, powerful page-formatting features, online help, outlining, paragraph numbering, widow and orphan control (keeps single lines from appearing on a page alone), and WYSIWYG or formatting code display. Automatic backup, merge, sort, multiple columns, undelete, and powerful macro functions are also featured. The newest revision supports sophisticated desktop publishing

software and almost every printer imaginable. It comes with spell-checker and thesaurus.
Information: WordPerfect Corporation, 288 West Center St., Orem, UT 84057.

WORDSTAR PROFESSIONAL 5.0
The second incarnation of WordStar has added a lot of features for desktop publishing and enhanced its WYSIWYG display. It's also easier to use and far faster than earlier versions. Supports several hundred printers and offers almost every WP feature of use to writers (dozens of vital features—like undelete—have been added). Spell-checker, thesaurus, indexing, and merge capability are included.
Information: MicroPro Corporation, 33 San Pablo Avenue, San Rafael, CA 94903.

XyWRITE III PLUS
XyWrite III Plus is probably the fastest WP program available (in speed of cursor movement and spell-checking, among other operations). It's command-driven, with online help available. All important WP features are included, and it's particularly strong in macro capability. Page formatting display is WYSIWYG or code display. Up to ten documents can be edited simultaneously (split-screen or separate windows), and there's no limit on file size. Of particular interest is the fact that the program can be customized in various ways to emulate almost any other MS-DOS WP program. XyWrite comes with a spell-checker, thesaurus, sorter, and more. The only major drawback is that it's difficult or impossible to use with some RAM-resident programs like Sidekick.
Information: XyQuest, Inc., 44 Manning Road, Billerica, MA 01821.

Appendix B: Online Service Contacts

If you're new to the world of online services, here's contact information for the major networks:

FULL-SERVICE NETWORKS

BIX
One Phoenix Mill Lane
Peterborough, NH 03458
(800) 227-2983

CompuServe
5000 Arlington Centre Blvd.
Columbus, OH 43220
(614) 457-0802

DELPHI
Three Blackstone Street
Cambridge, MA 02139
(800) 544-4005

GEnie
401 N. Washington Street
Rockville, MD 20850
(800) 638-9636

The Source
P.O. Box 1305
McLean, VA 22102
(800) 336-3366

UNISON
2174 Seymour Avenue
Cincinnati, OH 45237
(800) 334-6122

E-MAIL SERVICES

AT&T Mail
307 Middletown-Lincroft Rd.
Lincroft, NJ 07738
(800) 367-7225

DASnet
1503 E. Campbell Ave.
Campbell, CA 95008
(408) 559-7434

MCI Mail
Box 1001
1900 M Street, NW
Washington, DC 20036
(800) 624-6245

NEWS AND INFORMATION SERVICES

Dow Jones News/Retrieval Service
P.O. Box 300
Princeton, NJ 08543-0300
(609) 520-4649

Dialog & Knowledge-Index
Dialog Information Services
3460 Hillview Ave.
Palo Alto, CA 94304
(800) 334-2564

NewsNet
945 Havorford Road
Bryn Mawr, PA 19010
(215) 527-8030

I N D E X

A

after/asides files. *See* files, special

archive software. *See* software, utilities

archiving, 48-49, 90, 91-92; *see also* saving

ASCII, 143-145

B

backups
automatic, 83-84
compressing data during. *See* archiving
floppy disks used for making, 12
how many are enough, 83, 84
how WP programs make, 82-83
the importance of making, 12
leaving adequate disk space to hold, 83
recovering, 86-87
timing, 84

bin feeder. *See* printer, paper delivery methods for

bit, 52-53

block
and copy, 126
defined, 27-28
deleting a, 125, 127
disasters, avoiding, 127-128, 130-131
marking a, 125
and move, 125
pockets, 125
and save, 126-127
and scraps files, 117, 129-130

blues, the blank screen, 86-87

boot, warm. *See* reset

buffer. *See* printer, buffers for

byte
application to printer, 52-53
defined, 13

C

cables, extra long, for printers and other peripherals, 75

calculators, onscreen. *See* software, memory-resident

calendars, onscreen. *See* software, memory-resident

card
clock/calendar, 76
emulation, 76
"hard," 11, 76
memory expansion, 76
"speed up," 76
video (graphics), 14, 76

cast files. *See* files, special

CD ROM, 77-78, 147-148

character. *See* byte

checklist, computer selection, 16

checklist, word processing software selection, 35-36

codes
format. *See* format
marker. *See* markers

comments, including in a document, 131

computers. *See* hardware

cursor, desirable movement of, 25

cut and block. *See* block

D

data recovery. *See* delete

database
building a, 105
composed of records, 102
customizing articles with a, 109-111
defined, 102
discarding a temporary, 106
divided into fields, 103-105
adding fields to, 108
"F codes" in, 103
possible contents of, 103-107, 109-110

primary document merged with, 102
secondary merge document as, 103
and sort, 102-112
stand-alone vs. built-in, 102

defaults, resetting factory-set, 139

deleting
a block. *See* block
methods
delete key, 8, 127
delete to end of line, 127
delete to end of page, 127
overwrite mode, 25, 127
search and destroy, 94-95
park as an alternative to, 128-130
pockets, 128
recovering deleted data
as a block, 127-128
by recalling original document, 127-128
through "undelete," 128
recovering deleted files, 49
unneeded files, 92

DIP switches (on printers). *See* printers, DIP switches for

disk drives, 11-12
add-on, 76-77
desirable number of, 12
hard, 11, 77; *see also* card
backing up/optimizing, 47-48, 91
desirable size of, 13

diskcopy, the dangers of, 91

diskettes, floppy, 11
compressing data on. *See* archiving
mailing, 146-147
sizes of, 22

display, features of. *See* monitor

documents
naming. *See* file names, creating
onscreen. *See* saving
markers used in. *See* markers

Other Books of Interest

Annual Market Books

Artist's Market, edited by Susan Conner $18.95

Children's Writer's & Illustrator's Market, edited by Connie Eidenier (paper) $14.95

Novel & Short Story Writer's Market, edited by Laurie Henry (paper) $17.95

Photographer's Market, edited by Connie Eidenier $19.95

Poet's Market, by Judson Jerome $17.95

Songwriter's Market, edited by Julie Whaley $17.95

Writer's Market, edited by Glenda Neff $22.95

General Writing Books

Beginning Writer's Answer Book, edited by Kirk Polking (paper) $12.95

Beyond Style: Mastering the Finer Points of Writing, by Gary Provost $15.95

Getting the Words Right: How to Revise, Edit and Rewrite, by Theodore A. Rees Cheney $15.95

How to Get Started in Writing, by Peggy Teeters (paper) $9.95

How to Increase Your Word Power, by the editors of Reader's Digest $19.95

How to Write a Book Proposal, by Michael Larsen $10.95

Knowing Where to Look: The Ultimate Guide to Research, by Lois Horowitz (paper) $15.95

Make Every Word Count, by Gary Provost (paper) $9.95

Pinckert's Practical Grammar, by Robert C. Pinckert $14.95

12 Keys to Writing Books that Sell, by Kathleen Krull (paper) $12.95

The 29 Most Common Writing Mistakes & How to Avoid Them, by Judy Delton $9.95

Writer's Block & How to Use It, by Victoria Nelson $14.95

The Writer's Digest Guide to Manuscript Formats, by Buchman & Groves $16.95

Writer's Encyclopedia, edited by Kirk Polking (paper) $16.95

Nonfiction Writing

Basic Magazine Writing, by Barbara Kevles $16.95

How to Sell Every Magazine Article You Write, by Lisa Collier Cool (paper) $11.95

How to Write & Sell the 8 Easiest Article Types, by Helene Schellenberg Barnhart $14.95

The Writer's Digest Handbook of Magazine Article Writing, edited by Jean M. Fredette $15.95

Writing Creative Nonfiction, by Theodore A. Rees Cheney $15.95

Writing Nonfiction that Sells, by Samm Sinclair Baker $14.95

Fiction Writing

The Art & Craft of Novel Writing, by Oakley Hall $16.95

Characters & Viewpoint, by Orson Scott Card $12.95

Creating Short Fiction, by Damon Knight (paper) $8.95

Dare to Be a Great Writer: 329 Keys to Powerful Fiction, by Leonard Bishop $15.95

Dialogue, by Lewis Turco $12.95

Fiction is Folks: How to Create Unforgettable Characters, by Robert Newton Peck (paper) $8.95

Handbook of Short Story Writing: Vol. I, by Dickson and Smythe (paper) $9.95

Handbook of Short Story Writing: Vol. II, edited by Jean M. Fredette $15.95

How to Write & Sell Your First Novel, by Oscar Collier with Frances Spatz Leighton $15.95

One Great Way to Write Short Stories, by Ben Nyberg $14.95

Plot, by Ansen Dibell $12.95

Revision, by Kit Reed $13.95

Spider Spin Me a Web: Lawrence Block on Writing Fiction, by Lawrence Block $16.95

Storycrafting, by Paul Darcy Boles (paper) $10.95

Writing the Novel: From Plot to Print, by Lawrence Block (paper) $9.95

Special Interest Writing Books

The Children's Picture Book: How to Write It, How to Sell It, by Ellen E.M. Roberts (paper) $15.95

Comedy Writing Secrets, by Melvin Helitzer $16.95
The Complete Book of Scriptwriting, by J. Michael Straczynski (paper) $10.95
The Craft of Lyric Writing, by Sheila Davis $18.95
Editing Your Newsletter, by Mark Beach (paper) $18.50
Families Writing, by Peter Stillman (paper) $15.95
Guide to Greeting Card Writing, edited by Larry Sandman (paper) $9.95
How to Write a Play, by Raymond Hull (paper) $10.95
How to Write & Sell A Column, by Raskin & Males $10.95
How to Write and Sell Your Personal Experiences, by Lois Duncan (paper) $9.95
How to Write Romances, by Phyllis Taylor Pianka $13.95
How to Write Tales of Horror, Fantasy & Science Fiction, edited by J.N. Williamson $15.95
How to Write the Story of Your Life, by Frank P. Thomas $14.95
How to Write Western Novels, by Matt Braun $13.95
How You Can Make $50,000 a Year as a Nature Photojournalist, by Bill Thomas (paper) $17.95
Mystery Writer's Handbook, by The Mystery Writers of America (paper) $10.95
Nonfiction for Children: How to Write It, How to Sell It, by Ellen E.M. Roberts $16.95
On Being a Poet, by Judson Jerome $14.95
The Poet's Handbook, by Judson Jerome (paper) $9.95
Successful Lyric Writing (workbook), by Sheila Davis (paper) $16.95
Successful Scriptwriting, by Jurgen Wolff & Kerry Cox $18.95
Travel Writer's Handbook, by Louise Zobel (paper) $11.95
TV Scriptwriter's Handbook, by Alfred Brenner (paper) $10.95
Writing After 50, by Leonard L. Knott $12.95
Writing for Children & Teenagers, 3rd Edition, by Lee Wyndham & Arnold Madison (paper) $12.95
Writing Short Stories for Young People, by George Edward Stanley $15.95
Writing the Modern Mystery, by Barbara Norville $15.95
Writing to Inspire, edited by William Gentz (paper) $14.95
Writing Young Adult Novels, by Hadley Irwin & Jeanette Eyerly $14.95

The Writing Business

A Beginner's Guide to Getting Published, edited by Kirk Polking $11.95
The Complete Guide to Self-Publishing, by Tom & Marilyn Ross (paper) $16.95
Editing for Print, by Geoffrey Rogers $14.95
How to Bulletproof Your Manuscript, by Bruce Henderson $9.95
How to Get Your Book Published, by Herbert W. Bell $15.95
How to Sell & Re-Sell Your Writing, by Duane Newcomb $11.95
How to Write Irresistible Query Letters, by Lisa Collier Cool $11.95
How to Write with a Collaborator, by Hal Bennett with Michael Larsen $11.95
How You Can Make $25,000 a Year Writing (No Matter Where You Live), by Nancy Edmonds Hanson $15.95
Literary Agents: How to Get & Work with the Right One for You, by Michael Larsen $9.95
Professional Etiquette for Writers, by William Brohaugh $9.95
Time Management for Writers, by Ted Schwarz $10.95

To order directly from the publisher, include $2.50 postage and handling for 1 book and 50¢ for each additional book. Allow 30 days for delivery.

Writer's Digest Books
1507 Dana Avenue, Cincinnati, Ohio 45207
Credit card orders call TOLL-FREE
1-800-543-4644 (Outside Ohio)
1-800-551-0884 (Ohio only)
Prices subject to change without notice.

Write to this same address for information on *Writer's Digest* magazine, Writer's Digest Book Club, Writer's Digest School, and Writer's Digest Criticism Service.